MODERNITY

Christianity's Estranged Child Reconstructed

MODERNITY

Christianity's Estranged Child Reconstructed

JOHN THORNHILL

William B. Eerdmans Publishing Company

Grand Rapids, Michigan / Cambridge, U.K.

© 2000 Wm. B. Eerdmans Publishing Co.
255 Jefferson Ave. S.E., Grand Rapids, Michigan 49503 /
P.O. Box 163, Cambridge CB3 9PU U.K.

Printed in the United States of America

05 04 03 02 01 00   7 6 5 4 3 2 1

Library of Congress Cataloging-in-Publication Data

Thornhill, John.
    Modernity: Christianity's estranged child reconstructed / John Thornhill.
        p.   cm.
    ISBN 0-8028-4694-7 (pbk.)
        1. Modernism (Christian theology).   2. Christianity and Culture.
        I. Title.
    BT82.T46   2000
    261 — dc21

                                                    99-462215

CONTENTS

v

100660

CONTENTS

INTRODUCTION

MODERNITY IS A FIVE-CENTURIES-LONG MOVEMENT within our Western tradition of such complexity that it would seem to defy the making of an overall interpretation. However, a great deal of light is shed upon the nature of this movement — as the present text sets out to show — when it is recognized that the central concern of its originating moment was emancipation from late medievalism's heavy reliance upon the authority of tradition. Modernity would replace this authority with the accountability of a shared intellectual inquiry.

Modernity's reaction against late medievalism was entirely justified and necessary. The effort to replace the dead hand of tradition with a genuine accountability was, in fact, an outstanding example of the quest for excellence and truth — with deep roots in the Judeo-Christian and Hellenistic traditions — which has been an outstanding characteristic of Western civilization.

It was an accident of history that modernity's project became identified with a set of methodological assumptions too constricting to fulfill the high hopes its founders had for it. Until the first half of the twentieth century, however, the immense achievements of modern science and technology seemed to provide a warrant for these assumptions, distracting attention from their inadequacy. The romanticism which has inspired so much of the creativity of our culture since the late eighteenth century was a reaction against this situation. Romanticism's concerns and the accepted canons of critical and "scientific" thought have never been reconciled, however, and they eventually came to have a somewhat uneasy coexistence in the Western psyche.

The culture of modernity has been forced by the accelerated developments and the upheavals of the twentieth century to look more closely at the intellectual assumptions it has long taken for granted. Today, these assumptions are coming under criticism from two opposing directions. The proponents of "postmodernism," on the one hand, would argue that the project of modernity has manifestly failed; it stands condemned of having replaced the "meta-narratives" of the mythologies and religions of past cultures with what were really perspectives of group (class, race, gender) interest and dominance. On the other hand, in the chapters which follow we shall hear a growing number of Western thinkers arguing that the project of modernity, far from being abandoned, must be carried forward upon the basis of a critical review of the assumptions of the "scientific" methodology which has so powerfully dominated its development. The present text identifies with this second point of view: our Western tradition, it would argue, must not turn away from a job half done.

For reasons which history can readily identify, those who shaped the assumptions of modernity had no expectation that the thought of the Middle Ages had anything to contribute to their shared intellectual inquiry. They disregarded, therefore, the intellectual and spiritual achievements of past ages. One of the aims of the present text is to indicate something of the contribution this neglected tradition can make toward modernity's review of its assumptions.

To this point, we speak of elements in our argument which are recognized more or less clearly by other interpreters of the present situation of modernity. If this text has an original contribution to make, it is in its exploration of the part played by *ideological consensus* in the development of modernity's distinctive culture. Ideology (the importance of which is today being increasingly emphasized) may be defined as a cognitive perspective which provides the effective consensus of a particular historical group. As Western thinkers sought to emancipate our civilized tradition from the cultural sclerosis of the late Middle Ages, ideological consensus was undoubtedly a fundamental factor in the emergence of modernity as a distinctive and influential cultural movement.

A recognition of the part played by ideological consensus in the emergence of modernity helps us understand the striking characteristics of this cultural movement: its dynamic impact upon the whole Western tradition, its resistance to criticism, and the difficulties it is experiencing in responding to its present problems.

Central to these problems is the lack of any fundamental agreement concerning the nature of reality and the meaning of human existence. If the intellectual principles upon which the project of modernity is built are no more than a shared ideology and the in-house discussions of a philosophy which has become so esoteric that it has no concern to make itself intelligible to ordinary people, then our cultural tradition is forced to live with an emptiness at its core which breeds the boredom, frustrations, and self-destructive violence which have come to be all-too-familiar problems in the Western world.

In this interpretation of modernity — it is worth remarking — my argument finds common cause with the advocates of postmodernism. There can be no doubt that our Western tradition's quest for truth has produced many ideologies — versions of "the truth," all-inclusive interpretative systems which have been shaped by, and have promoted the interests of, some dominant group. The advocates of postmodernism are right when they point out that such ideological interpretations will undermine modernity's shared intellectual inquiry if they are not recognized for what they are. But the radical solution they propose — that *all* claims to possessing something of the truth should be rejected — can only lead to a relativistic nihilism which makes the search for truth meaningless.

The recognition of the part played by ideological consensus in the history of ideas is an important element, nonetheless, in the reappraisal modernity must make of its assumptions, if it is to carry forward its project of accountability through a shared intellectual inquiry. The advocates of postmodernism have made their contribution to this reappraisal by presenting in stark clarity the alternative modernity faces: either a destructive nihilism or some metaphysical consensus concerning the nature of reality which can provide the measure validating modernity's genuine achievements.

INTRODUCTION

This book has three parts. *Part I* contains four chapters. *Chapters 1, 2, and 3* interpret modernity's development as an ideological movement inspired by a questing for excellence and truth which has long characterized the life of the Western tradition. *Chapter 4* reviews appraisals of modernity made by six thinkers from widely different intellectual backgrounds — interpretations which lend support to a great deal that has emerged in the discussion of the previous chapters.

Part II contains four chapters, each of which considers a significant issue which has been brought to light by the culture of modernity, and the challenge it implies. *Chapter 5* discusses the wisdom which this culture prizes yet acknowledges itself to be lacking. *Chapter 6* discusses "the affirmation of the ordinary," through which modernity reacts against the elitism of past ages. *Chapter 7* concerns the narrative form, which is an important expression of modernity's "turn to the subject" and an indispensable medium for the expression of existential truth, the ultimate measure of what it means to be human. *Chapter 8* evaluates the "free society" which has been established by modernity's demand for social accountability, and the problems it must resolve if this remarkable achievement is to flourish.

Part III takes up the question of the relationship between the project of modernity and the Christian tradition. As will already be clear, the suggestion that the two are incompatible is rejected. Properly understood, we shall argue, the essential concerns of both movements are not only compatible but also in accord in ways which have far-reaching implications. *Chapter 9* discusses the "witness" which is the medium of Christian faith as it conveys the full range of human truth which evades the methodological assumptions of modernity. *Chapter 10* discusses the message of the Christian gospel brought by this witness, and the relationship of its radical claims to the ultimate concerns of modernity. *Chapter 11* interprets the authentic spirit of "Catholicism" as reaching beyond partisanship and extending a hospitality to existential truth — the ultimate goal of modernity's quest — in all its forms.

PART I

Understanding Modernity and the Nature of Its Present Difficulties

CHAPTER 1

The Interpretation of Modernity as an Ideological Movement

OUR WESTERN TRADITION HAS BEEN REMARKABLE among humanity's cultural traditions for its vitality and creativity, and for the immense transformations this creativity has brought, particularly in recent centuries. Today, this culture is often characterized by a distinctive spirit which is critical of views which prevailed prior to the modern period. It is also patronizing and dismissive of the achievements of other cultural traditions, as these traditions succumb more and more to the attractions of the West's "scientific" approach and the immensely successful technology this approach has produced.

For all its dynamism and apparent success, however, our Western culture is now suffering a crisis of self-confidence. The optimistic expectations of an ever ascending "progress," with which the West entered the twentieth century, soon gave way to a very different mood. Though few people accepted the main thesis of Oswald Spengler's work *The Decline of the West,* published at the end of the First World War, the fact that it became a best-seller indicated that its title had captured an emerging cultural mood. It is a mood which, as the century has progressed, has become more and more somber, until today we are told that we are facing "the end of modernity," that a new era of "postmodernism" has begun. Despite its immense achievements — achievements which extend beyond science and

3

technology to the whole range of cultural and creative life of Western society — the project of modernity has been overtaken by uncertainty and seems to face the prospect of increasing fragmentation.

The central problem of modernity begins to emerge as soon as we seek to define it. In fact, modernity has no firm self-understanding or confident self-definition. In its origins it was a movement of reaction against the cultural assumptions of medievalism. As a movement of reaction it is difficult to define, for the simple reason that what it is reacting against must enter into the definition. And if what was being reacted against was a cultural reality, itself in the process of change, the difficulty is compounded.

Modernity's lack of confident self-understanding is confirmed by the etymology of the term by which this period has chosen to be known. The designation adopted by modernity to characterize the period which preceded it, "middle age," had obvious negative connotations: the long centuries of this era were seen as an interim period between the humanistic achievements of the ancient world and those of the age emerging, which understood itself as a "renaissance," a rebirth of humanism. "Modern," the word adopted to characterize the emerging order of things, had, however, a distinctly tentative ring: the term *modernum* is derived from the late Latin term *modo,* an adverb meaning "just recently." It thus served to describe "recent developments" — the culture which replaced that of the medievals. These developments have continued, of course, ever since, with the vigor which is characteristic of our Western tradition, producing the complex cultural achievements in which we all share. However, as we survey the vicissitudes of this long development, it becomes no easier than it was in the fifteenth century to point to any one factor or enduring achievement which defines what is peculiar to modernity.

It may well be argued that the essential concern of the culture which succeeded the Middle Ages was *an affirmation of the legitimate autonomy of the secular order.* For a whole complex of reasons, the sacralized culture of medieval Christendom resisted this claim. The church had played the role of midwife and guardian to a new Western civilization. When, in the fifteenth century, the creative energies of this new civilization had reached a stage of development which sought independent expression, it was not easy for the church to recognize the legitimacy of the demand for autonomy which this development implied. Within a broader cultural frame, other social forces worked to inhibit the vitality which was emerging. The securities of the status quo saw the new creative energies as a threat to the social fabric, and turned instinctively to a rationalization which appealed to an upholding of what was "traditional." With the passing of time, these two reactions formed a powerful alliance for the defense of the status quo, an alliance which endured in a variety of forms — as far as Catholicism was concerned — until the radical change of outlook adopted by the Second Vatican Council in its Pastoral Constitution on the Church in the Modern World, *Gaudium et spes* (1965).[1]

Fundamental to the argument of the present work is an interpretation of modernity as an essentially *ideological movement*. An ideology is a cognitive system which shapes the effective consensus of a particular historical group. The effectiveness of an ideology as a social force comes not so much from the intellectual rigor with which it provides support for its essential propositions as from the fact that these propositions further the interests and securities of the group in question. For this reason, it is rhetoric rather than philosophical argument which fosters the emergence of an effective ideology. The outcome of a sociological interaction and process, an ideological consensus will inevitably move toward an oversimplification of the issues faced by the group, presenting them in too black-and-white a fashion, because its essential function is to bring understanding and practical attitudes into a unified equilibrium which can be owned by the group at large as it carries forward its common project. The historical pressures faced by the groups which have produced them leave their unmistakable mark upon successful ideologies.

The situation of any group sharing in an ideological consensus is ambiguous, therefore. On the one hand, the group can only find its effective identity through the formation of ideological consensus, but on the other hand, this process runs the obvious danger of presenting an inadequate and distorted view of particular issues and situations. Examples are not difficult to find. Marx's social analysis makes us

---

1. See *Gaudium et spes*, pars. 41, 55, 56, 59, belatedly acknowledging the validity of the claim of autonomy for the secular order. For Christian faith, it must be acknowledged, this autonomy is one of the undeniable corollaries of God's taking created reality seriously in the incarnation.

aware of the place of ideology in the emergence of social classes. Nations engaged in war have rapidly adopted an ideological consensus — sometimes bordering on insanity. History is cluttered with examples which leave us in little doubt about the dangers inherent in the process and the distortions of which ideological consensus is capable.

In his critical analysis of contemporary Western culture, *The Unconscious Civilisation*,[2] John Ralston Saul bases his argument upon the limitations of ideology as a factor shaping social awareness. His penetrating analysis is worth summarizing: Ideology has appeal because it speaks to people's "need to believe in single-stroke, cure-all solutions." Its vision approximates that of a "utopia"; once established, it begets a sense of "passivity before the inevitable"; it creates "a conformity" characterized by "intolerance" of dissenters; it fosters an "unconsciousness" which has lost touch with the real issues facing society. In the end, ideologies engender an "unconscious form of self-contempt" — in a rank and file who are confronted by "elites" who "have the 'truth.'" This conviction gives rise in these elites to an outlook which may be likened to that of religious zealots; inspired by their vision of "the truth," ideological elites see themselves called to "convince the rest of us" — not by "democratic debate" but by any means which will "manipulate, trick or force the majority into acceptance." Not surprisingly, this often involves a "demonisation" of views which do not sit comfortably within the ideological perspective. As the effective promoter of a sectional interest, ideology breeds a class of "courtiers" who serve the cause in order to share in the benefits.[3]

It would be wrong, however, to judge ideological influences in purely negative terms, as Saul does — as if the ideal human situation were one in which ideological elements have been unmasked and eradicated. Ideology, it is clear, is an inevitable concomitant of human sociability and the common search this sociability involves. In fact, ideologies serve as the indispensable bearers of important cultural resources. A mature human awareness does not attempt to eradicate ideological influences, but is alive to the bias the ideological vehicle inevitably brings, seeking the more adequate understanding which

2. John Ralston Saul, *The Unconscious Civilisation* (Ringwood, Victoria: Penguin, 1997).
3. Saul, pp. 21-27, 95.

lies beyond this bias — and at the same time acknowledging that the complete eradication of bias deriving from existential investment in the issue under discussion is almost impossible. It may well be argued that all cultural movements which have affected the course of history have owed their essential dynamism to the emergence of an effective ideological consensus.

The application of what has just been said to the culture of modernity is not difficult to make. The situation of our Western tradition at the end of the medieval period brought a polarization of creative energies which gave rise to antithetical ideological movements. Western civilization had reached a state of maturity which led it to call into question fundamental assumptions of the culture of medievalism — in particular, a reverence for tradition which was exaggerated, giving its support to social and ecclesiastical systems of inherited power and privilege which were open to serious criticism, and providing the warrant for a scholarship which too often degenerated into an intellectual formalism. The development of the cultural tradition of the West had reached a stage at which its peculiar genius called for a more adequate accountability. It was inevitable that a questioning of assumptions which had become so fundamental to the ideological consensus which animated the hardy culture of medievalism and bolstered its securities would provoke defensive reactions. The creative energies of our Western tradition were thrown into a polarized configuration which must be understood if we are to find a satisfactory understanding of the development of the past five centuries.

*   *   *

Some soundings into the ongoing development of the "modern" period of Western history support the interpretation being suggested, of "modernity" as an ideological movement of reaction against medievalism.

It is not difficult to recognize that a successful process of ideology formation frequently produces epoch-making slogans. Three such slogans come readily to mind as we review the emergence and consolidation of the culture of modernity. We have already pointed to the ideological implications of the term "renaissance" and its obvious function in focusing the creative energies of the culture which saw itself as replacing that of medievalism. At a later stage of its development, modernity's dominant slogan was "Enlightenment," with its clear implication of reaction against the obscurantism of the intellectual fashions which had ruled the Middle Ages. "Emancipation" is probably the most powerful slogan in the modern world. It is clear that a reaction against the constraints of traditional social forms — for which, often, no justification was offered apart from the authority of long-established ways — gave rise to an ideology of "emancipation" which is far from spent and continues to give a strong coloring to political terms such as "reform," "liberal," and "conservative."

In his study of Western thought, *The Passion of the Western Mind*, Richard Tarnas argues that astronomical theory was one of the decisive factors in the collapse of the intellectual project of medievalism. Scholastic thought of the late Middle Ages had degenerated into a muddle of competing systems, closed in on themselves and characterized by a free-floating dogmatism which relied too heavily upon the authority of inherited traditions of teaching. The earth-centered astronomical doctrine of the Ptolemaic and Aristotelian tradition, with its cosmology of heavenly "spheres" comprised of material different in nature from mundane realities, was taken for granted by even the greatest minds of the Middle Ages.

Tarnas judges that the great influence of Dante's *Divina commedia* (ca. 1307) — which took for granted the numinous meaningfulness of the earth-centered universe of Aristotle — contributed, ironically, to disillusionment with medievalism. The discrediting of the massive symbolic creation which Dante had established at the center of cultural consciousness in the final moments of the medieval world led to an indiscriminate rejection of the Aristotelian tradition from which it was derived.[4]

Tarnas details the history of this disillusionment. The calculations of Copernicus (1473-1543), the Polish mathematician and astronomer, pointed to the indefensibility of the earth-centered universe of Aristotle and Ptolemy. Kepler's (1571-1630) interpretation of the elliptical motion of the planets provided confirmation of the interpretation proposed by Copernicus. In 1609, the year Kepler published his findings, Galileo (1564-1642) saw through his newly con-

---

4. Richard Tarnas, *The Passion of the Western Mind: Understanding the Ideas That Have Shaped Our World View* (New York: Ballantine, 1993), pp. 193-96.

structed telescope in Padua such things as the craters of the Moon, the moons of the planets, the phases of Venus, and the multitude of unsuspected stars of the Milky Way. The Aristotelian doctrine of the incorruptible heavenly bodies was empirically discredited.

We hear overtones of the strong ideological reaction against medievalism in the rhetoric of thinkers who have articulated the outlook of modernity. René Descartes (1596-1650) begins the first of his *Meditations on the First Philosophy* (1641) with the words:

> It is now some years since I detected how many were the false beliefs that I had from my earliest youth admitted as true, and how doubtful was everything I had since constructed on this basis; and from that time I was convinced that I must once for all seriously undertake to rid myself of all the opinions which I had formerly accepted, and commence to build anew from the foundation, if I wanted to establish any firm and permanent structure in the sciences.[5]

The thought of John Locke (1632-1704) is one of the most influential expressions of the outlook of modernity. As we shall see in a later chapter, the authors of a significant analysis of the contemporary culture of the United States describe Locke's political theory as "one of the most powerful ideologies ever invented, if not the most powerful."

Immanuel Kant's 1784 essay, "An Answer to the Question: What Is Enlightenment?" echoes the sense of reaction and emancipation which animated the emerging culture of modernity:

> *Enlightenment is man's emergence from his self-incurred immaturity. Immaturity* is the inability to use one's own understanding without the guidance of another. The immaturity is *self-incurred* if its cause is not lack of understanding, but lack of resolution and courage to use it without the guidance of another. The motto of enlightenment is therefore: *Sapere aude* (Dare to be wise)! Have the courage to use your *own* understanding! . . .

5. Cited by Lawrence Cahoone in his anthology, *From Modernism to Postmodernism* (Cambridge, Mass.: Blackwell, 1996), p. 29.

> . . . it is difficult for each individual to work his way out of the immaturity which has become almost second nature to him. . . . Dogmas and formulas, those mechanical instruments for rational use (or rather misuse) of his natural endowments, are the ball and chain of his permanent immaturity. . . .
>
> For enlightenment of this kind, all that is needed is *freedom*. And the freedom in question is the most innocuous form of all — freedom to make *public use* of one's reason in all matters. . . .[6]

If the Middle Ages were seen as withholding from the generality of people the information with which they could make public use of reason, the Enlightenment project would correct this situation. The French Enlightenment thinker the marquis de Condorcet (d. 1794) set out to do this through the publication of the *Encyclopedie* of all knowledge. His "Sketch for an Historical Picture of the Progress of the Human Mind" gives expression to a rhetoric at once inspired by and fostering the ideology of modernity:

> We have watched man's reason being slowly formed by the natural progress of civilisation; we have watched superstition seize upon it and corrupt it, and tyranny degrade and deaden the minds of man under the burden of misery and fear. . . .
>
> We have already seen reason lift her chains, shake herself free from some of them, and, all the time regaining strength, prepare for and advance the moment of her liberation. It remains for us to study the stage in which she finally succeeds in breaking these chains. . . .[7]

In the writings of Auguste Comte (1798-1857) we meet a full-blown ideological rhetoric which is embarrassing to contemporary sensibilities in its oversimplification of the intellectual issues facing the early nineteenth century. Comte's philosophy of positivism[8] claimed Descartes and Bacon as its precursors (p. 12); its "funda-

6. Cited in Cahoone, pp. 51-53.
7. Cited in Cahoone, pp. 72-73.
8. As explained in Comte, *A General View of Positivism,* trans. Bridges (New York: Speller, 1975). Page references which follow are to this text.

mental principle" he acknowledged to have been brought to light by developments in the fields of "mathematics and astronomy" (pp. 11-12). Comte claimed that his "system" had identified the principles of social evolution as a progression through three phases — a stage shaped by a "theological" outlook, a stage shaped by a "metaphysical" outlook, and the emerging stage of "positivist" outlook. With the zeal of an evangelist, Comte saw his thought as providing the basis for social planning and "regeneration"; in it philosophy undertakes "her highest and most essential mission" (p. 9). He saw himself as carrying forward Descartes's project of an all-embracing philosophy: "one comprehensive system in which our intellectual faculties and our social sympathy are brought into close correlation" (p. 1); this system must embrace "the three kinds of phenomena of which our life consists, Thought, Feelings and Actions . . . every department of human nature, whether speculative, effective or practical" (pp. 8-9). It is "the only logical and scientific" way of bringing "all our varied observations of phenomena . . . into one consistent whole"; indeed, it "is already adopted by all true thinkers" (p. 2). Comte's rhetoric dismisses theology as having no account of reality apart from the action of "more or less arbitrary" divine "Wills" (p. 10); its ultimate effect upon society is "degrading" (p. 20). Comte is conscious of medievalism, damning with faint praise "the noble but premature attempt of medieval Catholicism" to establish the "spiritual power" which only his positivistic system can bring to light (p. 3). He sees a metaphysical account of reality as having had the value of challenging the "retrograde" inadequacies of the theological outlook; in the end, however, a metaphysical point of view "constitutes only a transitory phase of mind, and is totally inadequate for any constructive purpose" (p. 11).

The best analyses of modernity point to the thought of Friedrich Nietzsche (1844-1900) as having great significance for those wishing to understand the culture of this period. According to Nietzsche, "the value of truth must for once be experimentally called into question."[9] Historian of philosophy James Collins speaks of Nietzsche's philosophical system as "an experiment concerning the world and truth," established upon a "hypothetical starting point," bent on exploring the ultimate consequences of the dangerous "perhaps" of God turning out

9. Nietzsche, *The Genealogy of Morals,* par. 24, cited in Cahoone, p. 122.

to be "our longest lie."[10] Nietzsche's thought may well be interpreted as a *Lebensphilosophie* in which his gift of rhetoric is enlisted to urge a taking seriously of the assumptions of the ideology of modernity.

*   *   *

We have been relating the implications of the thesis that modernity is essentially an ideological movement to the thought of some of modernity's influential thinkers. We may also consider the implications of this thesis within the broader canvas of human history. The philosopher of history Eric Voegelin suggests that the "differentiation of consciousness" provides the key to an interpretation of the movement of history, and its differentiation into distinct phases.[11] Though he does not explore the implications of the notion of "ideology,"[12] it is not difficult to see that his analysis invites reflection upon the implications of the dynamism we have been considering. According to Voegelin, consciousness is differentiated, and distinct orders of culture are engendered, by different manners of conceiving the "representation of truth." Using this index, he divides the history of our Western tradition into four epochs.

The first epoch is shaped by a representation of truth according to what Voegelin calls *a "cosmological" principle*. In making use of this principle, the mythological culture and its formative ideology seeks to reflect, "represent," the order of truth to be found in the cosmos (cf. p. 66).

Voegelin notes the remarkable fact that (at what Karl Jaspers has called the "axis time" of human history, 800-300 B.C.) there emerged independently, in different parts of the world, concern for an order of truth which lies beyond the scope of the cosmological principle

---

10. See James Collins, *God in Modern Philosophy* (London: Routledge & Kegan Paul, 1960), pp. 257-66.

11. Eric Voegelin, *The New Science of Politics* (Chicago: University of Chicago Press, 1960). References which follow are to this work. For a comprehensive study of Voegelin's thought, see K. Keulman, *The Balance of Consciousness: Eric Voegelin's Political Theory* (University Park, Pa.: Pennsylvania State University Press, 1990).

12. He merely notes its correspondence to Plato's *doxa* (opinion), and the looseness of contemporary use of the term, which "would even call Platonic-Aristotelian *episteme* an ideology" (Voegelin, p. 30).

(p. 60). This new differentiation of consciousness adopts a representation of truth which invokes what Voegelin calls *an "anthropological" principle*. In our Western culture, for instance, the Greeks understood the human psyche "as a new center in man at which he experiences himself as open towards transcendental reality" in the representation of truth (p. 67).[13]

Voegelin considers that a new differentiation of consciousness "appears with Christianity," shaped by *a "soteriological" principle*.[14] If the anthropological principle sees the transcendent measure of mundane reality as far beyond the possibility of a relationship of mutuality and friendship toward humanity, the soteriological principle sees the ultimate truth as identified with the God who "bends in grace" toward humanity: "The revelation of this grace in history (takes place) through the incarnation of the Logos in Christ" (pp. 77-78).[15]

We shall have occasion in later chapters to discuss further Voegelin's soteriological principle and the ambiguities which have arisen from a lack of clear understanding of its relationship to the cosmic and the anthropological principles in Western thought. For the moment, however, let us consider the relationship between the differentiation of consciousness shaped by these three principles and that of a modern culture which is shaped by an ideology of reaction against medievalism.

Voegelin makes an important observation concerning the impli-

---

13. Voegelin summarizes Plato's understanding of this principle: "the truth of man and the truth of God are inseparably one. Man will be in the truth of his existence when he has opened his psyche to the truth of God; and the truth of God will become manifest in history when it has formed the psyche of man into receptivity for the unseen measure. . . . The validity of the standards developed by Plato and Aristotle depends on the conception of a man who can be the measure of society because God is the measure of his soul" (pp. 69-70).

14. From the Greek *soteria* (deliverance, salvation).

15. Voegelin contrasts the *philia politike* (political friendship), which is "the substance of political society" for Aristotle, with the "experience of mutuality in the relation with God . . . *amicitia* (friendship) in the Thomistic sense" which is the gift of "grace" (pp. 77-78). It should be noted that in making this point, Voegelin (in a way which has been too common among Christian thinkers) does not do justice to the faith of Israel, which beyond all doubt anticipated the faith of Christians by representing the ultimate truth as expressed in the self-giving ways of the God of the Mosaic covenant.

cations of the soteriological principle. Related as it is to an acknowledgment of the divine initiative and freedom expressed in the incarnation, the differentiation of consciousness proper to the Christian
faith has, as Voegelin puts it, "uncertainty" as its "very essence"
(p. 122): having passed beyond the *cyclic* understanding of history
which characterized the "cosmological" outlook, and even the "anthropological" outlook of Plato and Aristotle (p. 118), this faith must
accept the radical mystery of the outcome of the *linear* understanding
of history demanded by the acknowledgment of a God who is active
in that history.[16]

According to Voegelin, the option of the secular order upon
which modernity is founded is the choice of an autonomy which has
been seen as incompatible with the acceptance of the transcendent
measure of human existence presupposed by our Western tradition in
both its Greek and its Judeo-Christian antecedents. Having thus deprived itself of such a measure, modernity must validate itself by a
complete "immanentizing" of the "meaning of existence" (cf. pp.
118, 122, 124, etc.). Voegelin describes the differentiation of consciousness produced by this option as a *"gnosis."* He draws a parallel
between this "gnosticism" of modernity and that inspired by an outlook redolent of the cosmic religions in the early Christian centuries:
"Gnostic experiences . . . are an expansion of the soul to the point
where God is drawn into the existence of man." They may be intellectual, as in Hegel's or Schelling's "speculative penetration of the mystery of creation and existence"; they may be "voluntaristic," assuming
the form of "activist redemption of man and society, as for Comte,
Marx and Hitler" (pp. 124-25). Voegelin adds, "the modern age has
been used by successive waves of humanist, Protestant and enlight-
ened intellectuals for expressing their consciousness of being repre-
sentatives of a new truth" (p. 134).

It is unfortunate that Voegelin does not reflect deeply upon the
nature of ideology. His criticism of modernity would have been tem-
pered and more open to its positive achievements if it had taken into
account the ideological nature of the outlook of modernity — which

16. See Robert Alter, *The Art of Biblical Literature* (New York: Basic Books,
1981), pp. 26, 32-33, and Paul Ricoeur, "Biblical Time," in *Figuring the Sacred*
(Minneapolis: Fortress, 1995), pp. 167-79.

we propose to explore more fully in the chapters which follow. Voegelin does contribute in an important way to our inquiry by pointing to the "immanentizing" of norms that is an essential feature of modernity. If all cultural movements depend upon an ideological consensus for the success with which they unite a human community and shape the course of its history, the ideologies of cultures prior to the emergence of modernity presupposed a dialectical relationship between the central propositions of the ideology and the truth the ideology sought to "represent." Voegelin alerts us to what is peculiar to modernity: its ideology presupposes no such dialectic. As we shall see, this situation helps us understand the nature of the peculiar problems of modernity.

In the next chapter we shall consider the "scientific" methodology which became the canonized expression of modernity's reaction to medievalism. Voegelin's interpretation of the march of history invites us to reflect critically upon this reaction. The bearers of a cultural tradition are many and complex: from shared attitudes and customs and the complex web of symbolism they engender, to reflective forms of intellectual inquiry expressed in writing, literature, and art in all its forms. The "methodological doubt" which sought to clear the ground for a new and fully accountable intellectual inquiry, it is evident, ran the risk of excluding from its purview important sources of enlightenment concerning the meaningfulness of human existence. Already in the nineteenth century, John Henry Newman was suggesting that a methodical *assumption* of what is widely accepted as true within a cultural tradition provides a more productive starting point for the process of an inquiry which is fully accountable as it thoroughly evaluates these positions.

CHAPTER 2

The Inspiration of Modernity: Our Western Tradition's Quest for Understanding and Excellence

IF, AS ERIC VOEGELIN HAS POINTED OUT, THE ASSUMP-tions of modernity present it with an unprecedented difficulty, this does not mean that the search for truth is not essential to the project of modernity. In fact, the present chapter will carry forward the interpretation of modernity by suggesting that the ideology of modernity is an expression of a search for truth which has shown itself to be one of the essential characteristics of our Western cultural tradition.

In the chapters which follow, we shall be confronted by the complexity and subtlety of the influences which have contributed to the civilization in which we share. The Western tradition came into existence through a remarkable cultural confluence. From the tradition of Judaism it derived a peculiar "conscience" awareness which is never entirely satisfied — a sense of destiny against which we measure all our accomplishments and situations, making us restless pilgrims in time. This Judeo-Christian outlook came to be united with another tradition remarkable for its pursuit of excellence. The Greek pursuit of excellence produced, at the popular level, the contests *(agones)* — dramatic, choral, and athletic — which were the hallmark of the Hellenic way of life and inspired many of its finest achievements. At another level this spirit showed itself in a sense of form, and an appreciation of intelligence or *reason* as the register which makes possible the exploration of order and excellence among forms.

In opening his work *Insight,* Bernard Lonergan writes, "when an animal has nothing to do it goes to sleep. When a man has nothing to do, he may ask questions." Lonergan made his life's work the exploration of what this "asking of questions" can lead to. Human existence has been shaped, from its prehistoric origins, by intelligence. But for long ages this intelligence was not aware of itself. The emergence of a reflexive awareness in human understanding, and the consequent recognition of the place of "reason" in the great quest which inspires human strivings, was to have immense consequences.

The employment of abstract thought is so established in our cultural awareness that we tend to take the achievement it represents for granted. Sir Richard Burton, the nineteenth-century British explorer, records as typical the frustrating conversation in which he sought to ascertain the terms used to express the numerals in the languages of central Africa:

> "Listen, O my brother! in the tongue of the shores (Swahili) we say 1, 2, 3, 4, 5 — "
>
> "Hi! Hi!" replies the wild man, "We say fingers."
>
> "By no means, that's not it. This white man wants to know how thou speakest 1, 2, 3?"
>
> "One, two, three what? Sheep, or goats, or women?" (expressing the numerals in Swahili).
>
> "By no means, only 1, 2, 3 sheep in thine own tongue, the tongue of the Wapoka."
>
> "Hi! Hi! What wants the white man with the Wapoka?"[1]

Reflexive understanding is to be found, certainly, in other great cultural traditions of the world. There can be little doubt, however, that the peculiar genius of the West is associated with the achievements of understanding that is aware of itself. In introducing his study of the ideas which have shaped our Western worldview, Richard Tarnas describes our indebtedness to ancient Greece in this develop-

---

1. Richard Burton, *The Source of the Nile, the Lake Regions of Central Africa* (London: Folio Society, 1993), p. 402.

ment: "It was some twenty-five centuries ago that the Hellenic world brought forth that extraordinary flowering of culture that marked the dawn of Western civilization. Endowed with seemingly primeval clarity and creativity, the ancient Greeks provided the Western mind with what has proved to be a perennial source of insight, inspiration and renewal."[2]

This emergence of mind conscious of itself characterized the genius of Greek culture and established the foundations of our Western civilization. The achievement of the ancient Greeks has provided the background of all the creative developments of our cultural tradition ever since. If it had its origins in Greek literature,[3] it was in the work of the philosophers of the fifth and fourth centuries B.C. that it emerged with full clarity. The philosopher Anaxagoras (ca. 500-428) declared that *nous* (mind or intelligence) is the pervasive formative principle of the world. Plato has Socrates complain, however, that this pioneer thinker failed to recognize the immense implications of his discovery (*Phaedo* 97). These implications were explored by later minds, especially by Socrates (469-399), Plato (428-348), and Aristotle (384-322).

A recognition of the ideological influences at work in the origins of modernity and its rejection of medievalism makes it possible to understand why these origins had the nature of a dislocation which had little concern to take up a dialogue with the great intellectual achievements of our Western tradition in the course of the previous two thousand years. In their rejection of medievalism, the founders of modernity had no desire to investigate an intellectual past which was represented by what they knew of the scholarship of the late Middle Ages. The thought of Thomas Aquinas, the greatest thinker of the medieval period, was virtually unknown to them. For this reason we shall consider the contribution he can make to our discussion in an *appendix* rather than in this chapter.[4]

2. Richard Tarnas, *The Passion of the Western Mind: Understanding the Ideas That Have Shaped Our World View* (New York: Ballantine, 1993), p. 2.

3. See B. Snell, *The Discovery of Mind* (New York: Harper Torchbook, 1960).

4. See appendix, "Aquinas on Understanding That Is Aware of Itself." Aquinas clarified his fundamental metaphysical principles by combining a refinement of Aristotle's metaphysical realism with an understanding of "participation" and "analogy" derived from the Platonic tradition's interpretation of the relationship between

As Richard Tarnas points out, while the Renaissance of the fifteenth century was "a direct outgrowth of the rich and burgeoning culture of the high Middle Ages," it also involved a kind of "quantum leap" and "the emphatic emergence of a new consciousness." In the historical consciousness of the medievals, their own time was "only vaguely separated from the Roman era of Christ's birth." Renaissance consciousness adopted a "decisively new perspective on the past."[5] An important element of the ideology of modernity was taking shape — history was divided into three sharply differentiated periods: the age of the ancients; the "middle age," a term having unmistakably negative connotations; and the "modern" age.

The scholarship of the late Middle Ages had little in fact to contribute to the concerns of the founders of modernity. The thought of William of Ockham (ca. 1285-1349), for instance, is representative of the final phase of a scholastic tradition which was becoming increasingly bankrupt as it degenerated into an empty formalism. Though Ockham claimed to represent the tradition of Aristotle, his basic "nominalism" (which denied that the universal "natures" so central to Aristotelianism were more than mental constructs) was an overturning of the basic principles of Aristotle. Aquinas's view of creation as having an intrinsic worth and autonomous dynamism intelligibly grounded in the divine reality found no support in the principles of Ockham's system. For the metaphysical analysis he proposed, the relationship between universal concepts and the particular things which

---

mundane reality and the transcendent (see R. J. Henley, *St. Thomas and Platonism* [The Hague: Nijhoff, 1956]). Aquinas surpassed the metaphysical achievement of Aristotle most notably in making the *act of existing ("esse")* the central reference of his metaphysical analysis. For Aristotle, *actuality* (especially that of "substance") — as distinct from real *potentiality* — constituted a central point of reference. Aquinas based his metaphysical analysis upon the distinction between *essence* and *existence* — the meaningfulness of *what* something *is* must be distinguished from the meaningfulness of *whether* something *is*, i.e., whether it has extramental reality. He pointed to the absolute uniqueness and ultimacy of *esse* in the order of actuality; for him it constitutes "the actuality of all actualities and the perfection of all perfections" in the metaphysical order (*De potentia* q. 7, art. 2 ad 9). On the lack of precision in Greek thought and language concerning the differentiation of "existence" and "essence," see Gregory Vlastos, *Socrates: Ironist and Moral Philosopher* (Cambridge: Cambridge University Press, 191), p. 74 n. 137 and additional note 2.3, pp. 254-55.

5. Tarnas, *Passion*, p. 231.

make up the real world became acutely problematical. And the rationale Ockham adopted, to defend the divine transcendence from trivialization, contributed further to this uncertainty: he taught that the world's reality is utterly contingent on God's exercise of omnipotence and freedom; any claim on the part of the human inquirer that the cosmos is an ordered expression of divine truth was therefore undermined.[6] The thought of Ockham was known in his day as the *"via moderna* (modern way)"* — as opposed to the *"via antiqua"* of earlier scholastics — a significant symptom of the change of mood taking place in Western culture and the emergence of the ideology this change was producing. The medievals themselves had begun to use our term to designate the new order of things which was emerging.

Hearing Ockham, we understand Descartes's impatience to undertake an intellectual project that would "build anew from the foundation" and be transparently accountable. Ironically, the proposals of Descartes (1596-1650), like those of his English contemporary Francis Bacon (1561-1626), reflect the pervasive influence in the later Middle Ages of the "nominalism" championed by Ockham.[7]

It is not surprising that Descartes's collaborators in the project of devising a methodology for this renewal of intellectual endeavor were the mathematicians and astronomers who discredited the astronomy of the Middle Ages. A fundamental principle of the methodology of modernity's "scientific" reason began to emerge with Galileo's suggestion, following his own successful experiments, that the accurate observation of nature should concern itself only with those characteristics of things which can be precisely *measured* — *quantitative* aspects such as weight and motion — and not with ephemeral and subjective characteristics such as color, sound, taste, and smell. The quantitative experiment was proposed as the final verification of scientific theory.[8] Aristotle's philosophy of nature had sought to understand also the *qualitative* aspects of reality, as providing evidence of the natures of things. If developments within the Aristotelian tradition along these lines were open to serious criticism, the remedy proposed by Galileo was a radical one, narrowing

6. Cf. Tarnas, *Passion,* p. 204.
7. Cf. Tarnas, *Passion,* pp. 272-81.
8. Cf. Tarnas, *Passion,* p. 263.

the scope of an investigation of nature in a way which was to have far-reaching consequences.

Ockham had separated the individual reality and its empirical characteristics from the understanding mind. Galileo now narrowed the methodology by which physical reality could be subjected to a disciplined investigation. Only a small step remained to the philosophical system whereby Descartes sought to clear up the muddle bequeathed to the beginnings of the modern era by late medieval scholasticism.[9]

Descartes made his own the distinction made by Galileo: a disciplined inquiry should concern itself only with those aspects of things which can be analyzed in quantitative terms. The study of reality became therefore a kind of "universal mathematics," in which the physical universe was seen as a gigantic machine which could be understood and brought into the service of humanity. The clarity of mathematical understanding provided, as a consequence, the basis of a complete faith in human reason.[10] The fundamental principles of the "scientific" methodology which has been so influential in the forming of our modern outlook were taking on an established shape.

John Locke (1632-1704) contributed to this development. He rejected Descartes's view that the mind (which Descartes had so severely distinguished from the physical world) was endowed by the Creator with "innate ideas." His view was similar to that of Ockham: the "ideas" of understanding were produced by the compounding of the data of sensible experience. At the same time, he made his own the distinction already stressed by Galileo and Descartes, between "primary" and "secondary" characteristics: those which can be objectively measured in quantitative terms and those which involve a subjectivized human experience (like taste, odor, and color).[11]

The discrediting of the Aristotelian understanding of the cosmos called for a comprehensive theory which would give coherence to a sun-centered universe. It was the English physicist Isaac Newton who provided this master theory: "It finally fell to Isaac Newton, born on Christmas Day the year of Galileo's death, to complete the Coper-

9. The dualism of Descartes — mind *(res cogitans)* and body *(res extensa)* only finding communality by having a common source in God — is reminiscent of Ockham's voluntaristic nominalism.

10. Cf. Tarnas, *Passion*, p. 279.

11. Cf. Tarnas, *Passion*, pp. 333, 335.

nican revolution by quantitatively establishing gravity as a universal force."[12] In fact, as Tarnas observes, the astronomy of Copernicus had replaced that of Ptolemy, and now Newton proposed a cosmological system which was able to replace that of Aristotle: "With an exemplary combination of empirical and deductive rigor, Newton had formulated a very few overarching laws that appeared to govern the entire cosmos."[13]

Today, three centuries later, the "scientific" methodology we have described still has a dominant place in the ideological assumptions of leading thinkers. In his recent critique of "postmodernism,"[14] the well-known philosopher and social anthropologist Ernest Gellner — arguing that a radical intellectual relativism must be rejected — appeals to the "ability of cognition to reach beyond the bounds of any one cultural cocoon, and attain forms of knowledge valid for *all*," through "an understanding of nature" which is validated by the successes of modern technology (p. 75). This form of knowledge, he points out, "has proved so overwhelmingly powerful, economically, militarily, administratively, that all societies have had to make their peace with it and adopt it," even though it has a "corrosive, unharmonious relationship" with other components of their cultures (pp. 60-61). But, as Gellner seeks an explanation for this remarkable influence, he is hampered by assumptions derived from the ideology of modernity.

These assumptions lead him to take it for granted that pre-Cartesian thought has little to offer as an explanation of this influence — he judges, for instance, that the "epistemological tradition" of the West began with Descartes (p. 37). In the end he acknowledges that a satisfactory explanation eludes him: "no one really knows just how and why this unbelievably powerful cognitive style works, and no one knows exactly how it emerged, and no one knows what its eventual social implications will be" (p. 78).

While the principles of Descartes were incapable of articulating issues of a metaphysical nature, the principles which will provide a solu-

---

12. Cf. Tarnas, *Passion,* p. 269.

13. Cf. Tarnas, *Passion,* pp. 261, 270. These laws were the three laws of motion (of inertia, force, and equal reaction) and the theory of universal gravitation.

14. Ernest Gellner, *Postmodernism, Reason, and Religion* (London: Routledge, 1992). References which follow are to this work.

tion to the question raised by Gellner had been clarified, long before the time of Descartes, by Aristotle and Aquinas. These thinkers discussed the differentiation of methodologies appropriate to various orders of intellectual investigation. They even pointed to the reductionist temptation arising from the unparalleled transparency of mathematical intelligibility.[15]

Our understanding of modernity as an ideological movement helps us evaluate the methodology we have described. The twentieth century has, in fact, brought a growing awareness within our Western tradition that the "scientific" methodology championed by modernity's ideology is open to serious criticism — it has too narrow a base to sustain the intellectual project envisaged by Descartes. It is often assumed that this "scientific" rationality constitutes the central principle of the culture of Western modernity. But is this really the case? The developments we have outlined suggest another interpretation. The methodology adopted by modernity provided the means whereby modernity's reaction against the established culture of medievalism could express its newfound independence.

What is essential to modernity is a rejection of medievalism, in the name of a proper human autonomy, an autonomy which calls the traditionally accepted ways of the Middle Ages to account. It was an accident of history that the project of modernity seized upon this particular methodology as its privileged instrument. Once this choice had been made, however, it was to play a very decisive part in modernity's further development. In the last analysis, however, these developments were an expression of the peculiar genius of our Western cultural tradition: its restless quest for the ideal, and its recognition of reason as essential to the pursuit of this ideal.

The immense scientific and technological successes of this methodology sustained a mood of optimism in the ideology of modernity until the early twentieth century. But it was inevitable that the methodology's limited scope would eventually give rise to tensions and frustrations within a cultural tradition remarkable for its bound-

15. Cf. appendix, p. 230. Eric Voegelin instances Aristotle's reminder to his contemporaries "that an 'educated man' will not expect exactness of the mathematical type in a treatise on politics" as an example of the methodological confusions which have occurred in the history of science (*The New Science of Politics* [Chicago: University of Chicago Press, 1960], p. 5).

less aspirations and idealism. Richard Tarnas sums up the narrow scope which was to give rise to these frustrations: "The modern mind has demanded a specific type of interpretation of the world: its scientific method has required explanations of phenomena that are concretely predictive, and therefore impersonal, mechanistic, structural. To fulfil their purposes, these explanations of the universe have been systematically 'cleansed' of all spiritual and human qualities."[16]

In other words, the methodology which became canonized in our tradition, as providing the index of critical understanding, excluded in principle concerns and aspirations which are essential to human existence. Incapable of even raising the questions of the meaningfulness of "reality" and "truth," this methodology makes no claim to providing an answer to these questions, and thus leaves a void at the heart of our cultural tradition which has given rise to an existential frustration and a fragmentation which seems almost impossible to contain. If "fundamentalism" is defined as taking out of context and absolutizing for ideological purposes certain elements of a broader system, this chosen methodology of modernity became, in the end, a reductionist fundamentalism which has hampered the project of modernity.[17]

As our discussion progresses, we shall come to appreciate the cultural movement of romanticism as a response within our Western culture to the frustrations attendant upon this reductionism.

$$* \qquad * \qquad *$$

True to its genius, our cultural tradition, in the course of the present century, has been prompted by these frustrations to seek a more adequate understanding of the nature and scope of reason.

The philosophical school of phenomenology, inspired by Edmund Husserl (1859-1938), was a critical response to the "scientific" outlook which had come to be taken for granted in Western thought. Husserl's *Crisis of European Sciences and Transcendental Phenomenology*, which he had been working on at the time of his death,

16. Tarnas, *Passion,* p. 421.
17. See J. Moltmann, "Fundamentalism and Modernity," *Concilium* (1992): 109-15.

24

spells out this criticism and at the same time makes a plea for a more adequate understanding of the nature of "reason."[18]

Husserl sees the early twentieth-century notion of "science" as a "residual concept" (p. 228), which can only be understood as a relic produced by an earlier intellectual history. Descartes and the founders of modern thought still took for granted, according to Husserl, an assumption they had inherited from the Renaissance, that the various "sciences" which make up the intellectual project as a whole are "dependent branches of the One Philosophy" (p. 228). The Renaissance, in its turn, had inherited this notion of a "perennial philosophy" from the Middle Ages (p. 229).[19] But, as Husserl points out, the methodology Descartes bequeathed to modernity was destined to undermine the very basis of unity among intellectual disciplines if it was unable to give an account of reason itself "in all its particular forms" (p. 228). Husserl spells out the implications of what he is saying: "Reason is the explicit theme in the disciplines concerning knowledge (i.e. of true and genuine rational knowledge), of true and genuine valuation (genuine values as values of reason), of ethical action (truly good acting, acting from practical reason); here reason is title for 'absolute,' 'eternal,' 'supertemporal,' 'unconditionally valid ideas and ideals'" (p. 228).

One response to the metaphysical vacuum left by a widespread

18. Sections of this work are included in Lawrence Cahoone's anthology, *From Modernism to Postmodernism* (Cambridge, Mass.: Blackwell, 1996). References which follow are to this text.

19. This development, incidentally, provides an interesting illustration of the ideological pressures present in the formative moment of modernity — in the Renaissance's choice of the principles of Platonism in the framing of a *philosophia perennis,* rather than those of the discredited Aristotelianism of late medieval thought (cf. Tarnas, *Passion,* pp. 209-19, on the Platonism of the Renaissance). An eloquent expression of this assumption is documented in the writings of Marsilio Ficino, a key figure in the early Renaissance (cf. *The Letters of Marsilio Ficino,* vols. 1-5 [London: Shepheard-Walwyn, 1978-94]; Marsilio writes, for instance: "It was the chief work of the divine Plato, as the dialogues of Parmenides and Epinomis show, to reveal the principle of unity in all things, which he called appropriately the One itself. He also asserted that in all things there is one truth, that is the light of the One itself, the light of God, which is poured into all minds and forms, presenting the forms to the minds and joining the minds to the forms. Whoever wishes to profess the study of Plato should therefore honour the one truth, which is the single ray of the one God" [vol. 1, letter 42]).

acceptance of the Cartesian methodology is to argue that the "unconditionally valid" truth of which Husserl speaks — echoing what has been the basic assumption of the intellectual tradition of the West — is an illusion which must be abandoned. In his *Visions of the Future,* to be referred to in a later chapter, Robert Heilbroner proposes such a view. He seeks support in Thomas Kuhn's analysis of the "paradigm" shifts which condition "the ideas and theoretical structures of Science," and in Richard Rorty's suggestion that philosophy should abandon "a search for a non-existent truth" and see itself as "an ongoing 'conversation' about whatever matters it considers to be important."[20]

Ernest Gellner mounts a strong attack upon this position. He argues that the claim of C. J. Geertz that a relativism in anthropological analysis does not lead to nihilism is illogical: "Relativism *does* entail nihilism: if standards are inherently and inescapably expressions of something called culture, and can be nothing else, then no culture can be subjected to a standard, because *(ex hypothesi)* there cannot be a trans-cultural standard which would stand in judgment over it. No argument could be simpler or more conclusive."[21]

A methodology which abandons all claim to rendering an account of reason itself must lead, Husserl would argue, to the existential frustrations we referred to above. Its "scepticism about the possibility of metaphysics" constitutes "a collapse of belief in 'reason'"; and when the meaning of "truth" itself is problematical, the distinction so important to the ancients, between a critically validated understanding *(episteme)* and mere opinion *(doxa),* disappears. Husserl continues: "Along with this falls the faith in 'absolute' reason, through which the world has its meaning, the faith in the meaning of history, of humanity, the faith in man's freedom, that is, his capacity to secure rational meaning for his individual and common human existence. If man loses this faith, it means nothing less than the loss of faith 'in himself,' in his own true being" (p. 231). Husserl aims his remarks at Descartes's self-contained monad-subject when he continues: "This true being is not something he always already has, with the self-

20. Robert Heilbroner, *Visions of the Future* (New York: Oxford University Press, 1995), p. 76.

21. Gellner, pp. 49-50.

evidence of the 'I am,' but something he only has and can have in the form of the struggle for his truth, the struggle to make himself true. True being is *everywhere* an ideal goal, a task of *episteme* or 'reason' as opposed to being which through *doxa* is merely thought to be, unquestioned and 'obvious'" (p. 231).

As we shall see in the next chapter, the work of Charles Taylor confronts the frustrations engendered by an understanding of reason which is merely "procedural" and not the "substantive" reason Husserl is concerned to rehabilitate. Taylor's analysis of moral experience leads to the conclusion that a satisfactory account of moral experience is not possible in terms of a reason which is no more than "procedural"; it requires the invoking of "substantive" reason.[22] Taylor sees today's reliance upon "procedural" reason originating in Descartes: "Descartes offers a paradigm example of this with his model of clear distinct ideas."[23]

Though it does not use the term, the work of Bernard Lonergan, mentioned at the beginning of this chapter — which unfortunately is little known outside the circles of his enthusiastic disciples[24] — has as its object the rehabilitation of what Taylor calls "substantive reason." Lonergan, who situates himself within the Aristotelian tradition of Aquinas, is concerned to recover an expression of the realism of the perennial philosophy in terms which are accessible to the culture of modernity.[25] Lonergan's principle, "meaning mediates reality," presupposes "the scholastic tag, *ens per verum innotescit,* reality becomes

22. See Charles Taylor, *Sources of the Self: The Making of the Modern Identity* (Cambridge: Cambridge University Press, 1992), pp. 85-86: "I call a notion of reason substantive where we judge the rationality of agents or their thoughts and feelings in substantive terms. This means that the criterion for rationality is that one get it right. . . . By contrast, a procedural notion of reason breaks this connection. The rationality of an agent or his thought is judged by how he thinks, not in the first instance by whether the outcome is substantively correct. Good thinking is defined procedurally."

23. Taylor, pp. 85-86.

24. It is surprising that a writer as thorough as Tarnas makes no mention of Lonergan. He is not mentioned in two leading dictionaries of philosophy recently published.

25. See, for instance, Lonergan's "The Origins of Christian Realism," in *A Second Collection* (London: Darton, Longman & Todd, 1974), pp. 239-61. References which follow are to this text.

27

known through knowing what is true" (p. 250). He protests, however, that his is not a "naive realism" which assumes that knowing is "a matter of taking a good look": "the world mediated by meaning is not just given"; if it is to yield its truth, it must be "intended by questions," "organised by intelligence," "described by language that is enriched by tradition" — indeed, it is "an insecure world, for besides fact there is fiction, besides truth there is error, besides science there is myth, besides honesty there is deceit" (p. 241). This pursuit of truth, which Lonergan calls a "critical realism," is in fact the "struggle for truth" of which Husserl speaks.

The constricted perspective of modernity's "scientific" rationality had such practical success, however, that it effectively dominated the ideological consensus of our Western culture in the nineteenth and early twentieth centuries. As Husserl notes, the failure of modernity's project to achieve any understanding of how the many branches of "science" could be integrated contrasted with the "unquestionable successes" of the application of the methodology of "positive science" in research and technology (Husserl, p. 229). It is not difficult to understand how this momentous success diverted attention from the poverty of metaphysical resources available to modernity. The ideology of modernity assumed a new configuration as it looked forward with a naive confidence to a "Progress" in which the achievements of science and technology would solve all the problems of humanity.

At another level, as Husserl points out, these undoubted successes had a more subtle effect, seeming to render metaphysics superfluous, with "the surreptitious substitution of the mathematically substructed world of idealities for the only real world, the one that is actually given through perception, that is ever experienced and experienceable — our everyday life-world" (p. 233). It is at this point — when the "sciences" are unable to render a satisfactory account of the rationality they employ — that "science" becomes little more than a "residual concept": "Are science and its method not like a machine, reliable in accomplishing obviously very useful things, a machine everyone can learn to operate correctly without in the least understanding the inner possibility and necessity of this sort of accomplishment?" (p. 236).

Such an unsatisfactory situation had to provoke a reaction on the part of gifted thinkers. Analytical philosophy took up the challenge of attempting to rehabilitate a properly philosophical rationality. It is inter-

28

esting to compare Ludwig Wittgenstein's concluding words in his 1929 "Lecture on Ethics" with the judgment of Taylor quoted above, and to situate them within the analysis made by Husserl a decade later. Wittgenstein writes: "Ethics so far as it springs from the desire to say something about the ultimate meaning of life, the absolute good, the absolute valuable . . . does not add to our knowledge in any sense. But it is a document of a tendency in the human mind which I personally cannot help respecting deeply and I would not for my life ridicule it."[26] Wittgenstein's words call to mind Eric Voegelin's comment that Max Weber's choice of the word "disenchantment" to describe the irreversible process of modernity implies a regret which contrasts with Auguste Comte's enthusiastic and "distinctly progressive" understanding of the same process in the mid–nineteenth century.

Weber's thought — as explained in the "Author's Introduction" to his *Protestant Ethic and the Spirit of Capitalism*[27] — illustrates the problem faced by modernity as it carried on the intellectual project of the Western tradition within the constrictions of the methodology which had been canonized by the ideology of modernity. Weber saw the unique influence of Western civilization and its cultural achievements — of "*universal* significance and value" (p. 158) — as due to the "rationalisation" which constitutes an unprecedented achievement on the part of modernity. For Weber, the achievement of the West is essentially due to an instrumental rationality which has effectively adapted means to ends *(Zweckrationalitat)*. It is one of many forms of rationalization which have their meaningfulness from the adopting by human agents of "different ultimate values and ends." Weber lists as examples: "rationalization of mystical contemplation," "rationalizations of economic life, of technique, of scientific research, of military training, of law and administration" (p. 165). He offers no comparative judgment of these different rationalizations. They must all be evaluated internally according to how effectively they adapt means to their specific ends. To those who have opted for the end peculiar to one of these "rationalizations," the outlook determined by others "may well be irrational" (p. 165).

26. Cited in Cahoone, p. 198.
27. Reproduced in Cahoone, *From Modernism to Postmodernism*. References which follow are to this text.

Weber argues that the modern Western world has been shaped by options for an "economic rationalism" (p. 165) which has brought into existence a capitalistic system with "types, forms and directions which have never existed elsewhere" (p. 162).

Weber adverts to the question of the nature of "reason" itself. He recognized that the frequently made claim that science is "free from presuppositions" is false: "All scientific work presupposes that the rules of logic and method are valid. . . . In this, obviously, are contained all our problems. For this presupposition can not be proved by scientific means. It can only be *interpreted* with reference to its ultimate meaning, which we must reject or accept according to our ultimate position in life" (p. 171).

The "ultimate position" which gives validity to a particular rationalization is, for Weber, therefore, a matter of personal choice which is beyond the judgment of scientific method: "What man will take upon himself the attempt to 'refute scientifically' the ethic of the Sermon on the Mount? . . . According to our ultimate standpoint . . . the individual has to decide which is God for him and which is the devil. And so it goes through all the orders of life" (p. 174). Weber has no doubt that "magical and religious forces, and the ethical ideas of duty based upon them, have in the past always been among the most important formative influences on conduct" (p. 166), determining the "ultimate standpoint" which measures the rationalization of particular cultures. In fact, *The Protestant Ethic and the Spirit of Capitalism* belongs to a series of studies in the sociology of religion undertaken by Weber. But Weber frankly acknowledges that the methodology he has adopted has nothing to say on "the relative value of cultures" (p. 167), as they are differentiated by the adopting of different "ultimate standpoints." His evasive, ironic comment upon this fact leaves us disappointed that a sociologist of such talent and insight should find himself, by reason of the positivistic methodology he has adopted, unable to deliver any verdict on an issue of such ultimate significance for human existence. He writes:

> whoever wants a sermon should go to a conventicle. The question of the relative value of the cultures which are compared (in this study) . . . will not receive a single word. It is true that the path of human destiny cannot but appal him who surveys a section of it.

But he will do well to keep his small personal commentaries to himself, as one does at the sight of the sea or of majestic mountains, unless he knows himself to be called and gifted to give them expression in artistic or prophetic form. In most other cases the voluminous talk about intuition does nothing but conceal a lack of perspective toward the object. . . . (p. 167)

We meet once more the question raised by Husserl. It could be expressed in these terms: If the "presuppositions" of any rational account of the world and our existence in it are beyond validation by critical understanding, why do we continue to respect them and regret the "disenchantment" that makes them ineffective for us? Was not Nietzsche right when he claimed that we should acknowledge the consequences of the "death of God" and assume responsibility for a world which must ultimately be shaped by our human will? Nietzsche is, in fact, one of a significant group of Western thinkers who have sought to redress the inadequacies of the dominant assumptions of modernity by appealing to norms other than those of an impersonal rationality. Rousseau was an early spokesman for romanticism's attempt to give a proper place in the interpretation of human existence to the emotional and volitional orders, to the instinctive, the aesthetic, the symbolic, those dimensions of human existence which lie beyond the scope of the canonized methodology.

Nietzsche's essays show him to be a precursor to the existentialist movement of the mid–twentieth century. His parable of the madman who appeared with a lantern in the marketplace looking for God shows how profoundly he had grasped the option which confronted the culture of modernity.[28] This famous parable describes a dramatic confrontation between the madman and the people in the marketplace. Because they no longer believe in God, they scoff at him and ask ironically where God could have gone to. "Where has God gone?" shouts the madman, turning on them. "I will tell you. We have slain him — you and I. We are his murderers." And he confronts them with the stupendous thing they have done in excluding any notion of God from their understanding of their world: "But how did we do it? How could we drink up the sea? Who gave us the sponge to wipe out the

28. Nietzsche, *The Joyful Wisdom*, sec. 125.

whole horizon? What did we do when we unchained this earth from its sun? . . . Do we not now wander through an endless nothingness? Does empty space not breathe upon us? Is it not colder now? Is not night coming, and even more night? Must we not light lanterns at noon? God is dead. God stays dead. And we have slain him. . . ." His hearers can only vaguely grasp the implications of his terrible proclamation, and they gaze at him in shocked silence. "I came too early," the madman declares. "It is not my time. The monstrous event is still on its way. . . . This deed is still further from men than the remotest stars — and yet they have done it."

The parable is made all the more poignant because its author — who clearly identified with the madman who came before his time — ended his days in an asylum for the insane. Nietzsche had diagnosed the essence of the problem emerging in Western culture: the God of the religious cultures of previous ages was dying, and this development called for a revolutionary transformation of the worldview of the Western tradition. Nietzsche recognized the terrible responsibilities which devolved upon the human agent if — with the passing of sacralized cultures — the transcendent ground of all norms and values was removed from an understanding of human existence.

The question Nietzsche faced was ultimately the metaphysical question of the nature of reality and truth. It is interesting to hear leading exponents of the mathematically grounded scientific method raising questions which only metaphysics can answer. In his conversation with Australian journalist Phillip Adams, Paul Davies, physicist and winner of the prestigious Templeton Prize, the world's largest award for intellectual endeavor, discussed the rationality which — as Weber had recognized — is *presupposed* in any application of modernity's scientific method. Such rationality, he points out, is not "something that was there before" the existence of the universe; it is "something which is timeless, outside of time, indeed space, altogether." As he goes on to explain his point, Davies echoes the assumption which has given mathematical understanding a paramount place in the "scientific" methodology adopted by modernity:

> The closest analogy that I can get to the sort of timeless, abstract being — maybe it's more than just an analogy — is mathematics. If you ask the question, "Where is the number eleven?" well, it isn't

anywhere. It's not in space, it's not in time. Or consider the statement: eleven is a prime number. This is a true statement whether there is a universe here or not. Mathematical objects and statements reside in an abstract, timeless realm that transcends the physical universe, yet they apply to the physical universe too.[29]

In his *Origin of the Universe,* John Barrow makes the same point, drawing out some of its deeper implications. Noting that the recent discoveries which support the big bang theory of the origins of the universe have led some modern cosmologists to publish research papers bearing titles like "The Creation of the Universe out of Nothing," he urges caution. Modern scientific theory, he points out, assumes "a good deal more than one's everyday conception of 'nothing'":

> In the beginning there must exist laws of nature . . . energy, mass, geometry; and, of course underpinning everything seems to be the ubiquitous world of mathematics and logic. There needs to be a considerable substructure of rationality before any complete explanation of the universe can be erected and sustained. It is this underlying rationality that most modern theologians emphasise when questioned about the role of God in the universe. They do not regard the Deity as simply the Great Initiator of the expansion of the universe.[30]

Asked in a newspaper interview about the existence of God shortly after taking up a teaching post in South Australia, Paul Davies replied that the "deeper levels" of the principles involved in the interpretation of the universe must involve what is convenient for people to think of as "God." "I suppose I fall," he said, "more into a modern theologian's camp — or perhaps Thomas Aquinas' — I have a belief in an abstract, timeless God." Davies links human existence with this all-embracing rationality: "I think there must be something behind it

29. Davies, as quoted in Phillip Adams, *The Big Questions* (Ringwood, Victoria: Penguin, 1996), pp. 146-47.
30. John Barrow, *The Origin of the Universe* (London: Weidenfeld & Nicholson, 1994), p. 110.

all, and that human beings are a part of that meaning." He does not identify with the assumption of the founders of modernity's scientific method, that human dimensions and motivations have no place in the understanding of the scientist. The journalist conducting the interview left with the impression that, as far as Davies is concerned, "the more interaction between the arts, religion and science, the better."

It may well be argued that modernity is now coming to the end of an ideological phase which — from a sociopsychological point of view — was necessary for the emergence of a mature critical understanding. As Richard Tarnas puts it, in words which remind us of Voegelin's "differentiation of consciousness," the *participation mystique* which was for so long a dominant expression of humanity's relationship to "nature" had to be "outgrown"; and perhaps that could only be done by its being "disrupted and lost."[31] The immediate consequence, Tarnas writes, was that a

> fundamental sense of separation is . . . structured into the legitimated interpretive principles of the modern mind. It was no accident that the man who first systematically formulated the separate modern self, the rational ego, was also the man who first systematically formulated the mechanistic cosmos of modern science, with its assumption of an independent external world that must be investigated by an autonomous human reason, with its insistence on impersonal mechanistic explanation, its rejection of spiritual qualities

31. Richard Tarnas, "The Transfiguration of the Western Mind," *Cross Currents* (fall 1989): 270. He continues: "Here on both the individual and collective level can be seen the source of the profound dualism of the modern mind: between man and nature, between mind and matter, between self and the other, between experience and reality — that sense of a separate ego irrevocably divided from the encompassing world. Here is the painful separation from the timeless all-encompassing womb of nature, the development of human self-consciousness, the expulsion from the Garden, the disenchantment of the cosmos, the sense of total immersion in an impersonal material world. Here is the compulsive striving to liberate oneself from nature's power, to control and dominate the forces of nature, even to revenge oneself against nature. Here is the primal fear of losing control and dominance, rooted in the all-consuming awareness and fear of death — the inevitable accompaniment of the individual ego's emergence out of the collective matrix. But above all here is the profound sense of ontological and epistemological separation between self and world."

34

in the cosmos, its repudiation of any intrinsic meaning or purpose in nature, its demand for a univocal, literal interpretation of a world of hard facts — all of these ensure the construction of a disenchanted and alienating world view.[32]

Today's task, Tarnas argues, is one of overcoming the alienation which was the immediate price of differentiation.

Jürgen Habermas (1929-   ) is also convinced that the "Enlightenment" was an indispensable development in the history of Western thought. He judges, however, that the time has come to "enlighten the Enlightenment about its narrowness," as he puts it in his essay "An Alternative Way out of the Philosophy of the Subject: Communicative versus Subject-Centered Reason."[33] Habermas argues that Max Weber set up a "false alternative" in his assumption that there is an "opposition between substantive and formal rationality"; he does not accept "that the disenchantment of religious-metaphysical world views robs rationality, along with the contents of tradition, of all substantive connotations and thereby strips it of its power to have a structure-forming influence in the lifeworld beyond the purposive-rational organization of means" (p. 607). If the task of modernity is to be carried forward, this too-narrow post-Cartesian rationality must "drop the somewhat sentimental presupposition of metaphysical homelessness" which has served as the "paradigm of the philosophy of consciousness" — since this paradigm now shows itself to be "exhausted" (p. 591).

As the title of his essay suggests, Habermas understands rationality to be by nature "communicative"; its subject is not a monad of subjective consciousness but the mutuality of a community established by "the intersubjective relationship of individuals who are socialized through communication and reciprocally recognize one another" (p. 602). Instead of narrowly subject-centered understanding, communicative reason gives expression to "a decentered understanding of the world" (p. 606); it is capable of an openness to the "phenomena rediscovered by Romanticism — dreams, fantasies, madness,

32. Tarnas, "Transfiguration," pp. 270-71.
33. P. 596 in the reproduction of this essay in Cahoone, *From Modernism to Postmodernism*. References which follow are to this text.

orgiastic excitement, ecstasy . . . aesthetic body-centered experiences of a decentered subjectivity" (p. 599).

According to Habermas, the ultimate quest for truth is achieved by communicative reason in "a moment of *unconditionality*" which is "built into factual processes of mutual understanding" (p. 612). Though he does not make reference to the notion of ideology in this essay, Habermas is alive to the challenge it poses for critical awareness. In the "communicative" quest for truth, he writes,

> The tense interconnection of the ideal and the real is . . . clearly manifest in discourse itself. Once participants enter into argumentation, they cannot avoid supposing, in a reciprocal way, that the conditions of an ideal speech situation have been sufficiently met. And yet they realize that their discourse is never definitively "purified" of the motives and compulsions that have been filtered out. As little as we can do without the supposition of a purified discourse, we have equally to make do with "unpurified" discourse. (p. 613)

That the time is ripe for the more comprehensive understanding of rationality such as is proposed by Habermas is confirmed by the fact that, quite independently, thinkers from very different backgrounds, whom we are to cite in later chapters, make similar proposals. One of the principal arguments of Robert Bellah and the colleagues who collaborated with him in making a critique of the contemporary culture of the United States — as we shall see — is that this culture will only find a resolution to its emerging problems by the recovery of "an enlarged paradigm of knowledge": "we must critically recover the project of the classical American philosophies," they write, "following them in their willingness to see science as a social process that cannot be divorced from moral learning and imagination without impoverishment of every field."[34]

These thinkers identify with the argument we are to hear from Johann Baptist Metz, that authentic human subjectivity involves a solidarity and is inseparable from "collective memories." These memo-

---

34. Robert N. Bellah, Richard Madsen, William M. Sullivan, Ann Swidler, and Steven M. Tipton, *The Good Society* (New York: Random House, Vintage, 1992), p. 177.

ries, in the judgment of Bellah and companions, give expression to "important, but often barely conscious, patterns of meaning and self-definition."[35]

One of the key themes which will emerge in our discussion is the place of *wisdom* in a wholesome human culture. In an article, "The Debate about Modernity in the North Atlantic World and the Third World," Argentinian thinker Juan Carlos Scannone takes up this theme in words which serve well to summarize what is coming to light in modernity's critical reflection upon its own intellectual project.[36] Having considered sympathetically the suggestion of writers such as Habermas, that "the modern project — as formulated by the Enlightenment — is still unfinished" (p. 81), Scannone concludes:

> reason has to be understood in a broader and more radical way than (the Enlightenment's) critical theory does, and sapiential and symbolic rationality included. . . . Just as the understanding of the ego is relocated in terms of the "we" (the communicating community), so scientific rationality has to be relocated in terms of a . . . sapiential rationality, and analytical, transcendental and/or dialectical concepts in terms of symbols used anew post-critically. (p. 84)[37]

35. Bellah et al., p. 107.

36. Juan Carlos Scannone, "The Debate about Modernity in the North Atlantic World and the Third World," in *The Debate on Modernity,* a volume of *Concilium* 1992/6, ed. Geffre and Jossua (London: SCM, 1992). References which follow are to this text.

37. Scannone makes reference to the place of Paul Ricoeur's "second naivety" in this development. This is a theme we shall take up in a later chapter. It may be noted that Husserl introduced the notion of "naivety" in the text we have quoted — see Cahoone, p. 232 and p. 241: "It will gradually become clearer, and finally be completely clear, that the proper return to the naivete of life — but in a reflection which rises above this naivete — is the only possible way to overcome the philosophical naivete which lies in the (supposedly) 'scientific' character of traditional objectivist philosophy."

CHAPTER 3

The Uncertainties of an Ideology Which Calls Its Own Propositions into Question

THINKERS WHO SET OUT TO INTERPRET THE CUL-ture of modernity and the challenges it faces — from Karl Marx and Max Weber to the contemporaries we shall cite in later chapters — all acknowledge modernity's immense achievements. These achievements have transformed irreversibly the human situation of virtually every inhabitant of our planet: science and technology have brought benefits ranging from the eradication of disease to undreamt-of means of transport and communication; the political ideals of modernity challenge the age-old ways of all the world's traditions; an explosion of artistic and cultural self-expression is reshaping human consciousness. As we saw in the last chapter, our Western tradition's capacity for self-criticism has begun to reassert itself in a recognition of the inadequacy of the "scientific" outlook of early modernity.

Why, however, has this corrective not been able to revive the optimism of a movement which can lay claim to such achievements? Why is our culture experiencing a profound loss of confidence in itself?

The answer to this question is to be found, it will be suggested, in a fuller exploration of the implications of our suggestion that the animating principle of modernity has been a distinctive ideological consensus. But before we pursue this line of thought, we propose to extend our critical analysis by hearing some critical interpreters of modernity who come from very different backgrounds.

Kenneth Clark's thirteen-episode television documentary *Civilisation: A Personal View,*[1] which surveys the development of Western culture with art as its interpretative index, can help us set Western modernity within a larger context. As Clark concludes his immense survey, he is convinced that — despite the momentous developments which have taken place — human beings "haven't changed much in the last two thousand years" (p. 347). Clark points, however, to the peculiar genius of the West we have referred to: "the great, the unique, merit of European civilisation" is that "it has never ceased to develop and change" (p. 74).

If Western culture has always been characterized by development and change, it has known moments of extraordinary creativity. One was in the High Middle Ages, "about the year 1100," when there was "an intensification of existence," an outpouring of "heroic energy, confidence, strength of will and intellect" which, for Clark, is "still visible to us" in the Gothic cathedrals of Europe (p. 35). Another of these moments occurred in the fifteenth-century Renaissance, when "suddenly out of the dark, narrow streets there arose light, sunny arcades with their round arches 'running races in their mirth' under their straight cornices" (p. 89).

By comparison, the cultural developments which have taken place in the modern period tend to have, in Clark's judgment, the character of revolutionary reversals. In the sixteenth-century Protestant Reformation, "for the first time since the great thaw civilised values were questioned and defied" (p. 139). With the passing of time, developments within this new civilization brought disillusionment with the Christian tradition itself: "For almost a thousand years the chief creative force in Western civilisation was Christianity. Then, in about the year 1725, it suddenly declined and in intellectual society practically disappeared" (p. 269).

Clark is uneasy as he contemplates the underlying structures of the culture of modernity. If he makes a positive assessment of the Reformation upheaval, he recognizes that its emphasis upon the word

---

1. Kenneth Clark, *Civilisation: A Personal View* (London: BBC, 1969). References which follow are to this text.

was at the expense of image and symbol: "If civilisation was not to wither, or petrify . . . it had to draw life from deeper roots than those which had nourished the intellectual and artistic triumph of the Renaissance. And ultimately a new civilisation was created — but it was a civilisation not of the image, but of the word" (p. 159).[2]

Clark recognizes that the triumph of reason in modern culture was not without its ambiguity: "the smile of reason (on the face of Voltaire) may seem to betray a certain incomprehension of the deeper human emotions; but it didn't preclude some strongly held beliefs — belief in natural law, belief in justice, belief in tolerance" (p. 245). He acknowledges the paradox of romanticism's powerful influence in a culture which prized reason so highly: "that cluster of ideas and sentiments which surround the words 'romantic' and 'romance'" which "evade definition" (p. 68). He sees the ultimate expression of this movement, "a belief in the divinity of nature," as something which seems "irrational" to us; he acknowledges, nonetheless, that it "has added a great deal to our civilisation" (p. 269).

In the end, however, Clark is overtaken by the somber mood of late modernity. He asks himself, in words which echo those of Weber, whether the world which has been submitted to the control of reason may not now run the danger of becoming "a prison of the spirit," so that European culture is "once more reaching for something beyond its grasp." He sums up the situation of Western culture in this moment of late modernity: "We must leave the trim, finite interiors of eighteenth-century classicism and go to confront the infinite. We have a long, rough voyage ahead of us, and I cannot say where it will end, because it is not over yet. We are still victims of the Fallacies of Hope" of late modernity (p. 293).

If the prospect is bleak, Clark gives expression to the irrepressible spirit which seems to characterize our Western tradition, finding grounds for hope: "when I look at the world about me in the light of this series, I don't feel that we are entering a new period of barbarism. . . . Western civilisation has been a series of rebirths. Surely this should give us confidence in ourselves." He is aware of the metaphysi-

2. On the influence of Protestantism on Western culture, see Richard Tarnas, *The Passion of the Western Mind: Understanding the Ideas That Have Shaped Our World View* (New York: Ballantine, 1993), index under "Protestantism."

cal poverty with which we must undertake this task: "The trouble is that there is still no centre . . . one may be optimistic, but one can't exactly be joyful at the prospect before us" (pp. 346-47).

Clark used the history of art as a mirror in which the achievements and concerns of Western culture may be recognized. Richard Tarnas, whose work *The Passion of the Western Mind* we have already referred to,[3] has followed the history of intellectual development. There is a great deal of correspondence in the views the two arrive at. In particular, both underline the coexistence in modern culture of two mentalities, that of the "scientific revolution" and that inspired by the movement of romanticism.[4]

This split at the heart of Western culture is the principal instance of a fragmentation which seems to have become a feature of the culture of late modernity. In the last chapter Tarnas spoke of "estrangement" and "alienation" as characterizing this culture. He writes that "the cosmological estrangement of modern consciousness initiated by Copernicus and the ontological estrangement initiated by Descartes were completed by the epistemological estrangement initiated by Kant: a threefold mutually enforced prison of modern alienation" (p. 419). Tarnas summarizes the outcome of the "scientific" project initiated by Descartes: "the Scientific Revolution and the Enlightenment" ultimately tended "to undermine the human being's existential situation on virtually every front: metaphysical and cosmological, epistemological, psychological, and finally even biological" (p. 325).

Tarnas places the origin of these alienations in Cartesian assumptions. Descartes saw the human mind as "in some sense fundamentally distinct from the world," and as a consequence he assumed that "the human mind can claim no direct mirrorlike knowledge of the objective world" — human beings know "not the world-in-itself but the world-as-rendered-by-the-human-mind." Tarnas sees Descartes's taking of this position as setting in motion "a train of philosophical events — leading from Locke to Berkeley and Hume and culminating in Kant" — which have given rise to the epistemological problem faced by contemporary Western philosophy (p. 417; cf. pp. 227, 342).

3. References which follow are to this work.
4. Cf. Tarnas, pp. 282-90, for a summary of the "modern" outlook.

With Charles Darwin's theory of evolution, Tarnas points out, the modern mind suffered a further unsettling alienation. This time it was from the previously accepted assumptions of "the world's divine government," of the "special spiritual status" of humanity, and of an "indefinite success" for the human species (p. 327). Sigmund Freud's pioneering work in depth psychology further undermined traditional views concerning the dignity of the human agent, with its "dark, deflating vision" of the unconscious forces influencing human motivation (p. 328).[5] Karl Marx's analysis of the dynamics of human society seemed to go hand in hand with the work of Freud. According to this analysis, the "philosophical, religious and moral values" of a culture are "determined by economic and political factors," and the outlook which has united Western civilization is shown to be essentially "a self-deceiving bourgeois imperialist" ideology (p. 329).

The project of the Enlightenment was imploding. Its very cornerstone, "modern man's optimistic self-estimate," found itself "subject to repeated contradictions and diminution" as the project expanded its intellectual horizons (p. 329). It is not surprising that those seeking to address the existential plight of modern men and women looked to the movement of romanticism for inspiration, or that we find the two cultures of the scientific revolution and romanticism "present in varying proportions in every reflective individual of the modern West"; as Tarnas concludes, "The alienations which have shaped our culture have left the human being a divided animal, inexplicably self-aware in an indifferent universe" (p. 378).

Max Weber, the great sociologist, as we have seen, speaks of the experience of this world of estrangement as a "disillusionment." Eric Voegelin summarizes the outlook of Weber, whom he describes as the framer of "the last of the great positivistic systems." It is an outlook which reflects the beginnings of the somber mood which was to overtake modernity in the course of the twentieth century:

In Weber's execution of the plan, however, there can be sensed a new tone. The evolution of mankind toward the rationality of posi-

---

5. As Tarnas points out, Freud's interpretation of human consciousness tended to undermine what was central to the Enlightenment project itself: its exaltation of human reason.

tive science was for Comte a distinctly progressive development; for Weber it was a process of disenchantment *(Entzauberung)* and dedivinisation *(Entgottlichung)* of the world. By the overtones of his regret that divine enchantment had seeped out of the world, by his resignation to rationalism as a fate to be borne but not desired, by the occasional complaint that his soul was not attuned to the divine *(religios unmusikalisch),* he rather betrayed his brotherhood in the sufferings of Nietzsche — though, in spite of his confession, his soul was sufficiently attuned to the divine not to follow Nietzsche into his tragic revolt. He knew what he wanted but somehow could not break through to it. He saw the promised land but was not permitted to enter it.[6]

Tarnas sums up Weber's often-quoted evaluation of the effects of the Enlightenment as the creation of "an iron cage of bureaucratic rationality that permeates every aspect of modern existence," citing Weber's own words:

> No one knows who will live in this cage in the future, or whether at the end of this tremendous development entirely new prophets will arise, or there will be a great rebirth of old ideas and ideals, or if neither, mechanized petrification, embellished with a sort of convulsive self-importance. For the last stage of this cultural development, it might well be said: "Specialists without spirit, sensualists without heart; this nullity imagines that it has attained a level of civilisation never before achieved." (Tarnas, p. 412)

As Tarnas eloquently points out, the creative arts of Western modernity reflect a situation not unlike that which Weber foretold, manifesting itself in "despair, or self-annihilating defiance," or in "fragmentation, dislocation, and self-parody," whose only truths are "those of irony and dark paradox," to be brought to light in "the absurd and surreal." As a consequence, the "traditional artistic canon" of Western civilization has begun to dissolve, and the lack of consensus concerning the nature of reality and truth has produced a situa-

---

6. Eric Voegelin, *The New Science of Politics* (Chicago: University of Chicago Press, 1960), p. 22.

tion in which "artists became realists of a new reality — or an ever-growing multiplicity of realities — lacking any precedent" — "meaning seemed to be no more than an arbitrary construct, truth only a convention, reality undiscoverable," and "man," it has begun to be said, is no more than "a futile passion" (pp. 390-93).

The tragic irony of this outcome becomes apparent, Tarnas continues, when one considers its antecedents. Humanity had taken up the project of the modern era with "a near boundless confidence" in its "powers," in its "spiritual potential," in its "capacity for certain knowledge," in its "mastery over nature," in its confidence concerning its "progressive destiny." In the end the outcome was "a debilitating sense of metaphysical insignificance and personal futility, spiritual loss of faith, uncertainty in knowledge, a mutually destructive relationship with nature, and an intense insecurity concerning the human future"; Bacon and Descartes had been succeeded by Kafka and Beckett (pp. 393-94).[7]

If the ideological consensus which has emerged in our late modern period has a defining characteristic, it may well be a despair of finding a unified meaning in reality. To quote Tarnas again:

> The underlying intellectual ethos is one of disassembling established structures, deflating pretensions, exploding beliefs, unmasking appearances — a "hermeneutics of suspicion" in the spirit of Marx, Nietzsche, and Freud. Postmodernism in this sense is "an antinomian movement that assumes a vast unmaking in the Western mind . . . deconstruction, decentering, disappearance, dissemination, demystification, discontinuity, *difference*, fragments or fractures, and a corresponding ideological commitment to minorities in politics, sex, and language. To think well, to feel well, to act well, to read well, according to the *episteme* of unmaking, is to refuse the tyranny of wholes; totalisation in any human endeavour is potentially totalitarian" (Ihab Hassan). The pretence of any form of omniscience — philosophical, religious, scientific — must be aban-

7. See Tarnas, pp. 395-96, "The Postmodern Mind," and pp. 398-402 on "deconstructionism." Charles Taylor discusses this latter development (*Sources of the Self: The Making of the Modern Identity* [Cambridge: Cambridge University Press, 1992], pp. 487-90).

doned. Grand theories and universal overviews cannot be sustained without producing empirical falsification and intellectual authoritarianism. To assert general truths is to impose a spurious dogma on the chaos of phenomena. Respect for contingency and discontinuity limits knowledge to the local and specific. Any alleged comprehensive, coherent outlook is at best no more than a temporarily useful fiction masking chaos, at worst an oppressive fiction masking relationships of power, violence, and subordination. (p. 401)[8]

Charles Taylor is an original thinker who has avoided identifying himself with any particular philosophical tradition. His evaluation of modernity — in which, by following a quite different path, he arrives at conclusions similar to those of Tarnas — contributes to our understanding of contemporary Western culture. Taylor's immediate concern, in his *Sources of the Self: The Making of the Modern Identity,*[9] is an evaluation of modernity's account of the moral dimension of human experience. He argues that modern ethical theory is unable to provide a satisfactory rationale for this experience. And behind this failure he detects unresolved issues which remind us of the discussion of the previous chapter.

Taylor judges the intellectual climate of modernity to have "layers of suppression" which obscure something we take for granted in our daily "moral life and thinking." This suppression — which reminds us of the dynamisms characteristic of an ideological movement — makes his task, he judges, an "uphill fight" (p. 90), as he seeks to construe his "phenomenology" of moral experience. He finds that this experience is grounded in moral "intuitions" (such as "respect for the life, integrity and well-being, even flourishing of others") which "stand independent" of our actions, as the "standard" against which these actions are evaluated (p. 4). This phenomenological description recognizes a "strong evaluation" (p. 4) given to "hypergoods" which involve independent standards, commanding "awe, respect and admiration" (p. 20), and establishing the very roots of one's

8. Reference has already been made to Ernest Gellner's trenchant criticism of this "postmodernity" outlook in *Postmodernism, Reason, and Religion* (London: Routledge, 1992).

9. References which follow are to this text.

"being as a person," standing "incomparably above other life goods," and providing the measure according to which "these must be weighed, judged, decided upon" (p. 63). Taylor's phenomenological exploration leads him to conclude "that living with such strongly qualified horizons is constitutive of human agency, that stepping outside these limits would be tantamount to stepping outside what we would recognise as integral, that is undamaged human personhood" (p. 27).

Taylor links the modern sense of "identity" with the findings of his phenomenological analysis: identity is "defined" by "strongly valued preference." The lack of this produces the "disorienting lack" which constitutes an "identity crisis": in the individual, social group, or culture. The personal disorientation which results can be so complete that one sees oneself as having to "invent the questions as well as the answers" fundamental to personhood (p. 30).

According to Taylor, ethical theory of modernity shows itself incapable of rendering a satisfactory account of the experience he has described. His analysis brings to light ambiguities and inconsistencies underlying the complexities of modern culture, leading him to criticize modern ethical theory on two levels. In the first place, he looks at a group of acknowledged theoretical positions which he finds incapable, in principle, of rendering a satisfactory account of moral experience. And secondly, he considers the hidden assumptions and motivations which are often at work in the modern thinker's taking of a position, and which, ironically, are ultimately incompatible with that position.

Taylor criticizes two theoretical positions explicitly espoused by modern ethical theory — "naturalism" and "classical utilitarianism." *Naturalism* directly denies any meaningfulness to the essentials of his "phenomenology" of moral experience — its "ontology of the human" (p. 5) and its "qualitative" differences (p. 19) — by a *reductionism* which would ultimately assign these essentials to some category outside the moral order (such as pleasure seeking or utility) (cf. pp. 22, 5, 19, 25, 26, etc.). Classical *utilitarianism* (pp. 22-24, etc.) proposes a rationale which seeks to vindicate the "naturalist" position, rejecting "all qualitative distinctions . . . to construe all human goals as on the same footing, susceptible of common qualification and calculation according to some common 'currency'" (pp. 22-23).

The link with the "scientific" procedures which modernity has adopted, in opposition to the Aristotelian tradition, is evident enough. In fact, Taylor directly challenges modern thought's *distrust of goods and values,* and hence of the qualitative distinctions which are fundamental to his argument (pp. 53-56). He sees these positions as influenced by the assumption that the quantitative methodology of modern science provides the normative model of all critical understanding.

Taylor also points to the hidden metaphysical assumptions which make it impossible for modern ethical theory to give a satisfactory account of personal experience. He often refers to *epistemological problems* as exerting a great influence and leading to a "suppression of moral ontology among our contemporaries" (p. 10). Taylor makes a distinction, as we have seen, between what he calls "procedural reason" and what he calls "substantive reason" (pp. 85-86): the post-Cartesian thought of modernity concerns itself with "procedural reason," whereas the moral philosophers of antiquity and the medieval period took for granted that their explanations must be grounded in "substantive reason."

This assumption — so important in the ideology of modernity — Taylor links with *the model of natural science* which, by reason of its great "success," has dominated Western thought since the seventeenth century (p. 5). This Enlightenment norm of "disengaged reason" has produced "the ideal of the disengaged self, capable of objectifying not only the surrounding world but also" the human subject's "own emotions and inclinations, fears and compulsions, and achieving thereby a kind of distance and self-possession which allows" the subject "to act 'rationally'" (p. 21). Taylor relates this outlook to the "great revolution" in natural science of the seventeenth century, which involves the judgment that Aristotelian presuppositions should be abandoned and "we should cease trying to explain the world around us in subjective, anthropocentric, or 'secondary' properties" (p. 34). Taylor reminds us of Weber as he describes this stance of disinterested reason:

> the disengaged agent has taken a once-for-all stance in favour of objectification; he has broken with religion, superstition, resisted the blandishments of those pleasing and flattering world-views

47

which hide the austere reality of the human condition in a disenchanted universe. He has taken up the scientific attitude. The direction of his life is set, however little mastery he may have actually
achieved. And this is a source of deep satisfaction and pride to him.
(p. 46)

Taylor cites Iris Murdoch's ironic description of a "recognisable and
familiar" modern who, "confronted even with Christ[,] turns away
to consider the judgment of his own conscience and to hear the
voice of his own reason. Stripped of the exiguous metaphysical
background which Kant was prepared to allow him, this man is with
us still, free, independent, lonely, powerful, rational, responsible,
brave, the hero of so many novels and books of moral philosophy"
(p. 84).

Modernity's assumptions concerning the nature of a critical, or
"objective," investigation of reality, Taylor points out, are really a
"begging of the question" (when they are applied to an inquiry into
the meaning of the human situation). Such a rationale can never
"make sense" of human existence; at best it can come up with "some
theoretical language which purports to explain behaviour from the
observer's standpoint but is of no use to the agent in making sense of
his own thinking, feeling and action. . . . We cannot just leap outside
of these terms (such as 'freedom' and 'dignity') altogether, on the
grounds that their logic doesn't fit some model of 'science.' This begs
the question. How can we ever know that humans can be explained by
any scientific theory *until* we actually explain how they live their lives
in its terms?" (pp. 57-58).

In the end, Taylor skillfully turns the "scientific" model against
those who appeal to it to exclude the qualitative:

This (position I am advocating) is the complement to the anti-
Aristotelian purge of natural science in the seventeenth century.
Just as physical science is no longer anthropocentric, so human science can no longer be couched in the terms of physics. Our value
terms purport to give us insight into what it is to live in the universe
as a human being, and this is a quite different matter from that
which physical science claims to reveal and explain. This reality is,
of course, dependent on us, in the sense that a condition for its exis-

tence is our existence. But once granted that we exist, it is no more a subjective projection than what physics deals with. (p. 59)[10]

Taylor echoes Weber when he speaks of a "disenchantment" of modern consciousness, which makes modernity distrustful of the foundations which sustain the "moral ontology" and "frameworks" essential to any satisfactory account of the human condition. This disenchantment, in Taylor's judgment, has far-reaching consequences, leading to "the dissipation of our sense of the cosmos as a meaningful order," a development which "has allegedly destroyed the horizons in which people previously lived their spiritual lives" (p. 17). In this context, he recalls Nietzsche's parable of the madman who proclaimed "the death of God." Citing the words "How could we drink up the sea? Who gave us the sponge to wipe away the whole horizon?" he comments, "the loss of horizon described by Nietzsche's fool undoubtedly corresponds to something very widely felt in our culture" (p. 17), so that there arises for us "the problem of meaning" (p. 26).

Though his criticism of modernity is hard-hitting, Taylor's objective is ultimately conciliatory, and he seeks to make a positive contribution to modernity's struggle to give expression to the truth of human existence and to carry forward the project of the Enlightenment. He argues that, despite their disclaimers, modern ethical theories are motivated in fact by such qualitatively higher goods as "freedom," "a suspicion of strong goods" (as implying an elitism which is inimical to personal well-being), and a "stress on practical benevolence" (p. 84). He therefore sees the moral theories of modernity as strangely inconsistent, and as alienating modern culture from the very sources of its authenticity:

> It seems that they are motivated by the strongest moral ideals, such as freedom, altruism, and universalism. These are among the central moral aspirations of modern culture, the hypergoods which are distinctive to it. And yet what these ideals drive the theorists to-

10. Cf. Tarnas, p. 274, on Francis Bacon's reaction to an anthropomorphizing of reality in the originating moment of modern "scientific" theory, to which Taylor is referring.

wards is a denial of all such goods. They are caught in a strange pragmatic contradiction, whereby the very goods which move them push them to deny or denature all such goods. They are constitutionally incapable of coming clean about the deeper sources of their own thinking. (p. 88; cf. p. 95)

Taylor wants to clear up this inconsistency in order to defend what is assumed in "the great unsaid that underlies widespread attitudes in our civilisation" (p. 104).

*   *   *

The culture of late modernity has entered a phase of uncertainty and fragmentation. What we have seen to this point increases our understanding of the nature of this crisis. Modernity's project of providing a shared way of life which left behind the undeniable shortcomings of medievalism was both wholesome and necessary. The fact that such a movement could only be carried forward by the formation of an ideological consensus meant that it must face the hazards of this sociological process. In fact, those who shaped the ideology which emerged made the miscalculation of adopting a methodology which was too narrow for their ambitious plan to be immediately successful. The dynamics characteristic of ideology formation — particularly reluctance to abandon securities which have been achieved by cultural consensus — help us understand something of the difficulty modernity experiences in making the necessary adjustments to the methodological assumptions of its formative period.

　　More, however, needs to be explained. Throughout its history, our cultural tradition has given itself to an unending quest for existential truth. It was this critical spirit which inspired the project of modernity itself. In the latter part of this century, in this same spirit, leading thinkers have undertaken a critical review of the assumptions of modernity's "scientific" methodology. These reactions seem powerless, however, to reverse our cultural tradition's slide toward a mood bordering on nihilism. To understand this paradoxical situation, we must take a closer look at the essential propositions of the specific ideology which have animated the project of modernity.

　　Charles Taylor gives us a clue as to the peculiar difficulty the ideology of modernity must overcome when he points to the contradiction at work at the heart of modern ethical theory: though those who elaborate this theory are in fact motivated by the highest moral values, the theory itself robs these values of any sustainable validity. Taylor's instance is in fact a particular instance of a problem which confronts the ideological consensus of modernity as a whole *by reason of its key proposition.*

The ideology of modernity is essentially a reactionary movement. In response to the shortcomings of the intellectual climate of late medievalism, this movement established *accountability* as its essential proposition: the proper autonomy of our human existence demands that all propositions laying claim to an authority to shape the life of our cultural tradition must give a critical account of themselves before the bar of a shared understanding. Notwithstanding the opposition it has experienced from the ideologies of the status quo, this proposition is unexceptionable. It is the expression of the true genius of the cultural heritage of the West; it should be seen as irreversible. But this proposition will inevitably find itself lost in a vicious, self-destructive circle if it does not refer to a warrant which lies beyond the ideological order. Called to account, an ideological consensus, by reason of the motivations of group self-interest and group securities which are essential to its effectiveness, will always be found open to criticism. The ideology of modernity, calling *all* positions to critically validate themselves, inevitably finds itself "hoisted with its own petard" unless it acknowledges a measure which is not essentially ideological.

Looking back over our inquiry to this point, we may well recognize that those discussing the problems of modernity have pointed to this issue.

Voegelin is raising it when he observes that modernity, in rejecting any claim to "represent" any identifiable order of truth, was left with the arbitrary instability of an immanentized "gnosis." As we have pointed out, his evaluation of modernity would have been more positive if he had introduced the dimension of ideology to his analysis. (Voegelin must concede that the immanentizing of norms demands by an authentic human autonomy is not incompatible with an objective grounding of such norms — proper distinctions being made. Moreover, the proposition championed by an ideology does not nec-

51

essarily lose its objective validity by the fact that it is presented through the medium of an ideological consensus.) But Voegelin's essential criticism stands: an ideology will find itself in a self-destructive circle if it cannot ground the validity of its operative propositions beyond the ideological order. An ideology is critically acceptable only if it enters into the dialectic established by a reflective awareness of its inherent limitations.

Jürgen Habermas recognizes the need for such a dialectic when he interprets the goal of "communicative reason" as the "moment of unconditionality." For Bernard Lonergan, the "asking of questions" — which is the soul of any intellectual inquiry — is governed by the implications of the same dialectic: "in the world mediated by meaning and motivated by value, objectivity is simply the consequence of authentic subjectivity, of genuine attention, genuine intelligence, genuine reasonableness, genuine responsibility."[11] When Edmund Husserl pointed to the indispensable nature of the distinction made by the "perennial philosophy," between *episteme* (critically measured knowledge) and *doxa* (mere opinion), and expressed a concern that, in the culture of modernity, all intellectual positions are in danger of degenerating into *doxa,* he was naming this issue as central to the problems faced by the thought of modernity.

The fact that the authorities who have shaped the intellectual life of late modernity are known as the "masters of suspicion" echoes the logic of the argument we are making. Is this not illustrated by the fact that the points of view which assume a basis in objective truth, described as "meta-narratives," are seen by "postmodernism" as having as their essential function the maintaining of the ideology of some "closed" system?

As we have already noted, that remarkable nineteenth-century thinker John Henry Newman pointed to the unfortunate consequences for a cultural tradition that made the "methodological doubt" of Descartes the normative model of intellectual inquiry. His suggestion that a properly conceived "methodological assumption" would be a more fruitful starting point probably sounded too much like a return to the outlook of the Middle Ages to be appreciated by

11. Bernard Lonergan, *Method in Theology* (London: Darton, Longman & Todd, 1972), p. 265.

the ideology of modernity. More recently, however, Robert Bellah and the authors of *The Good Society* have suggested a more conciliatory form of the proposal Newman had in mind:

> We are not likely to give up what some philosophers call the hermeneutics of suspicion — the tendency in the West since the Enlightenment to call all received traditions into question. But without a hermeneutics of recovery, through which we can understand what a living tradition is in the first place, a hermeneutics of suspicion is apt to be an exercise in nihilism, which, far from liberating students, merely disorients them.[12]

When Richard Tarnas's inquiry leads to the judgment that "the contemporary intellectual milieu" of the West "is riddled with tension, irresolution, and perplexity" and links this situation with the contrast which exists between the "unprecedented wealth of perspectives" available to us and the lack of a "consensus in the nature of reality," and Charles Taylor argues that "procedural" reason is not enough to give us a satisfactory account of moral responsibility, they are raising the issue we are discussing. Kenneth Clark expresses in more simple terms the problem of modernity as it lives under the thrall of an ideology which lacks the register against which its propositions must be measured: "The trouble is that there is still no centre."

In other words, our Western tradition stands at a turning point; we face the alternative so clearly formulated by Nietzsche, between identifying a measure which lies beyond the ideological order or accepting an ultimate responsibility for defining the order which rules human existence. As the twentieth century has progressed, the instability and self-doubt at the heart of our cultural tradition have produced what Tarnas has described as "a pervasive spiritual crisis";[13] the philosophical movement of "existentialism" emerged as a reminder that modernity had left the Western tradition uncertain before the most fundamental human questions: suffering and death, freedom

---

12. Robert N. Bellah, Richard Madsen, William M. Sullivan, Ann Swidler, and Steven M. Tipton, *The Good Society* (New York: Random House, Vintage, 1992), p. 174.

13. Tarnas, p. 389.

and guilt, humanity's boundless aspirations and spiritual powerlessness. Nietzsche's call to accept the responsibilities arising from the "death of God" made him the prophet of dramatically contradictory movements: a despairing nihilism on the one hand, and a utopianism founded on the totalitarian exercise of political power on the other.

*　　*　　*

It must be acknowledged that the "deconstruction" of false systems of totalization, and of the false absolutes their ideologies are tempted to produce, is a concern of unquestionable validity if we are to carry forward the essential project of modernity. Having become aware of the ideologies which promote these false absolutes, however, our response should not be a despair which settles for a human existence knowing no ultimate values and standards, but a radical reevaluation of the assumptions upon which the intellectual project of modernity was founded — in the spirit of Edmund Husserl, Jürgen Habermas, and Bernard Lonergan.

In his *Theology and the Dialectics of History,*[14] Robert Doran, a disciple of Bernard Lonergan, argues that the threshold upon which modernity now finds itself confronts us with an option. On the one hand, our Western tradition may choose "deconstructive normlessness" (p. 5), with the "death of God" leading to "the loss of self, the end of history, and, for some, the closure of the book . . . a fated acceptance of absurdity as the final word . . . the celebration of the derisory, the cynical, the senseless . . . the ultimate upshot of a longer cycle of decline: the end of . . . creative world-constitutive responsibility as historical agency" (pp. 461-64). On the other hand, one may recognize that it is possible to respond to the crisis faced by the outlook of late modernity by opting, not for "the dissolution of the subject," but for "the self-appropriation of the subject" by the rediscovery together of "norms of human genuineness that fully respect modern insights into historicity" (pp. 6, 461).

If the analysis we have proposed is sound, it may well imply that today's talk of "the end of modernity" and of a new culture of "post-

14. Robert Doran, *Theology and the Dialectics of History* (Toronto: University Press, 1990). References which follow are to this text.

54

modernism" is an evasion of the real issue. Should we not recognize, with Habermas, that the essential task of modernity and the Enlightenment is still to be completed?

Reactionary movements which change the shape of history normally have, as might be expected, two phases. In the first phase, reaction to the status quo is of necessity excessive and heavily ideological, as it achieves a general acceptance of the change of consciousness which is called for. In a second phase, the excesses of the first phase are critically recognized and corrected. The crisis modernity now faces may well be interpreted as signaling the end of the first phase of modernity as a revolutionary cultural movement, heavily ideological in its cognitive content. At the same time, this crisis constitutes an invitation to embark upon the second phase of modernity as a reactionary movement. The Enlightenment's demand that *all* claims of truth and wisdom be weighed before the bar of human reason's "scientific" spirit was itself unreasonable, in that it failed to be sufficiently open to the full range of sapiential and existential truth. Modernity's first phase must now be followed by a phase in which its undoubted achievements are balanced by cultural elements neglected by the ideology of the reactionary phase.

Today the mood of our Western tradition is feeling its way toward a more balanced frame of mind. The chapters which follow, it is hoped, will make it clear that our Western tradition possesses the resources necessary to resolve the problems it faces.

CHAPTER 4

Some Contemporary Reactions to Modernity

(Historian, J. M. Roberts;
Philosopher, Alasdair MacIntyre;
Economists, Paul Ormerod and Robert Heilbroner;
Statesman, Václav Havel;
Theologian, Johann Baptist Metz)

IN THE PREVIOUS CHAPTERS, THE OVERVIEWS OF RICH-
ard Tarnas, Kenneth Clark, and Charles Taylor have helped us to situate the project of modernity. Let us now consider some other representative reactions to the situation of the modern Western world. Our
discussion to this point provides a frame of reference within which to
weigh what these thinkers have to say. At the same time, their various
points of view remind us of the rich manifold of human experience
which the narrowness of modernity's "scientific" spirit has tended to
neglect.

In a television series and text, published under the title *The Triumph of the West*,[1] J. M. Roberts, a leading English historian, provides
an overview of history rich in interpretative reflection and insight as
he seeks to answer the question implied in his title. The Western cultural tradition has exerted an influence which has irreversibly
changed the existence of virtually every human being on the planet;
how is this unprecedented influence of our culture upon the other
cultures to be explained? Since this development has taken place during the modern period of Western history, what Roberts has to say of-

---

1. References which follow are to J. M. Roberts, *The Triumph of the West*
(London: BBC, 1985).

56

ten implies an interpretation and evaluation of the culture of modernity.

This text is also relevant to our inquiry in that it exemplifies one of the great achievements of modernity, of fundamental importance to the critical spirit it values so highly: the development of a mature historical awareness. This awareness acknowledges the immense number of factors which give rise to the ambiguities to be encountered in any portrayal of the events of the past; it also recognizes the many factors which limit the possibility of adequate interpretation on the part of an observer far removed both temporally and culturally from those events.

Because human existence has an irreducibly historical character, this awareness raises the question of the validity of an ahistorical understanding of human nature. If such an understanding has any validity, it must be recognized that this validity is severely qualified. The text of *The Triumph of the West,* in fact, exemplifies the struggle of modern Western thought to come to terms with the full implications of this historical awareness. Roberts clearly intends to avoid identifying himself with any of the multitude of theoretical positions which come to light in the history he is portraying. He warns the reader against a false absolutizing of notions familiar in our cultural tradition: "the very idea of civilisation is a European idea" (p. 37); "Africa is a Western idea" (p. 38); in large part "the world exists in the minds of men" (p. 188); "the West first invented modern politics" (p. 278); such ideas as "the imperative of equality . . . arose solely in the secular, progressive culture of modern Europe" and are difficult to harmonize "with the ethical precepts of other civilisations" (p. 295).

But does this mean that, for Roberts, there exists no measure against which the changing realities of history can be understood? Our study has already made it clear that modernity has no clear answer to this question. In fact, many thinkers in the Western tradition would be drawn toward a form of "historicism,"[2] seeing such notions as "human nature" as only having a critically acceptable meaningfulness *through some philosophical interpretation of the genesis of historical knowledge.*

The reader of Roberts's text is left with the impression that he

2. Cf. *Cambridge Dictionary of Philosophy,* ed. Audi, s.v. "historicism."

inclines to such a view. Explaining his statement that civilization is "a European idea," he describes this idea as "a cultural artefact which helps to illuminate our data — though on the basis of certain European assumptions" (p. 37). In the concluding pages of his study, however, after reviewing the many ideas and standards which the West has given to the broader world, he is hesitant, writing: "This does not imply any intrinsic merit, even if that seems likely to be part of the story" (p. 413).

Roberts finds that the Judeo-Christian tradition has played an all-important part in the development of our Western culture. "The church," he writes, "was a major instrument both in the forging of Europe and in the alchemy which produced its civilisation" (p. 84). The master ideas which recur time and again in his telling of the story of our cultural tradition, as the sources of its remarkable energies and influence, have their original inspiration in the Judeo-Christian tradition: "certain central, very important elements in western civilisation" have a religious inspiration, "above all the non-rational faith that life should be directed by overriding transcendental values which legitimise goals in the here and now" (p. 288). Western culture inherited from the Jewish traditions the self-awareness of a people with a destiny, an awareness which has "generated a nagging sense of inadequacy which has often stirred up western thought and stopped it from settling down into immobility" (p. 56; cf. pp. 76, 225). Roberts places the roots of the West's attitude to the value and dignity of the individual human being in the same Judeo-Christian tradition: from the medieval culture "the world was to inherit a certain idea of the individual as a creature of potentially limitless spiritual value" (p. 116). This tradition is grounded in "the inherently individualist message of the Gospels" (p. 109) and in "the transcendent principle" contained in Christianity (p. 76). Roberts judges that "the moral imperative of equality" finds its antecedents in Christian thought (p. 295), as does the all-important sense of direction in the movement of history: Western civilization's energizing "sense of direction and purpose" and its "confidence in its destiny as a chosen vessel" have their origins in Christianity (p. 248).

Roberts's description of our culture points in other ways to the openness of human existence to a religious dimension. He sees some of the most influential movements of modernity as taking the place of the Christian faith of earlier ages: "science" becomes in the nineteenth century a "popular faith" engendering "almost boundless enthusiasm" (pp. 246-47); our tradition has given itself to an "idolisation of nationalism" (p. 292); "nationalism and socialism" have great influence as "secular creeds" (p. 288; cf. p. 295); Marxism is seen as "essentially a Christian heresy" (p. 79).

Roberts frequently uses the term "myth" to describe influential movements in cultural traditions: civilizations create their peculiar myths (pp. 46, 47, 49); "democracy," "nationalism," "human rights," and "progress" are all described as "myths" (pp. 38, 280, 294, 425). Other cultures are tempted to adopt "the mythologies of the West, whether Christian, Marxist, or merely vaguely materially progressive" (p. 403). This choice of terms, we may well assume, implies a significance which is nourished by the author's historical awareness, and goes far beyond the superficial meaning of the term in popular usage: while Roberts's evident sympathy with the presuppositions of historicism preclude any philosophical judgments concerning the openness of human nature to the transcendent, he clearly portrays human experience as typically acknowledging a relationship to something akin to the *numinous,* even if it is disguised in the secular forms of modernity. In the opening pages of his text, in fact, he links "faith and myth" in the great influence they have upon our human history: "faiths and myths profoundly divide and differentiate human beings" (p. 16).

This historical study provides us with valuable material toward a critical assessment of modernity. It makes us aware of the great achievements which have made the West so influential in the contemporary world. But it also considers the fact that "a great dream has faded," and that to many in the West "their civilisation appears to have gone wrong" (p. 367). In this time of questioning and uncertainty, Roberts's survey helps us to understand the foundations upon which the achievements of the West were established and to reflect upon their durability.

The achievements of the modern Western world are immense. Roberts's pages provide countless examples. Some are obvious and tangible: "Western technology is now the property of the entire human race" (p. 262). The affordable consumer goods it has produced enable our contemporaries to "take the idea of abundance for granted" (p. 263). Scientific advances have made "effective medicine" available to all and have brought a dramatic "decline in infectious diseases" (pp. 276-77).

But behind these very tangible contributions to human welfare are others less easy to define. Roberts judges that history must pronounce Western civilization the "champion of humanity" (p. 431); its "humanitarianism" (p. 254) has engendered "gentler standards of behaviour towards the weak, the ideal of a more objective justice, the intellectual rigour of science" (p. 430), and the championing of "fundamental rights" (p. 287; cf. p. 76).

The political ideas of the West have had and continue to have a profound influence upon all the cultural traditions of the world: "the West first invented modern politics and then exported them to the rest of the world" (p. 278) — "a way of managing collective affairs so that different interests could be given a hand in them without falling into violent conflict . . . some kind of forum or marketplace for arguing and bargaining," and agreement "that there is an area of collective activities," "that there exists a public good which is more than a mere summary of individuals' appetites" (p. 279; cf. p. 285). These political processes have provided a "new ideology of Revolution," making possible a process of peaceful change, in which the issue is no longer, as it was in the Middle Ages, one of entitlement and privilege according to antecedent "law and tradition," but the "single central issue" of changing the conditions of humanity for the better (p. 285).

As we have seen, Roberts makes clear the background and development of the master ideas deep in our cultural tradition which have inspired and sustained these achievements. Three of these stand out: an immensely productive scientific methodology, the sense of change and direction as essential to human existence, and the recognition of the dignity and value of the individual. Let us consider each of these in turn, insofar as they can help us toward a critical assessment of modernity.

Roberts judges modernity's "intellectual rigour of science" as one of its greatest gifts to the world at large. Although his account of the emergence of this "scientific" approach reminds us of much that has already come to light in our discussion, we will not be surprised to find that he unconsciously reflects attitudes typical of modernity.

He recognizes the continuing effect of the achievement of the

Greeks, singling out the Greek "ideal of excellence" as giving rise to a legacy which "has been renewed time and time again" in the history of the West: "we are constantly rediscovering it, reinterpreting it, and reusing it" (p. 53). The scientific methodology of Western modernity was established upon the basis of another Greek conviction, that "the world is essentially rational and explicable" (p. 242). Roberts acknowledges that "natural science" was "virtually founded" in the sixth-century B.C. "beginning of Greek rationalism" (p. 53). He makes no reference, however, to the founders of modernity making no attempt to enter into dialogue with the intellectual achievements of the previous two thousand years of our Western tradition. The intellectual life of the medievals, in fact, is comprehensively dismissed as "bemused awe" in the presence of "God's mysterious ways" (p. 241). And he leaves us with the impression that he sees the establishing of a "precise line of demarcation between the scientist and the philosopher" as a liberating advance which brought the intelligibility of the world to light almost for the first time (p. 242).

Roberts's description of Isaac Newton as the embodiment of modernity's new scientific approach, giving "grounds for hope that the mysteries of nature could, given time, all be explained, because they must be manifestations not of incomprehensible, arbitrary will, but of ordered, regular principles" (pp. 242-43), may well sum up the ideological stance of the Enlightenment and its reaction against the nominalism and voluntarism of the late Middle Ages, but it is scarcely just in what it implies concerning the best intellectual tradition of the West prior to the modern period.

Roberts's instinct as a gifted historian, however, makes him aware of the ambiguities of modernity's scientific project. He can speak with a late twentieth-century irony of Francis Bacon's vision of this project as "nothing less than the redemption of mankind from the consequences of Adam's fall" (p. 241). In the same tone he quotes "an English scientist in the 1660s" as declaring: "The management of this great machine of the world can be explained only by the experimental and mechanical philosopher" (p. 242).

Roberts reflects today's disillusionment in the concluding pages of his work, speaking of the "intellectual hegemony of Western science, buttressed by its sheer size and scale," making it today "a major religion, perhaps *the* religion of our civilisation, for most men and women one of the few remaining unquestioned verities." He calls into question the widespread "assumption that its ends are good" and speaks ironically of the way the spokesmen of "science" have tended to assume the role of a kind of "new priesthood" (pp. 417-18). "It would be bitter to have to concede," he reflects, "that the manipulation of man as a part of nature was the logical end of the western dream" (p. 418).

Romanticism, we have suggested, may be seen as a reaction against the inability of modernity's "scientific" approach to address the deepest concerns of human existence. There can be little doubt that some of the greatest achievements of modernity have come from this movement, in particular the resources of self-awareness and self-expression it has brought to light in Western culture. It is surprising that Roberts has little to say of this movement. He notes that Rousseau "foreshadows that profound welling up of human energies and creativity which we call Romanticism" (p. 253), but he gives little attention to the degree to which the influence of our Western culture upon the other cultural traditions of the world is indebted to this movement. It may well be argued that artistic self-expression promoted by this movement has been an important vehicle for humanitarian and social ideas of the West — through the communications explosion at present taking place.

Roberts links the achievement of the technology which was the outcome of modernity's scientific rigor with the remarkable fact that Western civilization has "proved more enterprising, adaptable and confident than any other" (p. 262). His discussion of our Western tradition's attitude to change is one of the most telling and enlightening themes of his study. He contrasts it with other cultural traditions and their tendency toward a stagnation from which the West has aroused them: "European civilisation was the first to escape the age-old fatalism" which has tended to characterize the cultural traditions of humanity (p. 414; cf. p. 317). In the last analysis, Roberts judges that "the essence of what was done by Western civilisation" has been "the implanting of the idea that willed change was possible" (p. 431). It is not surprising that the ideological mood engendered by this recognition is one of *liberation* — making "emancipation" one of the most powerful themes in the ideology of modernity. As we shall see, Alasdair MacIntyre and J. B. Metz also point to the importance of this theme.

The "enterprising, adaptable and confident" mood of our cultural tradition has engendered a momentum which is contagious. This mood has been associated with a sense of "immense adaptability" and a sense "that change was progressive and marked the way history was going" (p. 262). The Western tradition's "seemingly unique powers of continuous self-transformation" (p. 233) have energized its great achievements and produced the "prestigious, progressive stream of ideas" (p. 296; cf. p. 345) which have changed the world.

This Western movement of self-transformation has been inspired by a remarkable, if paradoxical, optimism: "the Western world seems perversely to remain optimistic on one subject on which there may be less ground for optimism than any other: the innate improvability of man" (p. 425). In the end Roberts finds it impossible to shake off this optimism, even if he expresses himself in measured terms: "There is no unquestionable ground for thinking that mankind is in a dead-end, or that the creativity it has derived from Western civilisation has been eclipsed. Both may be confronting no more than the end of their beginnings" (p. 431). His words remind us of the similar verdict made by Kenneth Clark.

The question of how the unique dynamism at the heart of our Western culture is to be accounted for is constantly in the background of Roberts's discussion. Could it be, he asks, that the boundless expectations which have inspired this project are "unsatisfiable in principle" (p. 425)? Though he does not make the connection, romanticism, as we have suggested, may well be interpreted as a reaction of frustration against the existential impasse set up by the Enlightenment's "scientific" assumptions. Roberts acknowledges that the West's powers of continuous innovation have antecedents which "can be discerned a long way back" (p. 233). He does not claim, however, to be capable of deciphering them fully: if these roots must be recognized as "owing much to the Judeo-Christian myths which stressed the direction and purposefulness of history," he judges that we are confronted by "a complicated idea with intellectual origins difficult to disentangle" (p. 259).

Roberts's discussion of what has inspired the West's vitality, continuous self-transformation, and boundless hopes is nonetheless enlightening. He places the origins of these characteristics in the achievement of the Greeks, their recognition of human beings as "unique" in their rationality, their spirit of "rational inquiry," and their embracing of "the idea of excellence" (p. 53). The reading of Roberts's pages points to the wedding of these powerful notions with the vision shaped by Judeo-Christian faith, as accounting for the peculiar genius of our Western culture. The prophetic tradition of Judaism, inherited by Christianity, invited an awareness of the human condition and its destiny which has as its background a "nagging sense of inadequacy," a sense which has often aroused Western thought and "stopped it from settling down into immobility" (p. 56).

With this awareness pervading medieval experience, even the disputes of the medieval period proved a "catalyst of liberties" and worked in the long run "in favour of liberty and pluralism," bringing a "self-critical adjustment within European civilisation" (p. 100). The culture which medievalism transmitted to the modern period "was an active, questing, striving religious culture . . . forever trying . . . to make things new." It never lost sight of the idea that "history was a pilgrimage." Indeed, the Christian tradition could be described as "almost obsessively self-critical"; it "never lost the capacity for self-renewal"; and it was this spirit which led to the upheaval of the Reformation (p. 108).

The "dynamic drive" of modernity cannot be properly understood except through the "sense of direction and purpose," and "a confidence in its destiny" which "came from Christianity" (p. 248). With the Enlightenment "the enormously influential idea of Progress emerged clearly for the first time . . . obviously owing much to Judeo-Christian myths" (p. 259). Grounded in this tradition, the Marxist view of history can be described as "essentially a Christian heresy" (p. 79). Such things as the Atlantic Charter (1941), which laid the foundations of the postcolonial world, are contemporary expressions of the "self-critical traditions" of the Western tradition (p. 381).

The third master idea which, according to Roberts, has had a pervasive influence in the Western tradition is the recognition of the dignity of the individual human being. Again, he places the roots of this Western ideal in the Judeo-Christian tradition.

As we have seen, Roberts judges that the modern expression of our Western culture has been "humanity's great champion," giving humanitarian values an essential place on the agenda of all the world's peoples (pp. 430-31). These ideals have their inspiration in Christian antecedents: "a certain idea of the individual as a creature of potentially limitless value" (p. 116); the "infinite value of the individual soul" as a concept "at the heart of Christianity" (p. 108); the "theological assertion" which opened the way to "the imperative of equality" (p. 295); the "transcendent principle" at the heart of Christianity, which implies "that the individual soul is of infinite value" and is at the same time "potentially a source of claims to rights" (p. 76).

Roberts's views of social order are influenced by the assumptions he shares with many who have been shaped by the culture of modernity — raising questions which must be discussed in a later chapter. He has difficulty providing a satisfactory understanding of themes which are fundamental to the political traditions of the West. His frustrations are made explicit when he weighs up the French Revolution's notion of the "right" of the individual person. He finds this concept to be illogical — he sees the notions of "fundamental rights" of individuals and "popular sovereignty" as incompatible (p. 287). As we shall see, Alasdair MacIntyre has a similar problem with the modern concept of "human right."

Roberts acknowledges the profound challenges facing contemporary modernity. Speaking in his introduction of "a loss of faith in a whole culture" and asking whether we should conclude "that our civilisation has, in any final sense, 'failed,'" he hesitates. If in the end he finds it hard to shake off the "perverse optimism" of the Western spirit (cf. p. 431), he nonetheless recognizes that during the present century "a great dream has faded" (p. 367). The "authorities" which sustained generations of the past have collapsed (p. 418). His final assessment of things reminds us of the discussion of the previous chapters. The "self-critical power" of our culture has had far-reaching consequences: "the fundamental ideas of the European tradition have been brought under question, many with irreparable consequences" (pp. 428-29).

*   *   *

The next reaction to the present culture of modernity we shall consider is that of a philosopher. Alasdair MacIntyre's influential work,

After Virtue,[3] is a critical study of the moral theory and practice of modernity. MacIntyre builds the essential argument of his essay upon the cultural and intellectual dislocation which he finds to have taken place with the emergence of modernity — calling to mind the discussion of the previous chapters. Though his approach is different, his conclusions are strikingly similar to those of Charles Taylor.

MacIntyre's evaluation of the present situation of Western culture is very somber. He points to what he judges to be the failure of our culture to provide a satisfactory rationale for the essentials of morality; this failure presents us with the prospect of a new Dark Age, in which people of good will turn aside from shoring up the institutions of our cultural tradition and cease to identify the continuation of civility and moral community with the maintenance of these institutions (p. 263).

MacIntyre argues that the cultural dislocation essential to his argument has reduced "moral utterance and practice" to no more than "a series of fragmented survivals from an older past" which give rise to "insoluble problems" (pp. 110-11) — to moral disagreements which can find no resolution because of "the conceptual incommensurability of the rival arguments," each based in a "quite different normative or evaluative concept" (p. 8). This impasse is difficult for those affected by it to understand, since it can only be resolved by exploring the history in which the cultural dislocation took place. MacIntyre interprets this history as essentially related to the full emergence of modernity in the Enlightenment — in "the later seventeenth century and the eighteenth century" when there developed, as "a received doctrine," a "distinguishing of the moral from the theological, the legal and the aesthetic." Morality thus became an issue which was removed from the cultural matrix in which it had lived, so that it could only be validated by a self-sufficient project of "independent rational justification" (p. 39).

Our discussion to this point has alerted us to the problems this project was destined to encounter because of the narrow methodological presuppositions canonized by the ideology of modernity. MacIntyre concludes that, in the end, this project of rational justification

---

3. References which follow are to Alasdair MacIntyre, *After Virtue,* 2nd ed. (Notre Dame, Ind.: University of Notre Dame Press, 1984).

failed, giving rise to "emotivism," an interpretation of the moral order which is, in effect, the denial of its very essentials.

Putting together the various components of MacIntyre's argument can assist us toward a fuller understanding of the implications of modernity. In what follows, therefore, we shall consider the following: (1) the relationship of the developments MacIntyre is discussing with the principles of the Enlightenment movement, in particular with its reaction to the Aristotelian tradition; (2) the failure of the project to find an independent rational justification of the moral standards of Western culture; (3) the unsatisfactory character of the moral "emotivism" which pervades our culture as a result of this failure; (4) what MacIntyre considers to be the ultimate choice of our culture — between the rationale of Friedrich Nietzsche and Max Weber, on the one hand, and a new appreciation, on the other hand, of the essential place of teleology or purposefulness in a satisfactory account of the moral order; (5) the historical and sociological essay in which MacIntyre sets out to rehabilitate a rationale of morality which is essentially Aristotelian.

MacIntyre's analysis reminds us of much that has already emerged in our text, as he makes clear the intellectual stance which characterized the Enlightenment movement and the manner in which this stance created a considerable problem for those who, at the beginning of the modern period, sought to provide a philosophical justification for the moral system taken for granted by Western society. He points to what we have recognized as the principal slogans of the ideology of modernity, "enlightenment" and "emancipation." For the ideology of the Enlightenment, *reason* and *authority* were seen as "mutually exclusive" (p. 42), and rational inquiry was seen as "a deliverance both from the burdens of traditional theism and the confusions of teleological modes of thought" (p. 60).

Protestant Calvinism and Catholic Jansenism, in their pessimism concerning fallen humanity's powers of reason, gave their support to the Enlightenment's rejection of medieval scholasticism: "it is (the Jansenist) Pascal who recognises that the Protestant-cum-Jansenist conception of reason is in important respects at one with the conception of reason at home in the most innovative seventeenth-century philosophy and science" (p. 54). For this new approach, as we have seen, the understanding of essences "belongs to the despised concep-

67

tual scheme of scholasticism" (p. 54). The new "anti-Aristotelian science" sees reason as having a very limited task: "it can assess truths of fact and mathematical relations but nothing more." It can say nothing of ends: "In the realm of practice it can speak only of means" (p. 54). Indeed, the recognition of *purposefulness* in nature is seen as a form of "superstition" (pp. 34, 62).

Having renounced any understanding of essences and purposes, the Enlightenment ideology had to establish a new methodology of experiential verification, grounded in the phenomenological order of experience, which MacIntyre describes in the following terms, bringing to mind what we said earlier about the salient characteristics of an ideology:

> The empiricist concept of experience was a cultural invention of the late seventeenth and eighteenth centuries . . . invented as a panacea for the epistemological crises of the seventeenth century; it was intended as a device to close the gap between *seems* and *is*, between appearance and reality. It was to close this gap by making every experiencing subject a closed realm; there is nothing beyond my experience for me to compare my experience with, so that the contrast between *seems to me* and *is in fact* can never be formulated. . . . The empiricist concept of experience was unknown for most of human history. It is understandable then that empiricism's linguistic history is one of continuous innovation and invention, culminating in the barbarous neologism "sense-datum." (p. 80; cf. p. 84)

In the end, the Enlightenment project has at its heart a fatal vulnerability, in that it failed "to address adequately, let alone to answer the question: what sort of person am I to become?" This question is inescapable if philosophy is to give a satisfactory account of human existence, "in that an answer to it is given *in practice* in each human life" (p. 118). The methodology canonized by the Enlightenment not only denied access to transcendent norms, it also moved inevitably toward a "mechanistic account of human action" which implied a "predictability of human behaviour" and invited the investigation of "ways to manipulate it" (p. 84; cf. p. 83).

The Enlightenment project, therefore, set itself the task of finding a rational justification for morality, while at the same time adopting a methodology which was fatally restricted in its scope. MacIntyre judges that this project has failed. He carries on a many-stranded debate with philosophical colleagues past and present, working in the field of moral theory. In his judgment contemporary "analytical moral philosophy," in its attempt to show "that the notion of rationality itself supplies morality with a basis," has failed (p. 21), leaving writers engaged in an interminable debate in which they "cannot agree among themselves either on what the character of moral rationality is or on the substance of the morality which is to be founded on that rationality" (p. 21).[4] Moreover, because of the failure of this philosophical project, "distinctively modern societies" have suffered a "moral calamity," in that it is no longer possible for them "to appeal to moral criteria in a way that had been possible in other times and places" (p. ix).

Reflecting upon this failure, MacIntyre makes a comment which could have significance for those seeking to understand one notable characteristic of the culture of modernity, which stands apart from other cultural traditions in the way it has marginalized philosophy, held in such honor in other cultures: "In a world of secular rationality religion could no longer provide . . . a shared background and foundation for moral discourse and action; and the failure of philosophy to provide what religion could no longer furnish was an important cause of philosophy losing its central cultural role and becoming a marginal, narrowly academic subject" (p. 50).

As we shall see, the remedy MacIntyre suggests for the problems created by modernity's inability to find a rational basis for moral principles is along the lines of a reappropriation of the historical and cultural resources of our Western tradition, a sapiential rationality grounded in the full human matrix of a traditional culture.

The next element of MacIntyre's analysis we must discuss is his judgment that, as a consequence of philosophy's failure to provide a satisfactory rational account of the principles of morality, "emotivism" is now established as the implicit rationale of modernity's worldview. Emotivism he defines as "the doctrine that all moral judg-

---

4. In the course of his text, MacIntyre makes a critical analysis of the moral philosophies of such modern authorities as Hume, Kant, Kierkegaard, Diderot, Nietzsche, Weber, Sartre, and Moore — cf. index of *After Virtue*.

ments are *nothing but* expressions of preference, attitude or feeling" (pp. 11-12).

If emotivism is easily criticized philosophically (pp. 12-13), and its essential thesis, that moral judgments are "neither true or false" (p. 12), should logically lead to the conclusion that "traditional or inherited moral language ought to be abandoned" (p. 20), this has not taken place, so that emotivism has now "become embodied in our culture" and "to a large degree people now think, talk and act *as if* emotivism were true" (p. 22).

This cultural situation is linked with the themes of the ideology of modernity, "liberation" and "autonomy." As a result, "the peculiarly modern self, the emotivist self, in acquiring sovereignty in its own realm" has "lost its traditional boundaries provided by a social identity and a view of human life as ordered to a given end" (p. 34). We are reminded of the problems of an ideology which cannot appeal to any measure beyond itself.

Despite these unresolved philosophical problems, our culture retains the language of morality, as it seeks "to uphold older traditions which have somehow or other survived into some sort of coexistence with modernity," so that the rhetoric of our culture "serves to conceal behind the masks of morality what are in fact the preferences of arbitrary will" (p. 71). MacIntyre points, moreover, to the manner in which emotivism is really the enemy of the autonomy which is so prized by modernity. According to emotivism's account of morality, moral assertions have a meaning equivalent to "I approve of this; do so as well." These assertions are made and defended as an expression of personal autonomy; in fact, however, they are manipulative and undermine the autonomy of others, "directing towards others those very manipulative modes of relationship which each of us aspires to resist" (p. 68).

MacIntyre situates the thought of Friedrich Nietzsche and Max Weber within this climate of emotivism. Nietzsche gives expression to what should be the logical outcome of the moral stance adopted by modernity: he "disposes of the Enlightenment project," understanding that "what purported to be appeals to objectivity were in fact expressions of subjective will"; his moral teaching is a "prophetic irrationalism," recognizing that the "rationally justified autonomous moral subject of the eighteenth century is a fiction, an illusion." In the end, Nietzsche is the moralist of modernity who must be taken seriously, "*the* moral philosopher of the present age" (pp. 113-14).

Our discussion has already made us aware of the representative importance of the thought of Max Weber in contemporary Western culture (cf. p. 109). MacIntyre sees Weber as putting the rationale of Nietzsche — that life has no form but what we project — into practice; MacIntyre cites Raymond Aron's summation of Weber's basic principle, "values are created by human decision," values rest "on a choice whose justification is purely subjective" (p. 26). Ultimately, for Weber, "no type of authority can appeal to rational criteria to vindicate itself except . . . its own effectiveness" (p. 26; cf. pp. 24-25). We are left, Weber recognized, with the bleak prospect of a "bureaucratic rationality" which has no justification except "the rationality of matching means to ends economically and efficiently" (p. 25).

The situation MacIntyre has analyzed is very disturbing, all the more so — if his interpretation is correct — because it has come about by a cultural dislocation which makes it very difficult for those sharing in it to appreciate fully. He uses two analogies to convey the situation he is suggesting. The first is a community in which natural sciences are blamed for a series of natural disasters, science is officially abolished, and its practitioners executed, so that scientific theory only survives in fragments which are deprived of their meaningful background (p. 1). The second he borrows from anthropology, appealing to the Polynesian concept of *taboo*. This concept, anthropologists have come to recognize, is the outcome of a sociohistorical process. In its initial stage, certain prohibitions have an intelligibility in the life of the cultural group; later — in a transformed social reality — the original rationale is no longer meaningful and the prohibitions become a set of arbitrary rules backed by nothing more than weight of custom and tradition (pp. 111-12). In the judgment of MacIntyre, the morality of modernity — now deprived of an accepted rational basis — survives in somewhat the same fashion: "why," he asks, "should we think about our modern uses of *good, right,* and *obligatory* in any different way from that in which we think about late eighteenth-century Polynesian uses of *taboo?*" (p. 113).

MacIntyre's analysis leaves us with an excessively pessimistic assessment of contemporary modernity's attitude to the foundations of morality. Because the established philosophies of late modernity in the West provide no adequate rationale to sustain these foundations, MacIntyre suggests that our continued use of basic notions such as "good," "right," and "obligation" with reference to human behavior becomes the equivalent of Polynesian taboos. One may reply, however, that the failure of *philosophies* to provide a satisfactory rationale in support of moral principles does not necessarily indicate that these moral principles are without *any* satisfactory rationale in contemporary Western culture.

With Aristotle, we may recognize that the spontaneous, pre-critical understanding of our culture — an understanding which is none the less real for being inarticulate — may well come to grips very profoundly with the issues raised by the basic principles of morality.[5] After all, as MacIntyre points out in his text, Aristotle was not inventing the concept of "virtue" but was giving a critical account of what was implicit in the life of the educated Athenian (pp. 147-48).[6]

MacIntyre's text certainly helps us understand the process of dislocation which has led to our present state of affairs (cf. pp. 18-19). He is arguing, in the end, for the rehabilitation of a rationale substantially at one with that which was commonly accepted before the Enlightenment. He suggests that the finding of a rationale which satisfactorily validates the moral concepts still taken for granted in our Western tradition calls for an appreciation of the historical processes which have produced the culture of modernity. We must find an understanding which "will *both* enable us to distinguish between what it is for a set of such rules and practices to have been fragmented and thrown into disorder *and* enable us to understand the historical transitions by which the latter state emerged from the former" (p. 113). The "classical" rationale he wishes to rehabilitate he judges to be essentially Aristotelian.

At the heart of MacIntyre's argument is a reasoning which calls

5. Cf. Aristotle's *Nicomachean Ethics* 1145b2-7; *Eudemian Ethics* 1216b26-35.

6. The point we are making is not unrelated to the distinction the social philosopher Sir Ernest Barker will make in a later chapter, between "society" and "state"; the British "common law" tradition has an obvious relationship to the moral awareness we refer to; it is an essential element in the "collective memory" of a culture which is to have an important place in the discussion of later chapters.

into question fundamental assumptions of the ideology of modernity. He understands the tradition of moral awareness which prevailed before the emergence of modernity as embracing three elements: "the conception of untutored human nature, the conception of the precepts of rational ethics and the conception of human-nature-as-it-could-be-if-it-realised-its-*telos*" (p. 53); modernity's "abandonment of any notion of a *telos* leaves behind a moral scheme composed of two remaining elements whose relationship becomes quite unclear" (p. 55).

As we have said, however, MacIntyre does not hope to establish his case by a philosophical reasoning, but by a study which brings to light the substance of his argument as it is embodied in the social and cultural reality of human history. The history MacIntyre studies is that which is embodied in the Western tradition's understanding of "virtue." He argues that virtue shows itself to be a "core concept" in our history which provides the Western tradition of morality with "its conceptual unity" (p. 186). His study shows this concept to have had a complex development, progressively assuming definition at different stages of the ongoing tradition, so that "the concept itself in some sense embodies the history of which it is the outcome" (p. 186). This tradition passes through three stages, each of which sees the *social* reality of human existence as a concomitant of the meaningfulness of the moral ideal it embraces.

The first stage is heroic societies, such as are portrayed in the Homeric poems or in similar sagas of other peoples. At this stage the basic values accepted by the society and the privileges and duties derived from these are expressed in the structure of the society and the roles assigned to its various members (p. 122).

In the second stage the Greek dramatists reflect Athenian society's maturing understanding of virtue, an understanding which goes beyond the awareness of heroic societies: "In Homer the question of honour is the question of what is due to a king; in Sophocles the question of honour has become the question of what is due to man" (p. 133).

In the third stage of MacIntyre's historical process, a moral tradition renders a critical account of itself. Among the Greeks this stage begins to emerge with Socrates' criticism of the Sophists; it is carried forward by Plato and Aristotle (pp. 139, 144, chap. 12).

The three elements of the paradigm at the heart of MacIntyre's argument, referred to above, find undeniable expression in the outlook of heroic societies: "The implied epistemology of the heroic world is a thorough-going realism" (p. 129). In subsequent stages these three elements remain essential to the understanding of morality: "the Sophoclean self differs from the emotivist self as much as does the heroic self"; if it "transcends the limitations of social roles and is able to put those roles in question . . . it remains accountable . . . there is an order which requires from us the pursuit of certain ends" (p. 145). MacIntyre sees Aristotle's achievement as the analysis of the intelligibility of this order to certain ends; in making this analysis, Aristotle sees himself not as inventing an account of what virtue is, but as "articulating an account that is implicit in the thought, utterance and action of an educated Athenian." He carries on his work in continuity with the historical tradition that has preceded him; his subject matter is "the pre-philosophical theory already implicit in and presupposed by the best contemporary practice of the virtues" (p. 148).

We can leave to professional philosophers the task of evaluating the details of MacIntyre's interpretation of Aristotle's account of human teleology.[7] For the sake of rehabilitating an essentially Aristotelian account of the principles of morality, as grounded in *telos* or purposefulness, he mounts a limited argument: every practice aims at some good, human nature as such pursues certain aims and goals, or a certain *telos;* this *telos*, according to the moral tradition Aristotle is giving an account of, is "the state of being well and doing well in being well, of a man's being well-favoured himself and in relation to the divine" (p. 148): "what constitutes the good for man is a complete human life lived at its best, and the exercise of the virtues is a necessary and central part of such a life" (p. 149; cf. pp. 194, 222-23).

MacIntyre acknowledges that Aristotle was hampered by his lack of "any sense of the specifically historical" (p. 147; cf. pp. 159, 180), something which offends the sensibilities of modernity. He makes a point of considerable significance for our Western tradition,

---

7. Acknowledging that he is parting company with such commentators as Jacques Maritain (p. 260), MacIntyre calls into question what he calls Aristotle's "metaphysical biology" (pp. 162-63, etc.).

however — that the medievals, influenced by the biblical tradition's essentially narrative form, brought an important complement to Aristotle's point of view (cf. pp. 147, 180).

Clearly the approach adopted by MacIntyre in his work owes much to this development, as he makes us aware of the ongoing story of our Western tradition. In a later chapter we shall discuss the importance of narrative as the medium of existential truth. *After Virtue* appeals to this function of narrative. The great cultures which preceded modernity have made "the telling of stories the chief means of moral education" (p. 121). "Stories are lived," MacIntyre reminds us, "before they are told" (p. 212). MacIntyre describes "a central thesis" of his text:

> man is in his actions and practice, as well as in his fictions, essentially a story-telling animal. He is not essentially, but becomes through his history, a teller of stories that aspire to truth. . . . I can only answer the question "What am I to do?" if I can answer the prior question "Of what story or stories do I find myself a part?" . . . Deprive children of stories and you leave them unscripted, anxious stutterers in their actions as in their words. Hence there is no way to give us an understanding of any society, including our own, except through the stock of stories which constitute its initial dramatic resources. Mythology, in its original sense, is at the heart of things. Vico was right and so was Joyce. And so too of course is that moral tradition from heroic society to its medieval heirs according to which the telling of stories has a key part in educating us into the virtues. (p. 216)[8]

Charles Taylor expressed this same argument: it is only in narrative that the existential truth of our human existence can be adequately signified. To the question "In what does the unity of an individual life consist?" MacIntyre replies: it consists in "the unity of a narrative . . . the unity of a narrative quest" (pp. 218-19). "Quest," of course, implies the *telos* or purposefulness which MacIntyre sees as essential to any satisfactory account of morality. We shall be reminded

---

8. Voegelin — through his "cosmic" principle — has already helped us recover the place of mythology, "in its original sense at the heart of things."

of what MacIntyre has to say as "wisdom" and "collective memory" emerge in later chapters as important themes in our discussion of modernity.

*   *   *

Thinkers in most Western countries are experiencing an uneasiness about the "economic rationalism" first spoken of by Max Weber, which has been so influential in shaping the government policies of nations in recent decades. There can be little doubt that this development reflects methodological assumptions of the ideology of modernity, and thus has an important place in our critical assessment of modernity. Paul Ormerod's *Death of Economics*[9] mounts a criticism of the economic orthodoxy which has tended to establish itself within our contemporary Western culture. His analysis clarifies the link between the present state of economic theory and the dominant ideology of modernity.

It is interesting to consider what he has to say against the background provided by MacIntyre's work. *After Virtue* sees the thought of Weber as providing "the key to much of the modern age" (p. 86): Weber's analysis of society looks to bureaucratic organization as its essential dynamism; the bureaucratic rationality which shapes society is judged according to its success in "matching means to ends economically and efficiently" (p. 25). It is Weberian assumptions, in the judgment of MacIntyre, which have made "expertise" one of the central themes of the ideology of modernity. Ormerod's book studies critically the "intellectual orthodoxy" which has established itself among economic experts, an orthodoxy which has great confidence in "the ability of economics to understand the world," and which "dominates political debate" in our Western countries (Ormerod, pp. 3-4). However, modernity's "expertise" is often "part of a masquerade of social controls rather than a reality" (p. 75).

If Weber's basic principle is followed, bureaucratic planners

9. References which follow are to Paul Ormerod, *The Death of Economics* (London: Faber & Faber, 1994). John Ralston Saul's works, *Voltaire's Bastards* (Ringwood, Victoria: Penguin, 1993) and *The Unconscious Civilisation* (Ringwood, Victoria: Penguin, 1997), express forcefully the growing dissatisfaction with the "economic rationalism" which is so influential in contemporary Western culture.

should be judged by the efficiency with which they manage the economy. Ormerod finds that in the area of macroeconomic planning they have clearly failed. He quotes an Organisation for Economic Cooperation and Development (OECD) study published in 1993, which found that forecasts of the OECD and the International Monetary Fund (1987-92), of output growth and inflation for the next year in the world's seven major economies, were no more accurate than the nonexpert's "naive projection that next year's growth of output or inflation would simply be equal to this year's" (p. 105).[10]

Ormerod's analysis of the factors which have given rise to the assumptions he is assessing, and his suggestions for a more satisfactory approach to economics, can contribute to our understanding of the ideology of modernity. He links the present state of economics with the importance given to mathematical conceptualization in the modern era: in the nineteenth century a desire to share "the status and prestige of the physical sciences in the Victorian era" gave rise to a desire "to raise the mathematical precision of economics"; ironically, this led to an identification with a "mechanistic view of the world" which has since been seen as "less and less relevant by today's biologists, chemists and physicists" (p. 9).

The mathematical model developed around 1870, by W. S. Jevons in England and Léon Walras in Switzerland, "adopted the then dominant view of the harder sciences, which saw the world as a smoothly functioning machine" (p. 45). In 1909 Vilfredo Pareto refined Walras's model of competitive equilibrium (p. 71). As this model came to dominate economic theory, the assumption of the early nineteenth-century founders of "political economy" — that the function of their discipline was to assist those making the prudential decisions of government "about how the world *might* operate" — was set aside, to be replaced by an apparently scientifically based assumption that economics applied "a set of discovered truths as to how the world *does* operate" (p. 4).

Upon this assumption, economic orthodoxy has "ruthlessly excluded" such things as the "institutional setting, the historical experience and the overall framework of behaviour" of the political commu-

10. MacIntyre cites a similar study of OECD predictions in his criticism of modernity's misplaced expectations of the "expertise" of social scientists (p. 89).

nity whose economy is being discussed (p. 14); it has concerned itself with a rational abstraction which "assumes a continuum of traders" (p. 43). We are reminded of the "cleansing" from scientific data of all that is "subjective" in modernity's desire to establish a truly objective "scientific" methodology.

Ormerod considers the appropriation by the promoters of this orthodoxy "of the word 'rational' to describe the basic postulates of orthodox economic theory" to be a highly successful "propaganda coup" (p. 111). He agrees with the American social scientist James Coleman, who describes "the economists' model of competitive equilibrium as a 'broadly perpetrated fiction'" (p. 91).

Ormerod points to other ideological factors which helped create the situation he is criticizing. The importance for the culture of modernity of the notion of "progress" is beyond question. Ormerod sees the linking of economics to the wagon of progress as influencing the adopting of a mechanistic model; the science and technology of the Victorian era was confident that it could transform the world: "they saw the physical world as a machine: a very complicated one, but a machine none the less, whose principles of working could be understood in the same way as the workings of a steam engine were" (p. 39).

The fact that the "Western market economies are clearly the most successful form of economic organisation ever invented" (p. 48) seemed to lend support to an unabated optimism, as economists continued to apply their mechanistic model in complete disregard of the gap which exists between this optimism and the results they were able to point to in macroeconomic planning. The fact that concern for the preservation of the environment has raised a radically new order of economic question seems to have little effect upon this situation.

Another supporting factor in recent decades has been the "ideological preconceptions of politicians":

> the political and social agendas of Ronald Reagan and Margaret Thatcher were powerfully motivated by the logic of free-market economics. Or, to be more precise, free-market economics was used to underpin the ideological preconceptions of these politicians. The deregulation of financial markets in the 1980s in the Anglo-Saxon economies; the deregulation of and increased flexibility in labour

> markets, a topic which is presently the subject of a fierce debate among the political classes of Europe; the privatisation of state-owned industries; reductions in welfare programmes — all these themes flow from the logic of the theory of competitive equilibrium. (p. 47)

As we all know, the agendas of many Western countries have been profoundly influenced by these policies (p. 68).

Ormerod has no intention of denying the valuable contribution mathematical analysis can make to the work of those responsible for fostering modern economies; understood "in its proper role, as servant, not as master, maths is an invention which can increase enormously the productivity of thinking" (p. 44). His target is the assumption that the economy functions like a machine and that this functioning can be captured by a type of "linear mathematical calculation which gives expression to the working of a machine" (cf. p. 36), and which disregards the other factors at work in a human community. Human society is "altogether too complex to be captured by a mechanistic approach" (p. 37).

In the course of Ormerod's study, he makes reference in fact to a great manifold of factors which influence systems of production and exchange in the world's economies. This influence is clearly decisive in a manner which is in no way registered in the abstract mathematical calculations of the competitive equilibrium model. It seems worth our while to list these factors. The fact that they are disregarded by thinkers responsible for economic planning shows how powerful the ideological stance of modernity is. They also illustrate the complexity of factors at work in a modern political community, something we shall discuss more fully in a later chapter.

Government decisions and policies concerning provisions for national defense have constituted an immense variable in national economies in the last half-century quite independent of the free-market equilibrium. The policies adopted by the government in the areas of education and public health can also vary considerably within a democratically governed community in a fashion quite independent of market forces. The changing attitude of the public to environmental issues is also independent of the market, as — for what is virtually the first time — the public weighs the benefits of modernity's industrial production against the costs in terms of deterioration of the environment (p. 30). Ormerod reports that economists who have concerned themselves with "whether the price mechanism could always be relied upon to save the world from running out of exhaustible resources" have concluded that it cannot be (p. 75).

These issues, like many others in modern political life, raise the vast question of the influence of cultural and social attitudes upon the functioning of the economy, a question to which Ormerod frequently returns. As he writes, most of us would instinctively react against the suggestion that human activities and human "free will" can be contained in any comprehensive mathematical formula (p. 42). The Green movement shows the impact a renewed appreciation of the "benefits of cooperative behaviour," as opposed to "self-interested rational calculation" (p. 35), can have upon the attitudes of those participating in the market. Ormerod cites the renowned economist J. K. Galbraith as declaring Thorstein Veblen's *Theory of the Leisure Class* as the book which most influenced his thinking. Veblen's work stresses the importance of social "institutions" and of "social and cultural values" in the functioning of the economy (p. 51).

Ormerod illustrates this, pointing to the difference changing attitudes to price and wage restraint can make (p. 82). Social solidarity can also affect the market mechanism: the oil-price rise (1973-74) had a much less damaging impact upon the German economy than it had in other parts of Europe. The German economy had developed a climate of collaboration "which emphasised the rights and responsibilities of both sides of industry"; in countries without such a climate, on the other hand, the crisis sparked industrial confrontation (pp. 134-35). Societies with a high degree of "social cohesion" have had a lower level of unemployment in recent decades (p. 203). Eastern European countries such as the Czech Republic, whose cultures have roots "in centuries of the Austro-Hungarian empire," have negotiated the dramatic changes in their economic organization far more successfully than countries like Russia and the Ukraine, whose roots were in thousands of years of "peasant economies" (p. 63).

The attitude to leisure in particular cultures is singled out by Ormerod as an important factor in the development of an economy insofar as it determines the way the benefits of growth will be utilized

(p. 23).[11] Apparent trivialities have an astounding impact on the functioning of the economy: in the United States, for example, around sixty billion dollars are spent each year on personal beauty care; in the United Kingdom over one billion pounds are spent each year on pet food (p. 25). Ormerod suggests that many people, confronted with the choice "dog-meat or taxes," would be prepared to pay higher taxes — provided they were convinced that the tax receipts would not be abused (p. 26). Again the outcome depends upon a complex mix of cultural factors operative in a particular society.

Investment policies, so influential in the functioning of an economy, will also be shaped by cultural and historical factors. Alfred Chandler's study of company development shows that the development of leading British companies fell behind those of America and Germany because a persistence of family control and management meant a tendency to disburse rather than invest profits (pp. 59, 61). Decisions to invest profits toward the development of personnel, and decisions concerning what portion of profits will be tied up in property, can vary greatly, with far-reaching results (pp. 64, 147).

Market strategies can reshape national economies. In the late nineteenth century, U.S. companies responded to the Sherman Antitrust Act (1890) by directly taking over potential rivals through mergers and acquisitions. Companies of enormous size were the result, most of which are household names today (p. 55). Such companies, rather than functioning as passive respondents to market forces, have used their "advantage of being big" to shape and structure the markets in which they operate (p. 59).

Ormerod refers to the unpredictability of the reactions of consumers. Many factors and the prevailing perceptions of these factors influence such reactions (p. 107). Studies have been made of the "apparent irrationality" in consumer behavior (p. 110). For example, one Cornell University study strikes at the first assumption of orthodox

11. Closer to home, the historian Geoffrey Blainey illustrates this factor in our Australian economy, noting that the disproportion of males to females in early nineteenth-century Australia contributed notably to the development of recreational sports, which led in turn to "a higher priority being given to shorter working hours and longer leisure rather than to higher wages" in the fight for better working conditions — in contrast to the United States, for example (*The Tyranny of Distance* [Sydney: Sun Books, 1966], p. 171).

economic theory, showing that most people "are far more cooperative and less competitive than the postulates of economic theory assert rational individuals should be" (p. 110). The part played by "conspicuous consumption" in the functioning of the market is in direct contradiction to one of the fundamental principles of orthodox economic theory (pp. 49-50).

Ormerod points to a miscellany of additional factors which affect the functioning of a national economy in a way which can in no way be included in the mechanistic mathematical model (p. 41): external "shocks" impossible to predict, such as the Organization of Petroleum Exporting Countries (OPEC) manipulation of oil prices (pp. 75, 211); technological breakthroughs and revolutions in communication (pp. 53-54).

We have listed the full range of these influences because they point to modernity's tendency to rely excessively upon a mathematical analysis as the norm of critical understanding to the neglect of the vast range of other dimensions essential to our human existence. Margaret Thatcher's statement, quoted more than once by Ormerod, that "there is no such thing as society, only the individuals who constitute it" (p. 34), epitomizes the intellectual impoverishment such a point of view has led to.

In the latter part of his work, Ormerod argues that the appropriate mathematical model for macroeconomics is a "non-linear" one similar to that used in the study of complex organic systems of interaction (pp. 168-69, 183). He shows that such a model goes beyond the limitations of the linear model of market equilibrium in the hands of those seeking a just distribution of work and benefit in the economy. It opens the way for responsible government to undertake the measures required for this just distribution when they are required (cf. pp. 204-12).

*   *   *

Robert Heilbroner's published lectures, *Visions of the Future*,[12] provide a complement to Paul Ormerod's study. Whereas Ormerod's

12. References which follow are to Robert Heilbroner, *Visions of the Future: The Distant Past, Yesterday, Today, and Tomorrow* (New York: Oxford University Press, 1995).

concern is narrowed down to economics as a discipline and criticism of its contemporary self-understanding, Heilbroner writes as a respected economist who wishes to set his discussion of the capitalistic system — one of the principal achievements of modernity — within a broader framework of social and historical issues.

Heilbroner makes a very definite periodization of history. What he calls "The Distant Past" extends from the origins of humanity until the eighteenth century. Its view of human existence was static; it expected that the future of humanity would be like the past. The period which follows he calls "Yesterday"; it extends from the eighteenth until the mid–twentieth century and is shaped by "the rise and flourishing of capitalism, with its sister forces of technology and science," and by "an emerging political consciousness" (p. 10). It looked to the future with optimism, as an ever ascending "Progress." The present period, which he calls "Today," cannot share in the naive optimism which inspired the hopes of "Yesterday": "the empowering gift of science, the relentless dynamics of a capitalist economy, and the spirit of mass politics still constitute the forces leading us into the future. The difference is that these forces are no longer regarded unambiguously as carriers of progress." While their "positive effects" cannot be disputed, these forces are now seen to have disturbingly "negative aspects" (p. 70).

It is interesting to note that Heilbroner's periodization has much in common with what has emerged in our own discussion. What characterizes his "Distant Past" is the traditionalist spirit of medievalism against which modernity has reacted. His "Yesterday" is essentially the period of modernity. While we have seen this period as beginning with the fifteenth century's reaction against medievalism, Heilbroner identifies it with the emergence of the Enlightenment as a fully self-conscious ideology of emancipation from medievalism. Like Heilbroner, we see an essential continuity between the era coming to an end and that which will be our future. For Heilbroner, the same three formative forces are at work, though the mood in which they are contemplated has changed. Our analysis has suggested that the more self-critical phase of modernity we are now entering is a carrying forward of the same essential project.

There is little doubt — as Max Weber recognized — that the emergence of capitalism in its modern form is one of the most powerful influences shaping the contemporary world. Heilbroner gives us a much clearer picture than Ormerod does of the dynamics of the capitalist economy: "the seismic pressure exerted by the accumulation of capital" (p. 53); capitalism's "relentless dynamics" directed toward "a pursuit of boundless extent" (p. 54); "the instability of the system itself, evidenced in constant worries over 'panics' and 'slumps'" which "reached a high point in the Great Depression" (p. 79); the emergence with the collapse of the socialist empire of a situation in which there is "no credible alternative" to challenge the capitalist system (p. 80) — so that one is tempted to make the judgment, "whereas socialism may have lost, it is not so clear that capitalism has won" (p. 82); the possibility that a "silent depression" may be emerging, as economies which appear to have been most successful find themselves with a growing problem of poverty (p. 81); the globalization of the capitalist system pointing to developments in which the "ensuing contest in the world market probably determines the political fate of nations more profoundly than anything but life-and-death conflict" (p. 86) — with this transnational system involving "the virtual exclusion of this all-important political contest from the direct responsibility or guidance of the state" (p. 83); the division of the world into a "Center," driven by the dynamics of capitalism, and a "Periphery" (which yesterday comprised colonial "servitors" and is today a zone where, "despite brave talk of economic development, crushing poverty is still the rule") (pp. 84-85).

Heilbroner's account of the place of capitalism in ongoing developments of the Western world contributes to our understanding of modernity. His capacity to suggest remedies to the problems involved is hampered, however, by his reductionist assumptions. The philosophical stance to which he inclines is that of "historicism," making it difficult for him to identify the measures according to which historical developments can be evaluated. "Science" should not be understood, he declares, as "a wholly disinterested inquiry into the nature of things . . . whose conceptual premises and modes of advance" rise "above the influence of their historical context"; on the contrary, science's "conceptual starting points, methods of inquiry, and indeed visions of science itself are inescapably embedded in their respective historical contexts" (p. 75). We quoted in a previous chapter his judgment that the notion of unconditional truth is an illusion which should be abandoned (p. 76). We also quoted Ernest Gellner's strong criticism of his position.

Heilbroner's discussion of the place of religion in human culture is disappointing. It is set within a framework reminiscent of Voegelin's periodization. In a first phase — reminiscent of Voegelin's "cosmic principle" — paramount concern is for the maintaining of personal and social harmony in tune with the cosmos. In the next phase — reminiscent of Voegelin's "anthropological principle" — recognition of the transcendent leads to "an obsession with propitiation and sacrifice"; "archaic religion is now succeeded by the still more anxiety-laden content of . . . the 'historic' period of religion, whose most important representative in the West is the Christian era" (pp. 33-34). This development inhibits, even paralyzes, expectations of historical and social change, producing a situation in which "only some new source of vitalizing energy, manifesting itself as powerfully as a force of nature and possessing something of the authority of religion," could resolve the impasse (p. 36). It was such a force which, according to Heilbroner, initiated the new era of "Yesterday" — the emergence of the capitalist system.

Such an interpretation is surprisingly simplistic. In a later chapter we shall cite Christopher Dawson's very different judgment of the influence of religion upon human cultures.[13] There can be little doubt that coming to terms with a recognition of the transcendent required a long period of adjustment. Factors such as what Heilbroner indicates, however, conditioned rather than determined developments. The long centuries in which Neoplatonism inhibited a full appreciation of the intrinsic value of mundane reality bear ample witness to this conditioning. This failure was due, not to an acceptance of the transcendent, but to Platonism's unsatisfactory account of the relationship between mundane reality and the transcendent. The High

---

13. Cf. Christopher Dawson, *Religion and Culture* (London: Sheed & Ward, 1949), p. 50. E. Evans-Pritchard, in *Theories of Comparative Religion* (Oxford: Oxford University Press, 1965), criticized fashionable accounts of the development of religion in the mid–twentieth century as not backed up by the facts available, and only to be explained by a climate of thought which was "a curious mixture of positivism, evolutionism and the remains of a sentimental religiosity" (pp. 4-5), and an "anti-religious bias reflecting a prevailing rationalism" (p. 11).

Middle Ages recognized this inadequacy.[14] In fact, the work of Max Weber and what we have heard from J. M. Roberts point toward the conclusion that capitalism itself, together with the other essential dynamics of modernity, was inspired by Western culture's deep roots in the Judeo-Christian tradition.

Heilbroner's study raises a question which has importance in any evaluation of modernity: What will the future hold? In raising this question, he cites the work of two "respected political analysts," Max Singer and Aaron Wildavsky, *The Real World Order: Zones of Peace/Zones of Turmoil*. These authors judge that much confusion arises when a single world is spoken of without the recognition that there are really two worlds, one "of peace, wealth and democracy" and the other "of turmoil, war and development" (cited p. 14). In the framework of our discussion, we would judge that the first zone is that part of the world which benefits from the achievements of modernity. Heilbroner judges that most of the world has not known these benefits: "neither science, nor capitalism, nor political emancipation opened vistas for most of the world, as they did in those relatively few areas in which these forces initially appeared" (p. 91). To the question of whether their prognosis for the world's future is optimistic or pessimistic, Singer and Wildavsky respond that this "depends on whether a century is a short time or a long time" (Heilbroner, p. 14) — they argue that "a process is well started that will make most of the world peaceful, democratic, and wealthy by historical standards by about a century from now, or perhaps two" (Heilbroner, p. 15).

We referred above to Heilbroner's concerns about the problems inherent in the dynamics of the capitalist system. Responding to Singer and Wildavsky, he urges caution, criticizing these authors for neglecting to incorporate into their view an analysis of capitalism. He chooses to discuss what the future holds in terms of possible developments in the three formative factors of "Yesterday" which he named: science, capitalism, and democratic politics. He is less optimistic than these authors, stressing the need for a more equitable distribution of wealth, as well as "the uncertain reliability

14. Cf. M.-D. Chenu, *Nature, Man, and Society in the Twelfth Century,* trans. and ed. Taylor and Little (Chicago: University of Chicago Press, 1968), pp. 239-69.

and crucial importance of political will" to manage the disturbances a divided world will bring (p. 92). In the end Heilbroner gives eloquent expression to the mood of our times and of its underlying ideological assumptions, as — in typical Western fashion — he refuses to give in to despair:

> Today's mood is somber rather than black; uncertain rather than despairing; and still strongly dependent on the forward momentum of the triad of forces in our midst, while newly mindful of their dangerous side — or even direct — effects. Thus I must stress as well as repeat that I assess our contemporary frame of mind as ambiguous, indeterminate, and apprehensive — a state of affairs that reflects, as did the mindsets of the past, the nature and developmental logic of the underlying social realities themselves. (pp. 70-71)

*   *   *

The next reaction we consider is that of a European statesman. Václav Havel played a major role in the dismantling of Czechoslovakia's Marxist regime. As president, first of Czechoslovakia and, from 1993, of the Czech Republic, he has wrestled with the problem of rebuilding a modern nation. As a playwright, he brings to this task talents and sensibilities not often found in today's political leaders. On 15 May 1996 Havel shared his reflections upon contemporary European culture in an address given at Aachen entitled "The Hope for Europe."[15]

The title is significant, pointing to what is probably the most fundamental problem facing Europe today, a problem not unrelated to the fragmentation of our late modern culture. Cardinal Carlo Martini, the archbishop of Milan who regularly addresses overflow gatherings of young people in his cathedral, is reported as saying, during a recent visit to Australia: "in Europe there is a great lack of hope. Many people are fearful for the future." He continued, "I think the great challenge for the church is to give hope to people and to heal wounds of fear and anger and division. I think the modern world has

15. Václav Havel, "The Hope for Europe," *New York Review,* 20 June 1996, pp. 38-40.

very much to give the church and the church has very much to give to the modern world."[16]

President Havel shows himself a perceptive and intelligent interpreter of our Western tradition in his awareness of the issues which have already emerged in our discussion. He appreciates, for instance, the way in which "categories of time and historicity" have been "introduced into human life" by our cultural tradition. He reminds us of Roberts when he refers to our cultural tradition's "spirit of endless searching" and the related discovery of "the idea of development, and ultimately of what we call progress as well." He points to the dangers of a wedding between this dynamism and the narrowness of modernity's pragmatic outlook — which has produced a culture in which "hands" took precedence over "minds," producing "the modern cult of beginnings, opening, advances, discoveries, growth, and prosperity, . . . a cult of industriousness, outward activity, expansion, and energy, that is, of the characteristically modern blind faith in quantitative indices." It is this approach which has produced the "huge social inequalities," the "arrogant anthropocentric treatment of the planet," the "cult of consumerism," and the "stockpiles of unbelievably destructive weapons" of today's world.

Havel develops the metaphor of "sunset," suggested by the Akkadian root of Europe's name. If the present moment of Europe's history sees the sun setting upon its era of world dominance, it may also prove "a time of quiet contemplation, reflection, evaluation, introspection — in other words of inwardly directed endeavor," such as is associated with the day's end. Havel is suggesting that the moment is ripe for Europe to find the wisdom which can be derived from its remarkably rich cultural heritage: "the time has come," he says, "for us to pause and reflect upon ourselves" and upon "the great historical challenge" this moment brings. Such a moment need not be one in which Europe is "estranged" from its true self and the world at large; it may be a moment in which Europe recognizes the true nature of the task which lies ahead of it in the coming century.

Havel echoes Roberts as he lists the immense achievement of Europe's period of modernity: "magnificent human endeavor, great

16. *Sydney Morning Herald,* 1 August 1996.

discoveries of the human mind. . . . From the secrets of Being and salvation, to the secrets of matter, from the discovery of treasures hidden on faraway continents to political achievements like the recognition of human dignity and liberty, the rule of law and the idea of equality before the law." He suggests, however, that these achievements must be set within the larger perspective of human history: in centuries to come "all European history may seem to have been no more than a single day filled with vigorous activity."

Europe's new role will be very different from that of yesterday: "Europe has ceased to be the center of colonial power or the control room of the world, and it no longer decides the world's fate." The fact that Europe is "no longer the conductor of the global orchestra," however, "does not mean that it has nothing more to say to the world." If it is to fulfill its role, Europe must "rediscover its conscience and its responsibility, in the deepest sense." Europe, if it wishes to do so, can find a new role in the world at large, "something more modest yet more beneficial"; it can become a "model for how different peoples can work together in peace without sacrificing their identity."

Havel speaks of the lack of hope which may defeat his optimism: the "loss of heart" which many Europeans experience before the immensity of the political task before them, the tendency to become lost in economic issues, the danger that discouragement will allow the "demons that have so fatally tormented European history" to reappear. In this context he makes reference to "fanatical nationalism" and "ethnic collectivism."

In the last analysis, Europe's deepest identity is grounded in "a common destiny, a common complex history, common values and a common culture and way of life." To find the authentic role it may have in the future, therefore, it must "revivify its best spiritual and intellectual traditions." The twilight reflection Havel calls for must concern itself with Europe's "spiritual and intellectual identity," with Europe's "soul": "the time of twilight taken as an opportunity for self-reflection, is a direct invitation to" a rededication to the "European tradition." Europe owes its existence to the "extraordinarily fortunate amalgamation of classical antiquity, Jewish religiosity, and Christianity, combined with the fresh energy of so-called barbarian tribes."

Havel is surprisingly forthright in expressing his view of what is called for as Europe reappropriates its authentic identity:

In my view relatively little is needed. We need only to remind ourselves of the anthem of the European Union. Does not Schiller's "Ode to Joy" offer an answer to this question? When it points out that life in the sacred circle of freedom requires giving allegiance and commitment to "the judge above the stars"? What else can this mean but that freedom and responsibility are two sides of the same coin and that freedom is thinkable only when it is based on a sense of responsibility toward an authority that transcends us?

He challenges a basic assumption of the ideology of modernity, judging that the "concept of a metaphysically anchored sense of responsibility has been the cornerstone of the values that underlie the European tradition"; the awakening of Europe's conscience, called for in its present moment of decision, is profoundly linked with this basis — through it Europe must reappropriate "one of the pillars of the European tradition: universalism, the commandment to think of everyone, to act as everyone should act, and to look for universally acceptable solutions."

Running through Havel's address is the theme of "peaceful and democratic cooperation" which must be presupposed if Europe is to find a common destiny for the future. He adopts an attitude different from that of historian J. M. Roberts on this issue. He is convinced that genuine social solidarity "has never meant limiting freedom in the sense that particular civil rights are expropriated by a power that is increasingly remote from the citizen." He believes that Europe has today "the opportunity to establish itself on democratic principles as a whole entity for the first time in its history." Havel's hope for Europe is that the present moment will "bring about a great renaissance of the civic principle as the only possible basis for truly peaceful cooperation among nations." If Europe finds its identity through an appropriation of its authentic traditions, it may become a "model for how different peoples can work together in peace without sacrificing any of their identity."

In evaluating Roberts's study of modern Europe's influence, we suggested that he may have neglected the importance of romanticism in his analysis of European influence in the broader world. Havel's essay seems to illustrate this point. Havel, the playwright, indicates something of the rich heritage this movement has given us in its concern to escape the narrowness of the "scientific" ideology which has so dominated modernity through the immense technological achievements which have transformed the contemporary world.

*   *   *

It comes as no surprise that Johann Baptist Metz, one of the most gifted European theologians of our day, adopts the standpoint of Christian faith as he makes his appraisal of contemporary Western culture. *Faith in History and Society*[17] is a work of "political theology," a "fundamental theology," aiming to provide a starting point of critical awareness for theological discussion, situating that discussion within the realities of society and culture (p. ix). In this relatively short but dense text, the author shows his originality and brilliance in a style rich in arresting epigrammatic statements.

To achieve his objective, Metz undertakes a penetrating criticism of the Enlightenment project and its continuing influence upon contemporary Western culture. He certainly appreciates the essential genius of the Enlightenment, defining this movement as "a process in which man ultimately became practical in his freedom in the face of the direct constraints of tradition," so that "tradition undoubtedly lost its power to determine human activity" (p. 36). He quotes Kant's definition of the Enlightenment as the acceptance of the critical spirit, giving the human agent the freedom "to make public use of reason in all things" (p. 42).

Metz judges, however, that the Enlightenment's reaction against the constraints of tradition assumed a form which was too extreme, depriving the new critical spirit of resources essential to the fostering of an authentic human existence. Ironically, what was intended to be the emancipation of humanity as a whole became the property of "a new elite or new aristocracy" in European society, the bourgeoisie (p. 43). In the hands of the middle class, the critical reason of modernity became "a technical reason which at once reduces everything to the level of an object and makes it marketable and profitable" (p. 44). He sees the pretended absoluteness of modernity's rationality as illusory, since moder-

---

17. References which follow are to Johann Baptist Metz, *Faith in History and Society* (New York: Seabury Crossroad, 1980; German original, 1977).

nity has its own unacknowledged mythologies — "evolution" for instance (pp. 6, 172). Metz suggests that the Enlightenment outlook has tended to undermine the very nature of genuine "politics." As a consequence, politics seems today to be "in its death throes" as it is "set over against technology and economics": "Are we not witnessing an increasing self-paralysis of political reason in the service of technological and economic processes and their anonymous 'power-systems'?" Contemporary politics, he judges, is showing itself incapable of controlling these systems and of extricating society "from the contradictions and catastrophes apparent today" (pp. 101-2).

Metz finds a similar irony in the outcome of the "criticism of metaphysics" which became fundamental to the ideology of modernity. The critical spirit of the Enlightenment served a good purpose when it brought to light the fact that the absolutism characteristic of metaphysics became an instrument of social powers — ecclesiastical and political — which remained "in the background" and not fully accountable (p. 42). But in the excessiveness of its reaction, the Enlightenment — appealing to a reason presumed to be "outside or above history" (p. 15) — found itself deprived of the complex cultural resources and the wisdom needed to deal with the problems which were to emerge in the modern world. Thus middle-class society, which has completely absorbed and become the embodiment of the Enlightenment spirit, "is no longer sustained by any all-embracing traditions, let alone religious traditions" (p. 35) with which to take up the challenges of the late modern world.

Like other commentators, Metz recognizes "liberation" as a theme of central importance in the ideology of modernity; he describes "emancipation" as "a kind of epoch-constituting catchword for our contemporary experience of the world" (p. 119). He too judges that a concept of "liberation" which has no transcendent measure is in real danger of moving "in the direction of a totalitarian control," if it does not "sink to the level of a commonplace idea of pure survival or cunning animal adaptation" (p. 91); in the end, its interpretation of the drama of human history may well be little more than "the apotheosis of banality" (p. 127).

Having adopted as its criterion a reason which pretends to be quite independent of social and historical reality, the Enlightenment brought about a situation in which "religion became a private affair of the middle class" (p. 46). The theology articulating this religion easily became alienated from the full theological significance of such notions as "the subject, the person or existence" (p. 46); shaped by the spirit of the Enlightenment, the thought of this theology was in danger of becoming "a purely theoretical intellectual process dissociated from human subjects" (p. 33). This middle class religion could easily degenerate into "a purely cultic spirituality," out of touch with "all the conflicts, repressions and challenges of everyday life," creating an "esoteric church, the opium of intellectuals" (p. 95).

Acknowledging the positive achievement of the Enlightenment in giving the authority of competence its due place, Metz argues that, as a bearer of existential wisdom, the Christian church can save the modern world from the "banality and collective obscurity" toward which it is heading. It must do this by developing a "type of authority which is backed by *religious* competence" (pp. 41-42).[18]

If the instrumental reason of the Enlightenment reduces everything to the level of "object," the existential truth which challenges its inadequacies is inseparable, in the judgment of Metz, from a true understanding of the "subject." This concept is the pivot upon which the essential argument of his study turns as it establishes a critical starting point for theology's discussion. Metz reminds us of the essays of Charles Taylor and Alasdair MacIntyre, and of the philosophy of Jürgen Habermas, as he directly challenges the assumptions of the Enlightenment concerning the place of the "subject" in our search for truth: "the word subject does not refer to the isolated individual, the monad who is only afterwards made sure of his co-existence with other subjects. Experiences of solidarity with, antagonism towards, liberation from and anxiety about other subjects form an essential part of the constitution of the . . . subject, not afterwards, but from the very beginning" (p. 61).

For Metz, therefore, existence-as-subject implies *solidarity,* another basic theme which emerges in the course of his pages. The Enlightenment's excessive reaction against human traditions alienated modern awareness from the symbols, stories, and collective memories that are the heritage of our solidarity as subjects (p. 150). Moreover,

18. Cf. Karl Rahner, *Theological Investigations* (New York: Crossroad, 1983), 19:115, 128, where a similar point is made.

for Metz, being a "subject" also implies the religious dimension of human existence: religion is essential to "the social constitution of the subject" (p. 46). The ultimate solidarity of humanity is established by "the possibility of all" human persons "becoming subject in the presence of God" (p. 229). As an alternative to a concept of truth measured by ahistorical reason, Metz offers a truth measured by the existence of the subject, what we are calling in these pages "existential truth" — "truth becomes the type of relevance that applies to all subjects"; he includes among these subjects "the dead and those who have been overcome or conquered" (p. 60).

Metz explores the implied link between his reflections upon the subject and another theme which is assuming importance in our discussion — which he refers to under the rubrics of "narrative" and "memory." Biblical religion he describes as "a history of the way in which a people and the individuals belonging to that people became subject in the presence of their God" (p. 60). Metz notes that the truth owned by Christian faith, which cannot be adequately expressed in abstract terms, calls for a narrative form: "Christ does not become universal via an idea, but via the intelligible power of a praxis, the praxis of following Christ. This intelligibility of Christianity cannot be transmitted theologically in a purely speculative way. It can only be transmitted in narrative — as a narrative and practical Christianity" (p. 165).

"Dangerous memory" is a phrase Metz has made part of the vocabulary of contemporary theology. The link with the narrative emphasized by MacIntyre and Taylor is clear. Metz notes that memories can serve different social purposes. Selective memories "in which we do not take the past seriously enough" — for which the past "becomes a paradise without danger, a refuge from our present disappointments" — easily become ideological, serving a "false consciousness" which is the enemy of the subject's truth and integrity. But there are also "dangerous memories" which "make demands on us," in which "earlier experiences break through to the center-point of our lives and reveal new and dangerous insights for the present," so that we see "for a few moments and with a harsh steady light the questionable nature of things we have apparently come to terms with" and are forced to acknowledge "the banality of our supposed 'realism'" (pp. 109-10). It is not surprising, Metz comments, "that the destruction of memory is a typical measure of totalitarian rule" (p. 110).

PART II

Some Fundamental Issues Raised by the Culture of Modernity

CHAPTER 5

Without Wisdom a Culture Disintegrates

MODERNITY IS BEING FORCED TO RECOGNIZE THAT IT must look beyond a too constricted notion of reason or understanding if it is to meet its present challenges. It has been suggested that we must come again to appreciate the place of "sapiential reason" in our Western culture. Several themes which have emerged in our discussion point in the same direction. Narrative, collective memory, and the community solidarity of those seeking the truth have been emphasized as important bearers of our cultural heritage; our neglect of the living continuity of this heritage has been judged as undermining the rationale supporting the moral principles we take for granted. It is not difficult to see that each of these themes brings to light the place of "wisdom" in our civilized tradition, the subject of the present chapter.

It is easier to recognize the importance of "wisdom" than to define it.[1] Clearly, however, "ideology" and "wisdom" are at opposite extremes of the intellectual spectrum. One could say that wisdom adds to the "two-dimensional" data of human experience and scientific reflection — resources immensely increased by the labors of mo-

---

1. The observations which follow are indebted to the essay "Wisdom," in *The Great Books*, vol. 3, *The Great Ideas: A Syntopicon*, ed. R. M. Hutchins et al. (Chicago: Britannica, 1952), pp. 1102-9.

dernity's Enlightenment and romantic movements — a "third dimension" of existentially satisfying interpretation. Though few of us would claim to possess wisdom, a consensus concerning its essential characteristics and its importance is not difficult to achieve — something which is not possible as far as art, science, or knowledge and learning in general are concerned.[2]

Though it would be generally agreed that belonging to a cultural tradition is an essential prerequisite to the finding of wisdom, wisdom does not advance cumulatively within a cultural tradition in the way knowledge in general does. It has the nature of a *personal* rather than a *group* achievement. Moreover, wisdom has no commonly recognized association with modernity; while the phrase "modern science" is immediately meaningful, most people would find "modern wisdom" a perplexing notion. "Ancient wisdom," on the other hand, has a familiar ring. The obvious implication is that, in the course of history, wisdom may diminish within a particular cultural tradition. Wisdom is recognizably different from "science" and "knowledge" in general in another way. While the latter can be misused, wisdom cannot; it somehow unites knowledge and goodness in a manner which makes its abuse unthinkable.

In his novel *War and Peace,* considered by some the greatest novel ever written, Tolstoy uses the narrative form to explore the ultimate questions of human existence. In more than one climactic passage, his characters echo what has just been said as they reflect upon the "wisdom" their experience has brought them — as for instance: "All we can know is that we know nothing. And that's the height of human wisdom"; "the highest wisdom is not founded on reason alone, nor on those worldly sciences of physics, chemistry, and the

2. This assertion finds confirmation in a 1975 survey of Australian attitudes and values carried out by Valerie Braithwaite, with 183 adults in Brisbane, to identify values which established their "personal and social goals" (cited by Gary L. Sturgess in a background paper presented at a "roundtable" organized by Australia's Constitutional Centenary Foundation, 25 January 1996). Of the fifty-four values itemized as having substantial support, "Wisdom (Having a mature understanding of life)" ranked with "The protection of human life (Taking care to preserve your own life and the life of others)" and "Human Dignity (Allowing each individual to be treated as someone of worth)" as owned by virtually 100 percent of respondents.

like into which intellectual knowledge is divided"; rather it is "but one science — the science of the whole — the science explaining the whole creation and man's place in it. To receive that science it is necessary to purify and renew one's inner self . . . and to attain this end, we have the light called conscience that God has implanted in our souls."

It seems, therefore, that wisdom is not so much a transmissible element of culture as the capacity to achieve a meaningful synthesis which integrates elements of the rich manifold of a cultural heritage. If this is so, the getting of wisdom presents a special challenge to new world cultures, particularly those which have a population coming from very diverse cultural backgrounds.

It was in the course of my efforts to interpret the characteristics of our Australian culture, for the writing of my text *Making Australia,* that I first became interested in the characteristics of new world cultures. In discussing culture as a human achievement whereby the common realities of human existence are put together "to constitute a world that is meaningful and bearable," I saw Australia as "a kind of remote seed-bed in which identifiable cultural elements brought from the old world found a life of their own, and in which indigenous growths eventually made their appearance."[3]

As I sought to identify what was peculiar to developments in the culture of white Australia — during its formative period prior to the Second World War — interpreters such as C. E. W. Bean[4] helped me see that the "frontier" spirit of the nineteenth century, such as was celebrated by Rudyard Kipling,[5] was an important formative element. This spirit released much of the energy which transformed the world map of the nineteenth century.[6] I formed the opinion that our new world culture has not been without its modest measure of "wisdom," titling one of the chapters in which I discussed an important part of our cultural heritage "A Wisdom Found in Adversity and Failure."

In *Making Australia* I also discussed the United States as provid-

3. John Thornhill, *Making Australia* (Newtown, New South Wales: Millennium, 1992), p. 32.
4. Cf. Thornhill, pp. 60-61.
5. Cf. Thornhill, p. 60.
6. Cf. Thornhill, pp. 53, 59-60, 63.

ing an important term of comparison in any effort to understand Australia's new world culture.[7] This is especially true of the Australia which has emerged from the massive immigration policy adopted after the Second World War. The relative homogeneity of early Australian culture — which produced the "wisdom" to which I refer — has been replaced by a far more challenging diversity.[8]

During the nineteenth century, the United States welcomed a huge intake of migrants from a wide variety of cultural backgrounds. As a consequence Americans do not share in any single age-old cultural tradition. The cultural unity they have achieved belongs to another order, that of the American ideal, the ideology whereby America interprets itself as the ultimate home of freedom, the greatest democracy the world has ever seen, with a "manifest destiny" to lead the world. This ideological ideal was more superficial, more open to self-serving and deception, than the cultural traditions in which the peoples of the old world found their identity — traditions with deep roots in values and ideals long nurtured in folk memory and symbolized in countless historical events, in national ritual, in literature, art, and architecture. The cultures of the old world had other "demons" to exorcise, as Václav Havel has reminded us.

In the culture of the United States, the most powerful nation the world has known, the culture of modernity assumes its most defined and militant form. Avery Dulles, one of America's most respected theologians, comments on the culture of the United States with words

---

7. Cf. Thornhill, pp. 28-29.

8. As I wrote in *Making Australia,* p. 19: "The community which developed in this country during the nineteenth century was one in which there coexisted distinct cultural traditions. The interchange between these cultures — those of England, Ireland and Scotland — in the first phase of Australian history, was an interchange which in all its diverse moods, ranging from common cause to distrust and antagonism, was grounded in the symbiotic relationship which had been produced by centuries of European cohabitation. Today's multiculturalism, in which juxtaposed cultural traditions enter into a new and unprecedented relationship, is of course very different. The antipodean transplant of the cultural interaction of the British Isles had, of course, its own distinctive features. For one thing, the Scots were no longer up in Scotland and the Irish were no longer across the Irish Sea, but these two groups were dispersed through the colonies, rubbing shoulders with fellow citizens of Anglo-Saxon extraction. There was also a considerable increase in the Irish component."

that bring to mind the characteristics of modernity with which our discussion has made us familiar. He judges that the United States suffered "a major incursion of individualistic utilitarian philosophy in the 19th century." He continues, "The common good was reconceived as the net result of a balancing of contrary interests. The pursuit of private gain by individuals and groups was seen as contributing, in the long run, to the prosperity of all. . . . The role of the Government was seen as that of an arbiter, laying down the conditions under which competition could be fairly conducted."[9]

Since writing *Making Australia,* I have become aware that the question of new world cultures has given rise to considerable discussion in the United States. F. J. Turner's "frontier thesis," first proposed in 1893, had an immense impact on the work of historians.[10] Turner was reacting against an interpretation of American history which made old world "germs," or cultural elements derived from Europe, the determining factors in America's development. For him the challenge of an expanding frontier was "the most important single influence" insofar as it "turned European things into American things."[11]

9. In "Catholicism and American Culture: The Uneasy Dialogue," *America,* 27 January 1990, p. 55. See also the remarkable U.S. study in self-criticism, Robert N. Bellah, Richard Madsen, William M. Sullivan, Ann Swidler, and Steven M. Tipton, *Habits of the Heart: Individualism and Commitment in American Life* (New York: Harper & Row, 1986), to which reference will be made in chap. 8.

10. Cf. *The Turner Thesis: Concerning the Role of the Frontier in American History,* ed. G. R. Taylor (Boston: Heath, 1956).

11. G. W. Pierson, in *The Turner Thesis,* p. 48. Turner first made an impact with a paper delivered in 1893. In a 1920 publication he summarized his position: "there was this gate of escape to the free conditions of the frontier. These free lands promoted individualism, economic equality, freedom to rise, democracy" (*The Turner Thesis,* p. 28). "It gave to the pioneer farmer and city builder a restless energy, a quick capacity for judgment and action, a belief in liberty, freedom of opportunity, and a resistance to the domination of class which infused a vitality and power into the individual atoms of this democratic mass" (p. 30). "American democracy is fundamentally the outcome of the experiences of the American people dealing with the West . . . the production of a society of which the most distinctive fact was the freedom of the individual to rise under conditions of social mobility, and whose ambition was the liberty and well-being of the masses" (pp. 31-32).

It was probably inevitable that the overwhelming success of Turner's thesis should be followed by a reassessment in which he was accused of oversimplifying the issues of U.S. history. With a single-minded concern for what was certainly a major influence, Turner neglected to take into account the other factors at work in America's formative period. A sympathetic critic of his work concludes that his major writings interpret the emergence of what characterizes America "without reference to Romanticism, to Evangelism, to the eighteenth-century Enlightenment, to the scientific discoveries and the secularization of thought that in varying degrees have overtaken all Western peoples since the discovery of America."[12] A reappraisal was necessary, especially through a clarification of the relationship between the new world culture of the United States and the European culture from which it was derived. In the words of one contributor to *The Turner Thesis,* "Continuity proved stronger than change. The transit of culture was not so much *from* as *to* the frontier."[13]

Louis Hartz has proposed an interpretation of new world cultures which comes to terms more adequately with the influence, in their formation, of cultural factors of the old world.[14] Hartz interprets new world cultures as incorporating "fragments of the larger whole of Europe" which are "detached" and "hurled outward onto new soil";[15] these cultural fragments lapse "into a kind of immobility" because they are deprived of "the stimulus toward change that the whole provides." His examples are illuminating. He sees Latin America and French Canada as embodying a "feudal" fragment which failed, subsequently, to evolve as did the European reality from which it came.[16] The United States embodies a "Whig" fragment which, in the absence of the symbiotic relationship it had with European traditions, developed into "a uniformly liberal culture which gathered peasants, 'petty bourgeois' and proletarians all into the ranks of democratic lib-

12. Pierson, p. 65.

13. C. J. H. Hayes, in *The Turner Thesis,* p. 71.

14. Cf. Louis Hartz, *The Founding of New Societies* (New York: Harcourt, Brace & World, 1964).

15. Hartz, p. 3.

16. In chap. 5 of *Founding of New Societies,* "The Heritage of Latin America," Richard M. Morse applies the principles of Hartz; and in chap. 7, "The Structure of Canadian History," Kenneth D. McRae does the same.

eralism" as an "egalitarian giant."[17] Australia embodies a fragment shaped by "the proletarian turmoil of the industrial revolution."[18] Hartz interprets late twentieth-century history as bringing an ironic impact of European modernity upon these fragments in the form their isolated life has given them.[19]

Hartz's hypothesis has much to commend it. It provides an important complement to Turner's thesis. Like Turner, however, he seems to make the mistake of seeking a single identifiable factor which provides the key to the interpretation of the history of new world societies. However, both Hartz's and Turner's factors are essential to a satisfactory understanding of American history. To see them as alternatives, as Hartz tends to do,[20] is to fail to recognize their complementarity.

If, as we have suggested, wisdom is found in achieving a synthesis which makes use of the rich manifold of a long-standing cultural tradition, Hartz's analysis of what has been involved in the removal of a "fragment" from the manifold in which it originated helps us toward a more satisfactory understanding of new world cultures. It helps us understand the seeming naïveté with which these cultures often seem to respond to the most basic of human questions — a naïveté which is very different from wisdom.

One would have to say that the public discussion in our Australian context of fundamental human questions — the discussion, for example, of the nature and function of the family, of the challenges brought by our "multicultural" society, and debate concerning such complex issues as abortion and euthanasia — is very disappointing for anyone who judges that only a genuine wisdom will provide the answers. More often than not, these and other political discussions become little more than an exchange of slogans, and their outcome seems to depend upon the effectiveness of lobby groups, political ex-

17. Hartz, p. 82.

18. Chap. 8 of *Founding of New Societies*, "The Radical Culture of Australia," in which Richard N. Rosencrance attempts an application of Hartz's principles to Australian culture, is somewhat disappointing. The developments of the three decades since Hartz's text was published, however, may well provide the material for a far more fruitful study.

19. Hartz, p. 3.

20. Cf. Hartz, p. 10 n, pp. 69-70 n.

pediency, and the trends of the latest opinion polls. The fact that, in the United States, the defense of traditional values relevant to these issues is in the hands of an alliance of fundamentalist Christians and the hard political right seems to provide confirmation for Hartz's interpretation of new world cultures as constituted by "fragments" of old world cultures which have become detached from the roots which give them vitality and resilience in their old world setting. The fact that, as we shall see in a later chapter, Harold Bloom finds it necessary to defend the "canon" of Western literature within the context of American culture seems to provide another illustration of the working out of the process suggested by Hartz.

Wisdom finds its defenders in our contemporary Western culture, however, in unexpected places — as a couple of Australian examples show. The cartoonist Michael Leunig has become a household name in Australia in recent years. The attention his work has been given provides clear evidence that in our Australian culture there is a deep yearning to recover the wisdom we seem to have lost. In a recent interview,[21] Leunig described himself as like "a monk in an old monastery." He spoke of what he is doing when he creates the cartoons which capture so poignantly the common experience of humanity: "you have to say the ritualistic words, almost, that other people feel but they don't have a chance to say, and sometimes you're like a therapist. Children need to hear mature people in society saying this is cruel or this is unfair, this is unjust." The wisdom he shares, in other words, is not esoteric but readily accessible to those who are in touch with their own humanity: "I think life is so full of choices that the great art of it is just to choose very little and make a lot of it."

The writings of our other example, acclaimed Australian author Tim Winton, have an inspiration very similar to Leunig's: to recover a readily accessible wisdom through a sensitive portrayal of the life-giving truth of common human experience. In a recent interview,[22] Winton shared some of the convictions which have inspired him as a writer, convictions with which — though they are far removed from modernity's "scientific" outlook — many Australians would identify.

21. With Fran Malley, *Sydney Weekly,* 21 November 1994.
22. With Michael McGirr, reproduced in the *Bulletin* of the Institute for Theology and the Arts, Paddington, New South Wales, no. 22 (summer 1996).

He judges that this unique continent has "changed" people coming here from the old world — from the moment he arrived in Europe he knew, he tells us, that he "wasn't a European at all." The symbolism of the Australian landscape is "important" for Winton "in a religious sense": "Landscape exists" for him "at the edge of consciousness, as an aspect of the divine."

Winton has wrestled with the issue raised by Kenneth Clark in his assessment of the origins of modernity: the Protestant tradition's creation of a "new civilisation . . . not of the image, but of the word." He was raised in a "non-conformist tradition" which was "appalled by any notion of representation of any form of spirituality." It was not a congenial environment for "a young boy totally affected by landscape and apprehending God through that, and through music and art and literature." In the end, he tells us, he had to leave the church of his childhood "in order to keep his faith." He now realizes that he was "hankering for liturgy" and its symbolism. He needed a "religious language" that was "sacramental."

If nature is an all-important religious symbol for Winton, he acknowledged nevertheless the importance of cultural forms as bearers of our human traditions. He was amazed to see his son responding to the architecture of Notre Dame in Paris: "For a kid, like myself, who was brought up in landscape, I was amazed at the way he responded to architecture. His eyes were out on sticks." From his childhood formation, Winton gratefully remembers "the richness of the life of story . . . the storiness of Scripture." Recalling the experience of sharing the story of Good Friday and Easter with his son, he reflected, "I realised what had sustained my faith as a child, apart from all the institutional frustrations, was the purity and power of all the stories which add up to the big story. And which I claim as my story."

Leunig and Winton illustrate something Robert Bellah and the coauthors of *The Good Society* will emphasize in a later chapter: the matrix of a cultural tradition is the bearer of a far richer diversity of resources than is commonly articulated. It is these resources of "collective memory" which provide the potential for the interpretative function of genuine wisdom. To those which Leunig and Winton have brought to light, we may well add the legends and heroes owned by the narrative traditions of particular traditions. The part played by

105

legends and heroes in the lives of people sharing in a cultural tradition illustrates the fact that resources of a tradition transmitted through an ideological medium — as legends and hero awareness certainly are — have a life-giving potential which is important for a healthy human community.

Cartoonist Michael Leunig and writer Tim Winton are representative of a broad movement without our contemporary culture which is seeking the wisdom to be found beyond the framework of the Enlightenment. Richard Eckersley, for instance, former science reporter for the *Sydney Morning Herald* and the author of important reports for *Australia's Commission for the Future,* reflects this concern among today's scientists themselves. He invites Australians to reflect on the "age-old philosophical questions" familiar to the world's wisdom traditions: "Who are we? Why are we here? Where are we going?" He judges that a narrow focus on "one aspect of science — as a source of practical innovation" and "new technologies" — has created a culture which "isolates us from ourselves, each other, society and nature." We need a "paradigm shift" of awareness which recovers an appreciation of the "undivided, flowing wholeness" of reality and "places humanity firmly within nature."[23] Elsewhere Eckersley takes up another of the themes of our discussion, noting the importance of the "narrative form" in the handing on of the wisdom potential of our cultural heritage to future generations. He judges that the neglect of "stories" which help young people to "construct a world view, a cultural context, to define who they are and what they believe" amounts to "the cultural abuse of an entire generation of young Australians."[24]

Michael McKernan, a distinguished academic who until recently administered the Australian War Memorial in Canberra, shares Eckersley's concern. He is alarmed at the small number of Australians studying history in our schools and universities. He believes that many of our young people are in danger of losing their culture because they do not know, historically, who they are: "it is very worrying," he declares, "that so few Australians know much at all about

23. "The New Science of Culture," *Sydney Morning Herald,* 7 July 1994.
24. "Apocalypse? No! Youth and the Challenge to Change," essay no. 1 in *Australia's Commission for the Future* (Carlton, Victoria, 1992).

what is the story of Australia. We stand the risk of being a nation without a collective memory."[25]

Wisdom is a personal rather than a group achievement, very different from the "cleverness" of the intellectual. Paul Ricoeur's frequently noted concept of a "second naivety" may well have considerable importance in helping us understand how wisdom can become a practical reality within the cultural traditions shaped by the awarenesses of modernity. Ricoeur suggests that the myths, symbols, and stories which have had a fundamental importance in the cultural traditions of the past may find a new meaningfulness, as a "dimension of modern thought" in our postscientific era, if — losing the "explanatory pretensions" they had in the "first naivety" of their origins — they are owned as having an "exploratory significance" for a symbolic and sapiential understanding.[26]

Louis Hartz's interpretation of the development of new world cultures suggests a comparison which may help us understand the culture of modernity. Modernity quite consciously created a "new world" to replace the world shaped by the traditional culture of the Middle Ages. It should not surprise us if this new world has some of the characteristics of the new world cultures analyzed by Hartz.

Just as new world cultures like those of the United States and Australia were constituted by the extrapolation of a fragment from the cultural matrix of their European origin, so too modernity created its new world by extrapolating the fragment of self-conscious rationality from the rich matrix of traditions, values, and wisdom potential in which that fragment had been nurtured by a thousand years of medievalism. In detaching its foundational fragments from their original cultural setting, a new world culture, Hartz suggests, paid the inevitable price of a development in isolation from its original nurturing matrix. The disintegration and existential frustration characteristic of contemporary modernity may be interpreted as evidence that modernity's "new world" paid a similar price. In fact, as we shall see in a later chapter, the famous U.S. columnist Walter Lippmann made this

25. As reported in the *Australian,* 21 August 1996. In Australia, at the present time, history is studied by less than 10 percent of students at tertiary level, and by less than 20 percent at secondary level.

26. Cf. Paul Ricoeur, *The Symbolism of Evil,* trans. Buchanan (Boston: Beacon Press, 1969), p. 5; see also introduction.

very point, commenting upon American society: "We are an uprooted people. . . . The modern man is not settled in his world. . . . We are blown hither and thither like litter before the wind."[27]

Those formed in the culture of Western modernity now look nostalgically at cultural traditions which have not been affected by the constricted assumptions of Western modernity. The words of Robert Bellah's *Habits of the Heart* concerning the culture of the United States illustrate this nostalgia, while at the same time lending support to Hartz's "fragment" theory of new world cultures: "Perhaps the truth lies in what most of the world outside the modern West has always believed, namely that there are practices of life, good in themselves, that are inherently fulfilling. . . . We have imagined ourselves a special creation, set apart from other humans. In the late twentieth century, we see that our poverty is as absolute as that of the poorest of nations."[28]

David Suzuki, one of the world's leading environmentalists, tells us that we have much to learn from the wisdom of cultures formed by the cosmic religions if we are to have a future on the planet.[29] There is a growing awareness among Australians that the culture of our indigenous people embodies, in its reverence for the environment, a wisdom from which we can learn. For all its bizarre aspects, the New Age movement's desire to find a new relationship with the dynamisms of nature may well prove in the end to be an awkward symptom of the existential frustrations of the closed world of modernity.

27. Quoted in Robert N. Bellah, Richard Madsen, William M. Sullivan, Ann Swidler, and Steven M. Tipton, *The Good Society* (New York: Random House, Vintage, 1992), p. 57.

28. Bellah et al., *Habits of the Heart*, pp. 295-96.

29. David Suzuki, *The Wisdom of the Elders* (New York: Bantam Books, 1993).

CHAPTER 6

Modernity's "Affirmation of the Ordinary" and Today's Mass Culture

THE PRESENT ERA HAS BEEN CHARACTERIZED AS "THE age of the common man and woman." Setting the ordinary man and woman at the center of the stage of life is an essential element of the ideology of modernity. Charles Taylor constantly refers to it in his discussion of contemporary ethical theories and, in fact, judges that an "affirmation of ordinary life has become one of the most powerful ideas in modern civilisation" (p. 14).[1] José Ortega y Gasset describes this development as "the most important fact in the public life of the West in modern times."[2]

Taylor discusses the paradoxical genesis of this modern attitude. He sees its contemporary form as the outcome of a reaction which was one of the driving forces of the Protestant Reformation. Ultimately, as he acknowledges, such an evaluation of ordinary life is grounded in "one of the most fundamental insights of the Jewish-Christian-Islamic religious tradition" (p. 218). Taylor suggests, however, that during the Middle Ages a hierarchical emphasis derived

---

1. Page references to Taylor are to *Sources of the Self: The Making of the Modern Identity* (Cambridge: Cambridge University Press, 1992).

2. José Ortega y Gasset, "The Crowd Phenomenon," cited in Lawrence Cahoone's anthology, *From Modernism to Postmodernism* (Cambridge, Mass.: Blackwell, 1996), p. 219; cf. also p. 225.

from Platonism tended to obscure this fundamental Christian value, giving rise to "a view of ascetic vocations as 'higher.'" The Reformation was, in part, a reaction against the elitism fostered by this hierarchical perspective: the Reformers rebelled against "the distorted notion of the monastic vocation, as the fully Christian life in contrast to the lay state as a half effort" (p. 220). This distorted view of the vocation of Christians was still influential in the early twentieth century: in 1935 Jacques Maritain ironically referred to the common assumption that the laity belonged to "a state of imperfection."[3] It was one of the issues which emerged in the debates of the Second Vatican Council.

It is not surprising that the "affirmation of the ordinary" became an important element in the ideology expressing modernity's reaction to medievalism. According to Taylor, there is a kinship between Protestantism's rejection of the elitism of the medieval culture and the beginnings of the experimental methodology of modern science, exemplified in the work of Francis Bacon: "the proponents of both . . . saw themselves as rebelling against a traditional authority" and "returning to neglected sources: Scripture on the one hand, experimental reality on the other." He continues: "Both appealed to what they saw as living experience against dead received doctrine . . . the paradigm figure against which both rebellions were levelled was the same," namely, Aristotle, "seen by both as the father of traditional physics . . . and as the philosophical mentor of the scholastic theologians" (p. 230).[4]

Taylor judges that this mentality undermined what had been the traditional basis of moral doctrine since the time of Plato; its rejection

3. Jacques Maritain, *True Humanism* (London: Geoffrey Bles, 1954), p. 116. Counter-Reformation Catholicism was slow to recognize that Protestantism's reaction to the elitism of medieval culture was justified. Maritain cites the views of the influential sixteenth-century theologian Melchior Cano: he opposed giving religious instruction such as was given to the clergy to the ordinary faithful; he opposed the reading of the Scriptures in the vernacular; and he saw the increased frequenting of the sacraments by the laity as one of the signs of the approach of the Antichrist!

4. Cf. Taylor, p. 231, where a link is suggested between the origins of modern science and Puritanism, as the goal of science shifted "from contemplation to productive efficacy . . . based on a biblical understanding of humans as stewards in God's creation." Max Weber drew attention to this factor in the shaping of modern Western culture with his study *The Protestant Ethic and the Spirit of Capitalism* (1904).

of what it saw as elitism fostered reductionist interpretations of moral values (p. 23). Later, the Enlightenment contributed to this process by denouncing Christianity for "laying a crushing burden on those in whom it inculcates a sense of sin," so that the libertarian mood of modernity's ideology experiences a breaking of an allegiance to certain traditionally accepted values as a "liberation" (p. 81). Taylor sees in this representative modern theme an instance of the paradox according to which the moral teaching of modernity covertly appeals to the very values it repudiates. The repudiation, early in the modern period, of supposedly "higher" goods and modes of activity was grounded in "a positive vision of ordinary life as hallowed by God." If it has repudiated this theistic basis, something of its inspiration is still present in the moral seriousness with which the value of ordinary life is affirmed today; to explain this seriousness, Taylor suggests, we must invoke this "predecessor" and also "raise the question to what degree" this seriousness "is still living from the spiritual insights of this predecessor which it claims to have repudiated" (p. 104).

The identification of the authentic message of the Judeo-Christian tradition with an affirmation of the ordinary was an established fact long before the Reformation. When Francis of Assisi embraced the gospel ideal of poverty, as Kenneth Clark reminds us, he did it "partly because he felt that it was discourteous to be in the company of anyone poorer than himself."[5] Erich Auerbach has analyzed the manner in which the New Testament registers a revolutionary change in our civilization's recognition of the place of the ordinary man and woman and their life concerns in the scheme of things. Auerbach sees this epitomized in Peter, who, in the gospel story, is "no accessory figure" but the "image" of humanity "in the highest and deepest and most tragic sense." This inspiring vision, Auerbach points out, is not the outcome of artistic creativity, but "was rooted from the beginning in the character of Jewish-Christian literature," which finds its ultimate inspiration in "God's incarnation in a human being of the humblest social station, through his existence on earth amid humble everyday people and conditions, and through his Passion, which, judged by earthly standards, was ignominious."

5. Kenneth Clark, *Civilisation: A Personal View* (London: BBC, 1969), p. 76.

This gospel story had "a most decisive bearing" upon our "concept of the tragic and the sublime." Peter and the other actors in the story of his denial are of the humblest background and human qualification. "A tragic figure from such a background, a hero of such weakness, who yet derives the highest force from his very weakness, such a to and fro of the pendulum" breaks out of the constraints of the "sublime style of classical antique literature." It arouses a sympathy and awareness in humanity "because it portrays something which neither the poets nor the historians of antiquity ever set out to portray: the birth of a spiritual movement in the depths of the common people, from within the everyday occurrences of contemporary life, which thus assumes an importance it could never have assumed in antique literature." This instance, Auerbach observes, is representative of the whole New Testament. Taking up, as it does, the universal concerns of humanity, it sets the whole world astir: "what we see here is a world which on the one hand is entirely real, average, identifiable as to place, time, and circumstances, but which on the other hand is shaken in its very foundations, is transforming and renewing itself before our eyes."[6]

Modernity's affirmation of the ordinary has had, it is clear, a complex development, and has found expression in very different ways. Great artists reflect the mood of their culture. If the Reformation was reacting to a theological elitism which had established itself in medieval culture, Clark finds another form of elitism reflected in the art of the Renaissance. The tapestry designs of Raphael, he points out, give expression to a convention according to which "the great events of biblical or secular history" are enacted only by "magnificent physical specimens." He judges that this convention proved a "deadening influence" in later art and, in the end, was to provoke today's "hideous reaction."[7] On the other hand, the mystical vision of a painter such as van Gogh was strongly drawn to the celebration of ordinary existence, and his expression of it went to the heart of the truth it encapsulates. The great acclaim van Gogh has received in our day, contrasted with the lack of recognition he was given during his life-

6. Erich Auerbach, *Mimesis: The Representation of Reality in Western Literature* (Princeton: Princeton University Press, 1974), pp. 41-42.
7. Clark, p. 133.

time, constitutes a tragic parable illustrating the emergence of our theme in late modern culture.

In 1875 van Gogh wrote to his brother: "Man is not on the earth merely to be happy, nor even to be simply upright. He is here to realise great things for society, to attain nobility and to rise above the vulgarity in which almost all individuals drag out their existence."[8] The work of Millet, who departed from convention in making peasants and workers his favored subject, was van Gogh's lifelong inspiration. Vincent took Millet's subjects and "translated" them, as he put it, through his own artistic expression. If Millet's portrayals — *The Gleaners* and *The Angelus* are familiar examples of his work — strike us today as "sentimental,"[9] Vincent's will stand for all time as an invitation to recognize the true dignity of the ordinary human beings he portrays.[10] It would not be difficult to find numerous parallels in Western literature. The stories of Guy de Maupassant, Flannery O'Connor, and Shusaku Endo come to mind. In our Australian tradition, we think of Henry Lawson's portrayal of the ordinary Australian "battler."[11]

The development of this theme in late modernity has a darker side, however. The German theologian Romano Guardini, writing in the aftermath of World War II, confronted in *The End of the Modern World: A Search for Orientation*[12] questions raised by recent developments in our Western culture. The editor's introduction calls it "the most sombre book to come out of Germany since the Third Reich died," a portrayal of "the end of our world" and the anticipation of the "world which is to come" (p. 3). It is not difficult to link Guardini's "grim picture of the new age of mass man" with his recent experience of the Nazi regime and its hold upon the German people.

8. *Van Gogh: His Sources, Genius, and Influence*, ed. Judith Ryan (Sydney: Art Exhibitions Aust. Ltd., 1993), p. 16.

9. *Van Gogh*, p. 40.

10. See, for example, *Worn Out* (1881), *The Sower* (1882, etc.), *Head of a Peasant* (1884), *Potato Eaters* (1885), *Head of a Man* (1886), *Portrait of the Postman, Joseph Roulin* (1886).

11. Cf. my *Making Australia* (Newtown, New South Wales: Millennium, 1992), index under "Henry Lawson."

12. Romano Guardini, *The End of the Modern World: A Search for Orientation* (London: Sheed & Ward, 1957; German ed., 1950). Page references which follow are to this text.

113

His description of "mass man" reminds us of Max Weber's "iron cage of rationalised bureaucracy." He links the emergence of this cultural type — which, ironically, "stands at the extreme pole from the autonomous" — with the bourgeoisie's pursuit of "rational clarity" and the "rise of technology." Indeed, this type is fashioned according to the "law of standardisation, a law dictated by the functional nature of the machine." Its vanguard "are not merely conscious of the influence of the machine; they deliberately imitate it, building its standards and rhythms into their own ethos" (p. 77). Guardini describes the regimentation of "mass man" in a way which reminds us of Taylor: "the regimented instincts of this new human type forbid him to appear distinctive, compel him to appear anonymous. Mass man acts almost as if he felt that to be one's self was both the source of all injustice and even a sign of peril" (p. 79).

Ortega y Gasset ironically describes the regimented existence of the contemporary world: "We can tell a mass-man when we see one. . . . The mass-man is anyone who does not value himself, for good or ill, by any particular criterion, and who says instead that he is 'just like everybody else.' Despite this ridiculous claim, he will not feel any disquiet, but rather feel reassured, smugly at ease, to be considered identical with all the others."[13] For Johann Baptist Metz, as we have seen, the culture shaped by such an outlook will be little more than "the apotheosis of banality."

The momentous technological developments of the decades since Guardini wrote this text have further accentuated the developments he describes. The "mass media" of communication, as they are called, are increasingly standardizing humanity's access to information and our possibilities for entertainment. The integration of the economies of the world places the decisions which shape so many features of our world in the hands of fewer and fewer individuals, and at the service of their self-interest. The demands of "economic rationalism," and the pursuit of expansion for technological empires depending upon immense resources of finance and manpower, foster a world of "competing and escalating imperialistic systems."[14]

13. Ortega y Gasset, p. 222.
14. Cf. Robert Doran, *Theology and the Dialectics of History* (Toronto: University Press, 1990), pp. 116-18 and index under "imperialism."

The political process of democratic society in the age of mass culture and standardized communication becomes more and more a manipulation of the media images of the protagonists, and an exploiting of the possibilities of influencing enormous audiences by subtle propaganda and innuendo. The standardization of entertainment makes boredom one of the pervasive problems of contemporary society. To meet this situation, those who devise this entertainment are increasingly tempted to have recourse to the outrageous, the violent, the bizarre. Increasing exposure to these things desensitizes the audience, and we see the emergence of a new species of antiheroes, iconoclasts who entertain through the shock of ridiculing the accepted standards of our cultural heritage. Dress fashions have always followed a pattern of standardization, but now, with the age of the common man and woman, the proletarian style has become the norm and fashion houses produce proletarian-style clothes with brand names! It may well be argued that this pervasive boredom, and the existential frustration it masks, contribute to the increasing problems of drug taking and irresponsible violence within contemporary society.

The form this theme has assumed in the ideology of modernity is a paradoxical instance of the problem inherent in an ideology which has not owned any measure beyond its own discourse. If our interpretation of modernity is sound, it is inspired by the restless quest for excellence which characterizes our cultural tradition. Yet the "affirmation of the ordinary" has assumed a form in the ideology of modernity which is the enemy of excellence. It is this contradiction that Ortega y Gasset confronts. He sees a healthy cultural community as "always a dynamic unity composed of two factors: masses and minorities." The special "qualifications" of excellence possessed by members of the minorities enrich and sustain the lives of the masses. If they are suppressed, the culture will inevitably degenerate.[15]

One would never suggest the life of ancient Athens or of the medieval towns which produced the great cathedrals as models for us to follow. But one is startled to reflect upon the astounding creativity of these communities — comparable in their population with the minor provincial centers of the contemporary world — as illustrations of the point Ortega y Gasset is making.

15. Ortega y Gasset, p. 221.

Modernity's distrust of traditionally accepted standards, as fostering elitism, assumes many shapes. In *The Western Canon: The Books and School of the Ages*,[16] the American literary scholar Harold Bloom has felt obliged to defend the enduring value for our Western tradition of the great achievements of the literature of the past. He finds himself contending against a "School of Resentment" which sees claims of aesthetic excellence in these works as coming from an unacknowledged desire to maintain elitist privilege in the ongoing "class struggle" (p. 23). He fears that a process has already begun, in which "What are now called 'Departments of English' will be re-named departments of 'Cultural Studies' where *Batman* comics, . . . theme parks, television, movies, and rock will replace Chaucer, Shakespeare, Milton . . ." (p. 519). Bloom employs the word "canon," which is "religious in its origins," because the "scandalous original-ity" of writers such as Shakespeare is denied by the "School of Re-sentment" because they have given themselves over to the "worship" of "the composite god of historical process" (p. 20).[17] Bloom is pessi-mistic concerning the short-term outcome of the leveling process of "resentment" — "the Balkanization of literary studies" (p. 517) — which is taking place in his own professional field. In fact, he de-scribes his work as an "elegy" for the canon (p. 517).

If he points to an order of value which is *existential* in his defense of the canon, Bloom's argument does not appeal to a shallow moral-ism: "The silliest way to defend the Western Canon," he writes, "is to insist that it incarnates all of the seven deadly virtues that make up our supposed range of normative values and democratic principles" (p. 29). Paradoxically, Bloom's defense of the canon may well be in-terpreted as a defense of the *ordinary* in its most authentic expression in our tradition, rather than as a bolstering of the elitism resented by the mood of modernity. He sees the *aesthetic* as having its own "power," "authority," and "dignity," urging that we must distinguish this authority "from whatever spiritual, political, or even moral conse-quences it may have fostered" (p. 36).

16. References which follow are to Harold Bloom, *The Western Canon: The Books and School of the Ages* (New York: Harcourt Brace & Co., 1994).
17. Bloom places Shakespeare at the center of the canon, affirming the "qualitative difference" (p. 25) by which he surpasses "every other writer": "no one has matched him as psychologist, thinker, or rhetorician" (p. 10).

116

We human beings need such an enduring existential authority "because we are mortal" (p. 30). The canon emerges in the process of "tradition" whereby we transcend our mortality. When it is authentic, this process "is not only a handing-down or process of benign transmission; it is also a conflict between past genius and present aspiration, in which the prize is literary survival or canonical inclusion" (pp. 8-9). The body of Bloom's work richly illustrates the subtle conflict which has shaped the literary tradition of our culture, as "greatness recognizes greatness and is shadowed by it" (p. 10). We shall return to this peculiar authority of literary narrative in a later chapter.

In the light of our own discussion of the differentiation of historical periods, it is interesting that Bloom's reflections upon the canon of literature and its fate in contemporary culture lead him to adopt the schema of historical periods suggested by Giambattista Vico (1668-1744), the Italian scholar who pioneered the philosophical interpretation of human history. Vico's treatise *The New Science* saw history as proceeding according to a cycle. "Theocratic," "Aristocratic," and "Democratic" ages succeed one another, and a "Chaotic" age follows, giving rise finally to the emergence of a new "Theocratic" age (Bloom, p. 1). Following Vico's schema, Bloom judges that we are at present entering a "Chaotic Age," and he would not be surprised, he tells us, to see the emergence of a new "Theocratic Age." He is apprehensive concerning the form the "Theocratic Age" may take, if the influence of the United States is to be a determining factor.

Bloom is critical of his own country, the United States: "the evening land is now in the West's evening time" (p. 38); "We dominate the Age of Chaos because we have always been chaotic, even in the Democratic Age" (p. 518). One must agree: a study of modernity, as we have seen, cannot escape reflection upon this nation of unprecedented power and influence.

The United States is a social experiment without precedent, produced by and reflecting the mobility and vitality of the Western tradition. It is a nation with a divided soul. On the one hand, its Puritan origins have left it with the sense of a God-given "manifest destiny" — leading G. K. Chesterton to describe it as "a nation with the soul of a church." On the other hand, it is a creature of the Enlightenment, an object lesson in the characteristics of Western mass culture, and the aggressive advocate of both of these.[18]

The American playwright Arthur Miller commented on the culture of his country when interviewed on the occasion of the publication of his play *The Last Yankee*.[19] Miller's views are of special interest in our discussion of the age of the common man and woman because with his play *The Death of a Salesman*, Miller is said to have portrayed the American theater's "definitive common man." His recent play takes up a similar theme. This perceptive observer has watched the United States develop in the course of the present century — he was seventy-nine when interviewed. He still has faith in the wisdom of which common man and woman are capable: judging that "people in general are searching for a sense of values"; insisting that "left to themselves people find their way . . . suddenly from somewhere, God knows where, I've seen it happen before: people suddenly draw themselves up and seem to find some source of just plain common sense."

Miller recognizes that powerful factors symptomatic of late modernity work against this basic goodness. He singles out consumerism as a dominant influence: "What we're always emphasising over here is consume. You exist only to consume." He is very critical of the effect of television upon the lives of ordinary people, as it becomes progressively "irritating" and "stupefying," spreading a "materialism of life" which "seems to overwhelm everything." He thinks television is making Americans "dumber," because "basically it is a superficial art" which "trains people to think superficially." He illustrates this by pointing to the astounding fact that "an enormous number of Americans don't even know we dropped the atom bomb on Japan."

Miller acknowledges that the United States is "the cutting edge of the world, sometimes in a bad way," and that because of its many unsolved social problems, "basically decent, ordinary Americans," such as those portrayed in *The Last Yankee*, "are struggling to keep

18. Cf. my *Making Australia*, pp. 27-31; and Robert N. Bellah, Richard Madsen, William M. Sullivan, Ann Swidler, and Steven M. Tipton, *Habits of the Heart: Individualism and Commitment in American Life* (New York: Harper & Row, 1986).

19. Interview with James Waites, "Speaking for the Drowning," *Sydney Morning Herald*, 8 March 1995.

their heads above the rising flooding waters of social madness." Miller is "appalled at the hypocrisy" within the political world. But he "is not pessimistic entirely," he says, "in the long run." He sees "a lot of creativity" coming out of the "vulgarity" of American life.

CHAPTER 7

Existential Truth, Narrative, and Modernity's "Turn to the Subject"

HAROLD BLOOM TAKES HIS STAND ON THE AUTHOR-
ity of the aesthetic excellence of great literature. We must agree with
him that an attempt to defend the canon by a moralizing argument
commending its function as a vehicle of ethical standards is out of
place. What he is claiming, in the end, is that great portrayals of reality
speak for themselves, through the truth they embody. Alexandr
Solzhenitsyn adopted a similar stand in the speech he prepared for re-
ceiving the Nobel Prize. He pointed to the manner in which great literature expresses the truth to be found in the living reality of its own
world: "The convincingness of a true work of art is completely irre-
futable, and it forces even an opposing heart to surrender."[1] Portrayals which manipulate or force the truth, he noted, do not endure,
and convince no one. But a true masterpiece "bears within itself its
own verification. . . . Those works of art which have scooped up the
truth and presented it to us as a living force — they take hold of us,
compel us, and nobody ever, not even in ages to come, will appear to
refute them."[2]

---

1. As reported in the *Sydney Morning Herald*, 2 September 1972.
2. Bloom makes the point that the "School of Resentment" does not apply
its criticism to music and the visual arts. Matisse and Stravinsky should, he points

120

The fundamental place of narrative in our understanding of the truth of human existence is essential to Solzhenitsyn's argument. It deserves to be carefully pondered as we carry forward our discussion. In the first place it is closely related to the "turn to the subject" which is one of the outstanding characteristics of modernity: its awareness of and exploration of the subjective dimension of human experience.

This development is in marked contrast with the previous outlook of our Western tradition. The outlook of the ancient Greeks and the medievals emphasized the *objective* dimension of experience, showing little inclination to explore the peculiar intelligibility of the experiencing subject. Aquinas, for example, acknowledges the central place of the human subject in the reality of our experience, writing "persona significat id quod est perfectissimum in tota natura" [person signifies that which is most perfect in the whole of nature] (*Summa theologiae* pars 1, q. 29, art. 3 in corp.). Yet his exploration of the implications of his statement is very meager when compared with the work of a thinker like Maurice Merleau-Ponty as he took up Edmund Husserl's challenge to contemporary philosophy.

One is tempted to suggest that the remarkable achievement represented by understanding that is aware of itself — to which reference was made in chapter 2 — tended to capture the attention of our tradition in these earlier periods. *Objective* knowledge became the total concern of the quest for truth, and a full exploration of the *subjective* dimension was not undertaken. Descartes's choice of subjective experience in the form of a doubt is clearly related to the skepticism of an age which was disillusioned with the bankrupt intellectual heritage of late medievalism; Descartes's near contemporary, Montaigne, was expressing the mood of the age when he suggested that the most sophisticated intellectual attitude was a universal doubt. But Descartes's option may well have deeper significance, reflecting the search for an autonomy which had completely emancipated itself from the constraints of medievalism.

---

out, "go down with Joyce and Proust as . . . dead white European males." He continues, "I gaze in wonder at the crowds of New Yorkers at the Matisse exhibition: are they truly there because of societal overconditioning?" (*The Western Canon: The Books and School of the Ages* [New York: Harcourt Brace & Co., 1994], p. 527). The paintings of van Gogh, to which reference has been made, provide an illustration of Solzhenitsyn's point.

In fact, the ideology of modernity which emerged came to see a genuine autonomy as incompatible with the social solidarity so emphasized by the previous cultures. Descartes's autonomous subject became an isolated and alienated monad, a lonely observer claiming (through the methodology provided by Descartes) to have no more than a severely qualified access to the objective world. The intellectual mood of modernity and that of the ages which went before it are thus very different. If the ancients and medievals became somewhat fixated by the dazzling prospects offered by objective knowledge, modernity has become almost lost in a boundless sea of subjectivity.

As we have seen, Western thinkers are today challenging the isolated subjectivity which has been a central component of the ideology of modernity. The corrective which is emerging is not an abandoning of what has been brought to light by modernity's unprecedented awareness of human subjectivity, but a more adequate understanding of that subjectivity — not the awareness of a monad, but an awareness which is most authentically realized in solidarity with others; not the awareness of a lonely arbiter making itself the central reference point in the intelligibility of reality, but a de-centered subjectivity, which shares in a limited and qualified way in the exploration of a boundless ocean of intelligibility and truth.[3]

In commending Bloom's appeal to the authority of aesthetic excellence in literature, we said he was taking his stand upon an "existential" order of truth. We use the term in a very precise and accessible sense. By the "existential" we are referring simply to *what is properly, ultimately, and comprehensively human*. Enlightenment methodologies have neglected constitutive dimensions of the human, running the risk of reductionism in their attempt to achieve scientific objectivity. It is here that the importance of narrative becomes clear. An *abstract* account of human existence and human destiny — even a sound metaphysical account — can achieve no more than an inadequate or analogous reference to the transcendent dimension which is essential to human destiny. Symbolism, metaphor, and rhetoric may convey considerably more. A narrative of the "story" of a human ex-

3. See Lawrence Cahoone's "What Postmodernism Means," pp. 13-21 in the introduction to his anthology, *From Modernism to Postmodernism* (Cambridge, Mass.: Blackwell, 1996).

istence, however, affirms the whole reality; even if its ultimate dimensions are obscure and mysterious, they are at least implicitly affirmed, ready to be brought to light more adequately once we have found the means. This recognition provides the essential background to the emphasis given by Alasdair MacIntyre and Charles Taylor to the place of narrative in a satisfactory account of human existence. As we have heard, when Václav Havel seeks to give expression to the wisdom needed by contemporary Europe, he does so by recounting its story.

In the light of this, it may be suggested that romanticism's frustration with the inadequacy of the "scientific" account of the mysterious depths of human existence has led in late modernity to a remarkable interest in the narrative; if it is only in the narrative form that the ultimate truth of human existence finds expression, perhaps we shall find important clues to the truth of our own personal existence in the lived and fictional stories which are available to us.

The narratives of past ages were often in an *epic* form, described by György Lukács, the Marxist philosopher and critic, as "literary products of integrated ages of faith." The critical awareness of modernity is unable, however, to share the assurance with which these cultures set their narratives within interpretative frameworks.[4] According to Lukács, ours is the age not of the epic but of the *novel* — "the expression in literary form of 'problematic' ages of doubt." "The novel," he writes, "is the epic of a world that has been abandoned by God."[5]

Richard Tarnas cites a description of the outlook of the author of late modernity:

> The contemporary writer . . . is forced to start from scratch: Reality doesn't exist, time doesn't exist, personality doesn't exist. God was the omniscient author, but he died; now no one knows the plot, and since our reality lacks the sanction of a creator, there's no guarantee as to the authenticity of the received version. Time is reduced to presence, the content of a series of discontinuous moments. Time is

4. The establishing and disestablishing of these frameworks of meaning involve the process of "sacralization" and its reversal in "secularization": cf. my *Christian Mystery in the Secular Age* (Westminster, Md.: Christian Classics, 1991), pp. 4-15.

5. Cited in T. R. Wright, *Theology and Literature* (Oxford: Blackwell, 1989), p. 111.

no longer purposive, and so there is no density, only chance. Reality is, simply, our experience, and objectivity is, of course, an illusion.[6]

Yet, as Tarnas observes, the hunger for existential truth has called forth a prodigious flood of fictional narratives: "Having lost belief in the theological and mythological master plots of earlier eras" and their epics, "the literate culture of the modern West turned its instinctive hunger for cosmic coherence, for existential order, to the narrative plots of imaginative fiction."[7]

There is a clear link between the place of narrative in our appreciation of human existence and the emergence of a mature historical consciousness in our reflection upon our human story, which is one of the outstanding achievements of modernity. It was inevitable that this critical awareness should present a challenge to the traditions of the world religions and the stories through which they present their interpretations of human destiny. The prediction of the great social thinker Ernst Troeltsch, that history would raise greater problems for Christian theology than natural science had done, has been proved right. But the resolution of these problems promises to clarify and confirm the importance of this achievement of modernity. The historian John W. O'Malley discusses these problems, distinguishing three "styles of historical thinking," the inadequacies of which must be recognized if one is to achieve a balanced historical consciousness.[8]

The first he calls "classicism," or "substantialism" (Collingwood). It interprets the past as "the voyage through history of some enduring substance which is really untouched by history" (pp. 590-91). As an example, he cites the approach adopted by Livy, the Roman historian of the time of the emperor Augustus — for whom "Rome" was such an entity enduring in history.[9] O'Malley quotes the

6. Richard Tarnas, *The Passion of the Western Mind: Understanding the Ideas That Have Shaped Our World View* (New York: Ballantine, 1993), pp. 392-93, citing Ronald Sukenick's *The Death of the Novel and Other Stories.*

7. Tarnas, p. 373.

8. Cf. John W. O'Malley, "Reform, Historical Consciousness, and Vatican II's Aggiornamento," *Theological Studies* 32 (1971): 573-601. References which follow are to this text.

9. It is important to distinguish "substances" such as were assumed by Livy from the "substances" which are central to the metaphysical analysis of Aristotle

scholastic Giles of Viterbo (1469-1532), echoing this view with reference to church reform: "Men must be changed by religion, not religion by men." It is not difficult to see how readily Christian theology's assumption of the enduring nature of the elements of Christian "tradition" has tended to identify with this approach. As O'Malley observes, this approach led — logically enough, when one reflects upon it — to a point of view according to which "the past was seen, not on its own terms, but exclusively according to the realities of the present," so that medieval "Englishmen, Frenchmen and Germans thought that they were Romans" (p. 592). M.-D. Chenu gives a striking example of this mentality, in the medieval assumption that the apostles were essentially monks, and that the way of life of the early church was one with the way of life to be found in a medieval monastery![10] Our astonishment at such a point of view provides clear evidence of the historical consciousness which has emerged in our Western culture.

A second approach, which has much in common with the "classicist" approach, O'Malley calls "primitivism." For this mentality, a "golden age" constitutes "a norm model, an ideal for all that follows" (pp. 592-93). The present is understood as a falling away from or recovery of this ideal reality of the beginning. The self-understanding of "Renaissance" culture illustrates this view (p. 593). Once more it is not difficult to see why this interpretative perspective has held attraction for Christian theology. Catholic theology's emphasis upon the "apostolic tradition" as an abiding norm seemed to invite identification with it; so, ironically, did Protestantism's criticism of the medieval church as not having kept faith with its New Testament origins (pp. 593-94).

The third interpretative approach to historical change described by O'Malley derives from the Enlightenment and takes "progress" as its measure. This point of view easily fails to take the past sufficiently

---

and Aquinas. Walter Kasper neglects this distinction in his discussion of the problem historical awareness poses for the theologian when he questions an understanding of history as involving "accidental changes in a permanent substance" (*An Introduction to Christian Faith* [New York: Paulist Press, 1980], p. 156). This distinction is of great importance if historical consciousness is not to dissolve awareness of the past into a relativity which has no common basis of interpretation.

10. M.-D. Chenu, *La théologie au douzième siècle* (Paris: Vrin, 1957), p. 228.

on its own terms; for it, "the present" is "the best explanation of the past," because it shows "where the past was naturally tending all the time" (p. 594).

Given these common assumptions, it is not surprising that O'Malley's survey of the understanding of reform and renewal taken for granted by all councils of the church prior to the Second Vatican Council shows them to be very inadequate. Prior to the First Vatican Council (1870), reform meant a "restoration" of what had existed but had become corrupted (pp. 580-83). This council was forced by the spirit of the times to make some acknowledgment of "doctrinal development or progress" (p. 584). The Second Vatican Council's adopting of *aggiornamento* (updating) as a major concern marked a "revolutionary shift." As O'Malley observes, the approach taken by the council directly contradicts the assumption of Giles of Viterbo, in that now "religion was" to be "changed by and for men in order to accommodate . . . new historical and cultural differences."

O'Malley's discussion of the implications of a historical consciousness which has transcended the shortcomings of previous approaches[11] leaves one somewhat dissatisfied. He defines "history" as "both past reality as it actually happened and the reconstruction or understanding of that reality as it takes place in the historian's mind and imagination" (p. 596). If the assumptions of the past tended to judge that the "past reality" could in some way be attained by the historian, this understanding must be modified: "the past is radically contingent and particular . . . every person, event, and document of the past is the product of very specific and unrepeatable contingencies . . . a reality of the past is not culturally relative, it is culturally absolute" (pp. 596-97). It follows that the historian must recognize that his or her study will be conditioned by his or her cultural awareness, for the historian brings to the task of interpretation "a mind filled with questions, methods, prejudices and personal quirks which are the result of . . . personal, cultural and psychological history" (p. 597). As Troeltsch foresaw, the fact that our interpretation of the past must be

11. Today's historical awareness demands that we relativize all doctrinal formulations and institutional forms, but this relativity must be understood as having a reference to a truth which provides the absolute measure of these human expressions, even if it cannot be *adequately* expressed by them.

recognized to be profoundly conditioned has constituted an immense problem for Christian theology — given its assumption that the divine self-disclosure which is the substance of Christian faith has taken place through historical events.[12]

In the end, the historical inquirer engages in *a dialogue with the past* in which the reality of that past is interpreted through the resources of insight which are available to a particular inquirer and the tradition to which that inquirer belongs. The nature and the limited achievement of this "dialogue" will be better appreciated, however, once it is recognized that a similar dialogue takes place every time we interpret the words and actions of other persons which are directly observable to us. In the end, even our interpretation of those human facts which constitute our immediate experience is the outcome of a process in which our own existential resources and experiences provide the measure of our interpretation. Whatever truth our interpretation contains, it will never be a complete expression of the truth which is there to be found.

Today, as we have seen, commentators on educational trends in the Western world express concern at the decline taking place in the study of history. As our discussion has made clear, history is an incomparable teacher. A people with no awareness of the struggles, achievements, and failures which have produced today's world has a very severely limited access to the resources available to it in its cultural tradition.

The fundamental challenge faced by Western thought today is the reconciling of a recognition of objective truth with a full acknowledgment of the vast range of subjective factors which condition our access to that truth.[13] While avoiding the relativism whereby a radical historicism sees the historical process itself as the ultimate constitutive of meaning, we must accept the point of view of a de-centered subjectivity, undertaking an exploration of the boundless sea of meaningfulness that constitutes what Husserl called our "life-world."

Late modern thought is unable to accept the "meta-narratives" which claim to explain the totality of this life-world. The choice of

12. Cf. my *Christian Mystery,* pp. 53-57.
13. The ancient Greeks first used the argument which points out that the denial of objective truth is self-defeating: see Cahoone, p. 17.

terminology is interesting — an evidence of awareness of the ultimacy of the narrative form in our interpretation of human existence. We must agree with the judgment that doctrinal systems claiming to explain the totality of our life-world cannot be sustained. Existential truth, the ultimate and comprehensive truth of human existence, must be open to what is beyond the measures of human reason; it cannot be contained in any closed system of human thought.[14]

14. The philosopher Nicholas Rescher (*The Strife of Systems: An Essay on the Grounds and Implications of Philosophical Diversity* [Pittsburgh: University of Pittsburgh Press, 1985]) takes up the problem faced by the fragmentation of post-Cartesian philosophy, a fragmentation which could seem to indicate that there is no one rational truth, throwing the whole project of interpreting human existence into jeopardy. He suggests that the subjective options of this plurality of philosophies must be more clearly acknowledged. The apparent impasse need not lead to the denial of a unified reality, nor to the abandonment of a genuine doctrinal debate. The "orientation pluralism" which Rescher proposes identifies the perspectives peculiar to modern philosophies, and the options they imply, and examines the coherence of the systems which have been developed within these various perspectives. In the enriching dialogue which may thus take place, we are brought back to the openness to truth in all its forms which is called for in late modernity, and also to a clearer awareness of the options upon which different philosophical positions are founded.

CHAPTER 8

The "Free Society" of Modernity and the Consolidation of What It Has Achieved

THERE IS PROBABLY NO MORE TELLING INDEX BY which a cultural ethos can be evaluated than the social system it has produced; it is in the political arena that various understandings of the meaning of human existence find expression. This is especially true of the culture of modernity, with "emancipation" as its dominant theme. The present chapter will explore what this index can tell us of modernity and its cultural presuppositions. After making this analysis I shall suggest that our Western tradition possesses resources which make possible a safeguarding of the remarkable achievement represented by modernity's free society.

Authors whose views we have already considered make it clear that the new social order created by modernity is not without its challenges. As J. M. Roberts puts it in his *Triumph of the West*,[1] "the West first invented modern politics" (p. 278) — a social process which applies a "new ideology of Revolution," according to which the "single central issue" of political debate is changing the conditions of humanity for the better (p. 285). But Roberts also calls into question one of the principles upon which this new social order is established: he sees

1. J. M. Roberts, *The Triumph of the West* (London: BBC, 1985). References which follow are to this text.

129

the upholding of "fundamental rights which could not be touched by popular will" as incompatible with the fact that the definition of these rights "rests on the popular will" (p. 287). In *After Virtue* Alasdair MacIntyre raises the same issue; indeed, he judges the "natural or human rights" seen as so important by modernity to be "fictions."[2] MacIntyre also suggests that a Nietzschean totalitarianism is the logical outcome of modernity's understanding of the moral order. J. B. Metz interprets the ideology of the Enlightenment as in danger of drifting toward totalitarian social manipulation. It is certainly a fact that the crises which have torn the world apart in late modernity have involved totalitarian regimes of both the right and the left.

If the United States is, as we have suggested, the embodiment in today's world of the spirit of modernity, a critical analysis of the political reality of that great nation should prove enlightening to those seeking to understand the culture of modernity and the liberal democratic state it has created. We are fortunate to have such a critical analysis in the two volumes produced by Robert Bellah and his colleagues, *Habits of the Heart: Individualism and Commitment in American Life*, published in 1985, and *The Good Society*, published in 1992.[3]

These authors derive the title *Habits of the Heart* from Tocqueville's remarkable 1830s study, *Democracy in America*. The "central problem" discussed in *Habits of the Heart* is "the American individualism that Tocqueville described with a mixture of admiration and anxiety" (p. vii). Writing in 1985, Bellah and his collaborators echo the somber evaluations of late modernity with which we are already familiar:

> There is a widespread feeling that the promise of the modern era is slipping away from us. A movement of enlightenment and liberation that was to have freed us from superstition and tyranny has led in the twentieth century to a world in which ideological fanaticism

2. Alasdair MacIntyre, *After Virtue*, 2nd ed. (Notre Dame, Ind.: University of Notre Dame Press, 1984), pp. 69-70.

3. References which follow are to Robert N. Bellah, Richard Madsen, William M. Sullivan, Ann Swidler, and Steven M. Tipton, *Habits of the Heart: Individualism and Commitment in American Life* (New York: Harper & Row, 1986), and Robert N. Bellah, Richard Madsen, William M. Sullivan, Ann Swidler, and Steven M. Tipton, *The Good Society* (New York: Random House, Vintage, 1992).

and political oppression have reached extremes unknown in previous history. Science, which was to have unlocked the bounties of nature, has given us the power to destroy all life on the earth. Progress, modernity's master idea, seems less compelling when it appears that it may be progress into the abyss. And the globe today is divided between a liberal world so incoherent that it seems to be losing the significance of its own ideals . . . and a poor, and often tyrannical, Third World reaching for the very first rungs of modernity. In the liberal world, the state, which was supposed to be a neutral night-watchman that would maintain order while individuals pursued their various interests, has become so overgrown and militarized that it threatens to become a universal policeman. (p. 277)

But, like other voices we have heard, these thinkers refuse to renounce hope that our cultural tradition may overcome its present difficulties: "Many of those we talked to arc still hopeful," they continue. Indeed, they are prepared to see the fragmentation and individuation of late modernity as something which may have been "necessary to free us from the tyrannical structures of the past." They argue, however, that these developments "must be balanced by a renewal of commitment and community if they are not to . . . turn into their opposites." There is "a world waiting to be born if we only had the courage to see it" (p. 277).

Habits of the Heart offers a diagnosis of the ills which today beset the United States. In the first place, this study links the individualism which leaves its authors so uneasy with the notion of the "unencumbered self" inherited from John Locke and the other founders of modernity, an understanding which "obscures personal reality, social reality and particularly the moral reality that links person and society" (p. 80).

With MacIntyre, these authors judge that the political climate of the United States has led to an accentuated reliance upon the bureaucratic expertise of Max Weber's social analysis: "Between them, the manager and the therapist largely define the outlines of twentieth-century American culture." At the center of the social awareness which at once fosters and is reinforced by this situation is "the autonomous individual, presumed able to choose the roles he will play and the commitments he will make, not on the basis of higher truths but

131

according to the criterion of life-effectiveness as the individual judges it" (p. 47).

The situation just described has been magnified by a loss of contact with previous cultural traditions — the logical outcome of Descartes's and Locke's autonomous self. "Breaking with the past is part of our past," they write. "Leaving tradition behind runs all the way through our tradition" (p. 75). *Habits of the Heart* takes its stand upon an understanding of culture which is at once dynamic and profound: "the cultural tradition of a people — its symbols, ideals, and ways of feeling — is always an argument about the meaning of the destiny its members share" (p. 27). These authors argue for a "reappropriation" of the traditions in which the American culture had its origins (p. 292). As we have seen, they look with a tinge of envy at the other cultural traditions of the world (pp. 295-96).

Some years later these authors took up again with remarkable passion and magnanimity the argument they had initiated in *Habits of the Heart*. They gave this new study the title *The Good Society*. As this title suggests, they adopt a position which directly contradicts the "value-free" methodology which Lockean assumptions bequeathed to the social science of modernity.

Before we pursue this valuable analysis, however, an important observation that provides the all-important background to their criticism should be made. The "reappropriation" of tradition advocated by Bellah and his colleagues in no way implies a failure to recognize the fact that modernity has brought into existence an unprecedented form of human society. They judge that "the emergence of modern science and the modern economy" have created "a radically new and rapidly changing kind of society" (p. 6). The "communitarian" approach they advocate in no way implies their reluctance to identify with this new social reality. They argue, however, that it will only become the "decent society" it is able to become through "more substantive ethical identities and a more active participation in the democratic polity" (p. 6).

One of the earliest inspirations of *The Good Society* was Karl Polanyi's *The Great Transformation*, and its suggestion that "the early capitalist economy disrupted traditional society everywhere, stimulating the growth of powerful nationalist states to cope with these disruptions, and set off destructive forces which by the middle of the twentieth century had come close to destroying civilization" (p. 291). Throughout their discussion, however, the authors identify with the views of such American thinkers as John Dewey and Walter Lippmann, in their recognition of the unprecedented opportunities available to the society created by the culture of modernity. They approve of Lippmann's judgment that we are experiencing, in the present era, "a vast period of global transformation, the greatest since the coming of settled agriculture" (p. 7). They identify, too, with Dewey, who "had no nostalgia for the old small communities" preceding the modern era, seeing them as "too enthralled by custom" to be able "to release the energies of individual and social growth" (p. 7). They see Dewey as advocating a development similar to what they have in mind: not "a mere revival of old small communities . . . but something new that would infuse public spirit and public consciousness into those now largely invisible structures" of the unprecedented society created by modernity. If "modernity itself is at the heart of our problems," the question is not of turning back the clock but of realizing the potential offered by modernity's achievements: we must learn "how to unite the tremendous possibilities opened by modern technological, economic, and administrative advances with a coherent pattern of living together" (p. 302).

The main concern of the authors of *The Good Society* is to promote this "coherent pattern of living together." They identify with novelist Saul Bellow's judgment on modern society: "There are displaced persons everywhere" (p. 57). They also claim, with Lippmann, "that we all, as Americans, as moderns, live in an uprooted condition." As Lippmann puts it:

> All of us are immigrants spiritually. We are all of us immigrants in the industrial world, and we have no authority to lean upon. We are an uprooted people, newly arrived, and *nouveau riche*. As a nation we have all the vulgarity that goes with that, all the scattering of soul. The modern man is not yet settled in his world. It is strange to him, terrifying, alluring, and incomprehensibly big. . . . We are blown hither and thither like litter before the wind. (pp. 293-94)

We are reminded of the analogy suggested in chapter 5, between the situation of new world societies and that of modernity in the "new world" with which it wished to replace the world of medievalism. There is no question, our authors make clear, of turning back. They share Lippmann's perplexity, however, as he contemplated the new society he saw taking shape: "No mariner ever entered upon a more uncharted sea than does the average human being born into the twentieth century. Our ancestors thought they knew their way from birth through all eternity: we are puzzled about the day after to-morrow" (p. 294).

The Good Society's critical appraisal of the society created by modernity looks first and foremost to the presuppositions derived from the social theory of John Locke. Its authors judge that these presuppositions have had a dominant influence in shaping the ethos of modern America.

There can be little doubt that Locke's thought has great significance for modernity as a whole. If the "divine right of kings" claim seemed to epitomize the autocratic structures upheld by the traditions of the past against which modernity was in reaction, the rationale with which Locke argued against this claim stood for the liberating spirit of modernity. This rationale provided the "new ideology of Revolution," as Roberts calls it, upholding familiar principles: the liberty of the individual, the rule of the majority, and constitutional law. Locke's teaching, according to *The Good Society*, provided the "public morality" which shaped the originating vision of the United States. This teaching is judged by Bellah and his associates to be

> one of the most powerful ideologies ever invented, if not the most powerful. It promises an unheard-of degree of individual freedom, and unlimited opportunity to compete for material well-being, and an unprecedented limitation on the arbitrary powers of government to interfere with individual initiative. In all these ways it expressed a modern liberal ideal that contrasted with the hierarchical domination and exclusiveness of most of the human past. . . . All limits in the freedom and autonomy of the individual, other than those he freely consents to in entering the (quite limited) social contract, are rejected. . . . Limited government, in the Lockean view, exists to provide a minimum of order for individuals to accumulate property. All traditional restraints are rejected, and nothing is taken for granted that has not been voluntarily agreed to on the basis of reason. (p. 67)

Locke's proposals for the organization of the new society of modernity, these authors call, with justification, an "ideology" — confirming our basic thesis. An ideology, as we have defined it, is *a notional system which fosters the interests of a social group;* its influence and authority is a function of its identification with those particular interests. The fact that Locke's theory had effects far beyond those he envisaged, as the authors of *The Good Society* point out, is consistent with this ideological dynamic. It was a theory with which the essential concerns of modernity readily identified. Locke saw his teaching as essentially "a protest against the social and cultural constrictions of the past"; he in no way anticipated, however, the widespread influence it was to have. He certainly did not envisage its being implemented "without the religious constraints that were basic to his thought" (p. 68).[4]

Locke's political theory not only identified with modernity's program of emancipation from the dead weight of tradition, it also appealed to the individualism of America's "frontier" spirit: "when you can see the smoke from your neighbor's chimney, it's time to move West" (p. 19). It is paradoxical, as *The Good Society* points out, that while Locke's rationale is patently open to criticism as an oversimplification of the relationship between the individual citizen and society at large, it has a tenacious hold on the American mind, embodying "the appealing but treacherous notion that we can create a good life simply by striving for individual comfort and security, and that by so doing we are indirectly enriching the lives of those around us" (p. 86). Like other successful ideologies, the Lockean rationale is extremely resistant to opposing views: "in politics and law, as in the economy, Americans seem caught in a conundrum: many realize that the old institutions and ways are working badly, but our inherited pattern is so powerful that it inhibits the quest for a new paradigm that would respond to present realities" (p. 110). Only this ideology can explain the naive hopes for a wholesome "world society based on consent" that are characteristic of the American outlook, and the as-

4. Cf. Bellah et al., *The Good Society*, p. 67: "the historian John Dunn has forcibly argued that Locke's thought was inseparable from his theology and from his stern Calvinist sense of obligation." In his *Letter concerning Toleration*, Locke made it clear that he judged belief in God to be essential to the existence of human society (cf. Bellah et al., *The Good Society*, p. 180).

sumption that "with proper enlightenment most people would come to think of themselves as Americans do, that is as individuals pragmatically concerned with their (basically economic) interests" (p. 228). These assumptions have inspired America's international politics in a way which puzzles observers attuned to the historical and cultural complexities of the contemporary world.

The Good Society lends its weight to an argument that has appeared already in our discussion; namely, that deprived of the traditional resources of the venerable cultural traditions from which it has originated, modernity has made it more difficult for the contemporary world to find the *wisdom* it needs to resolve its problems. With Lewis Mumford these authors see "the great gift of civilization" as only being able to flourish within a shared "orientation to past and future"; but they judge "the civilizing gift of historical orientation" to be severely impaired by "Lockeanism's lack of historical sense" (p. 86). They criticize the social sciences which have established themselves in American universities for not having remedied this defect: "A central part of our cultural endowment was severely diminished. Ethical reflection about the good life and the good society, drawing on the religious, philosophical, and literary heritage of the West, was no longer at the center of higher education." Instead, "the tendency of . . . Lockeanism to think of human beings as atomistic self-interest maximizers made the teachings of the 'new' social sciences quite comfortably familiar." Wisdom had no place as "the social sciences reinforced the language of utilitarian individualism, and its assumption that social problems are primarily technical rather than moral or political" (p. 163).

In the "central argument" of their book (p. 264), the authors contend that the situation produced by the Lockean ideology is a departure from the intention of those who first adopted that ideology as their rationale in establishing the United States. Originally, they argue, "the Lockean ideal" was

> embedded in a complex moral ecology that included family and church on the one hand and on the other a vigorous public sphere in which economic initiative, it was hoped, grew together with public spirit. Without overlooking its many injustices, we may note that it was still a society that operated on a humanly intelligible scale.

> Both the economy and the government were sufficiently small-scale
> as to be understandable to the ordinary citizen. (p. 265)

The immense industrial development of the nineteenth century confronted Americans with "two possibilities, which we may denote as 'cultivation' and 'exploitation.'" The former "involves the creation of regional cultures in some degree of harmony with the natural environment, where individuals, families, and local communities could grow in moral and cultural complexity . . . not inconsistent with autonomous individualism when this was supplemented by religious and republican understanding of the common good, and large scale institutions did not dominate individual decision" (p. 265).

However, as America's industrial economy developed, "the temptations of exploitation in so new and so rich a country proved irresistible." As a consequence, in the judgment of Lewis Mumford, a great many of the potentialities for an indigenous culture were frustrated — "The pattern of exploitation was destructive to both the natural environment and the life of the community" (p. 265).

The authors argue that, while the Lockean assumptions of the dominant American culture champion individual liberty and call for a minimum of governmental interference in the activities of citizens, an enormous economic development and the massive buildup of defense provisions during the Cold War have left Americans with a "most un-Lockean economy and government," so that "powerful forces affecting the lives of all" Americans "are not operating under the norm of democratic consent" (p. 79). Ironically, it was the transfer of Lockean assumptions concerning individual liberty to the huge industrial corporations which contributed significantly to this situation, so that these corporations now exercise a kind of "private government," and "it has been impossible, in spite of a long history of efforts to do so, to integrate them effectively into a democratic polity" (p. 71).

To redress this situation, in which Lockean assumptions no longer meet the needs of today's political reality, a new consciousness must be engendered to transform the nation's institutional life: "The goal must be nothing less then a shift from radical individualism to a notion of citizenship based on a more complex understanding of individual and social happiness" (p. 107). Václav Havel called for a reappropriation of "the civic principle" as the basis of hope for modern Europe. In fact, as we have already noted, *The Good Society* cites Havel: "As Vaclav Havel and the peaceful revolutions of Central Europe have eloquently reminded us, consciousness precedes being: raising consciousness is the premise for institutional reform" (p. 107).

To achieve its purpose, *The Good Society* develops three overlapping arguments. (1) It looks critically at other elements of the Enlightenment ideology which have been fostered by the Lockean assumptions of modern American culture. (2) It seeks ways in which American culture can reconnect with tradition and collective memory, as a source of the wisdom required if it is to meet its present challenges. (3) Its authors set out to initiate a discussion of the themes of which this wisdom must give a satisfactory account — such themes as "the good life," "the common good," "justice," "freedom" and its relationship to "solidarity," and of course the issue they have made central to their discussion, the meaning and healthy functioning of the "institutions" of the political community.

The Good Society's critical reflection upon the Enlightenment assumptions which have at once fostered and been confirmed by Lockean theory brings to mind issues we have already discussed. The history of the gradual ascendancy of the Enlightenment ideal of disinterested, value-free reason in American culture is outlined. Derek Bok, a president of Harvard University in the mid–twentieth century, is quoted as an advocate of the "scientific" approach of disinterested reason. The summary of his views provides an interesting illustration of the fragmentation which has resulted from this Enlightenment approach, with its appeal to "procedural" rather than "substantive" reason:

> He believed that science was the only reliable source of truth, yet he did not believe that science offered the values necessary for the survival of a free society — science would always be the province of an intellectually favored elite and had no answers outside its own special competences. . . . He notes the increased specialization within already specialized disciplines, and the loss of the capacity of anyone to put the pieces together, but he views those developments complacently: among the multiplicity of knowledge there are riches for everyone. . . . (In the end) what every student needs to learn are skills and methods in the natural and social sciences and in the humanities relative to which substance is simply illustrative. (p. 166)

Bok's views are the final outcome of the "sudden appearance of the research university in America" which took place in the latter part of the nineteenth century, as "a response to the emergence of the cultural paradigm of scientific knowledge" (p. 154). This development was inspired by the Enlightenment's program: "Isn't it the function of the university, after all, to sweep away the cobwebs of tradition and superstition and give its students the tools of clear critical inquiry?" (p. 156). The best American education became value-free: "its only norm is free inquiry" (p. 156). As a result, the research university, "rather than interpreting and integrating the larger society, came more and more to mirror it" (p. 155).

The situation created by this approach to education raises fundamental questions for these authors. They cite historian James Berlin as saying it has led to an outlook characterized by "sterile objectivity and disinterestedness" (p. 161). Theologian Mary Hatch's *cri de coeur* is cited sympathetically: This outlook assigns religion "to the private realm, along with art, sexuality and every kind of moral feeling that can't be reduced to a rule or a law . . . because it's not 'real knowledge.' Real knowledge rests on facts, not feelings. It's scientific. It's public because it's 'objective data' which yields real power to control things" (pp. 206-7). The dissatisfaction of Harvard students with their education, however, prompts serious questions concerning the success of this value-free approach to education. One graduate-student orator is quoted as saying, "They tell us that it is heresy to suggest the superiority of some value, fantasy to believe in moral argument, slavery to submit to a judgment sounder than your own. The freedom of our day is a freedom to devote ourselves to any values we please on the mere condition that we do not believe them to be true" (p. 44). As we have seen, *The Good Society* joins in the call for a recovery of "sapiential reason" in our Western culture, arguing that the health of American society calls for a removal of the "profound gap" which exists between "technical reason" and "practical or moral reason, the ways we understand how we should live" (p. 44; cf. p. 177).

Reinhold Niebuhr is cited, commenting upon the famous debate occasioned by state laws imposing a fundamentalist view of evolutionary theory: "If we must choose between types of fanaticism, is there any particular reason why we should prefer the fanatics who destroy a vital culture in the name of freedom and reason to those who

139

try to strangle a new culture at birth in the name of authority and dogma? The latter type of fanaticism is bound to end in futility. But the former type is dangerous because it easily enervates a rational culture with ennui and despair" (p. 157).

As we have seen, the authors advocate the recovery of "an enlarged paradigm of knowledge" to replace the narrow "scientific" paradigm which has established itself. Such a paradigm

> recognizes the value of science but acknowledges that other ways of knowing have equal dignity. Practical reason, in its classical sense of moral reason, must regain its importance in our educational life. We must give more than a token bow to art and literature as mere vessels of expressive values, for they can often give us deep moral insight. Ethos is the very subject matter of the humanities and social sciences; ethics cannot possibly be merely one more speciality or a set of procedures that can simply be sprinkled on wherever needed. We must critically recover the project of the classical American philosophers, following them in their willingness to see science as a social process that cannot be divorced from moral learning and imagination without the impoverishment of every field. The enormous pressure in the university to come up with something new, to revise the inherited view, makes it perilously easy to forget that, as Randolph Bourne put it, "the past is not yet over," and that the critical assimilation of it is a central task of education. (p. 177; cf. p. 158)

These authors judge that the individualism of American culture has inhibited a proper appreciation of the thought of the "classical American philosophers." Charles Peirce, in their judgment, is "probably the most brilliant and original of American philosophers" (p. 104). Peirce, adopting a perspective not unlike what Jürgen Habermas was to suggest later, argued that genuine science should be seen as "a social enterprise carried on by a community of inquirers, whose ideas develop in constant conversation with each other as to what the questions are and what the experimental results mean" (p. 163). Josiah Royce took up Peirce's ideas, broadening them to include "not only science but the whole moral life of mankind as necessarily carried on by what he called 'a community of interpreters,' reconsidering the heritage of the past in the light of the present reality in a continuing conversation about spiritual truth and moral good." The influential American thinker John Dewey made "a social understanding of individual development and human action . . . central to his entire project of educational and political reform" in America's new modern society (p. 164).

Modernity's "hermeneutics of suspicion" — "the tendency in the West since the Enlightenment to call all received tradition into question" — should not be abandoned, the authors argue. This approach, however, should be complemented by a "hermeneutics of recovery" — "through which we can understand what a living tradition is in the first place" — if education is not to become "an exercise in nihilism" which leaves young thinkers deprived of any intellectual orientation (p. 174). Bellah and his associates see rhetoric as having played an important part in the life of cultural traditions, a function which has been lost in the paradigm dislocation brought by the Enlightenment.

It is important to reemphasize *The Good Society*'s acknowledgment that modernity and its supportive ideologies have produced a new kind of society. Healthy provision for the future does not mean turning one's back upon modernity's achievement, but an integration which preserves these achievements and makes them more consonant with the best interests of humanity. Thus, in concluding the chapter in which they subject development in American education to severe criticism, these authors make this important acknowledgment, that the excessive narrowness of the assumptions of the Enlightenment may have been a necessary stage in the intellectual history of the West: "cognitive competence is essential for effective citizenship, in close interaction with moral sensitivity and imaginative insight. Perhaps specialization in (largely scientific) cognition, freed from older dogmatic and culturally parochial constraints, was an essential stage in the development of higher education; but now it is clearly time to reintegrate cognition with a more fully human understanding" (pp. 177-78).

Like other commentators on modernity, the authors acknowledge the pervasive influence of Max Weber's rationale of bureaucratic "rationalization" in contemporary political awareness: "a process of systematically organizing all social relations so as to make them the most efficient possible means to maximizing wealth and/or power. Its characteristic institutions . . . (being) the self-regulating market and the bureaucratic state" (p. 233; cf. pp. 10, 26).

This widespread acceptance leaves the authors uneasy. The complexity of the institutions of contemporary society easily gives the public the impression that these institutions are beyond their comprehension and must be left to bureaucrats; this complexity "should not be a cover beneath which undemocratic managers and experts can hide" (p. 20), giving rise to "some form of modern gnosticism" (p. 15). There is a danger that massive, unaccountable government structures which have developed in recent decades have created a situation in which "public and private managers have soothed" the public "into believing that they know what they are doing" (p. 80), and democracy becomes little more than "an ideological facade for what is fast becoming an administered society" (p. 27). *The Good Society* links this situation with its essential argument. The great temptation "is to believe that technical fine-tuning will solve the problem. Yet the very meaning of 'effectiveness' raises value questions — effective for what purposes? — that should lead to moral debate" (p. 23; cf. p. 43).

The Good Society points to "the self-regulating market" as one of the most powerful institutions of the society of modernity. Milton Friedman and the Chicago school of economics he founded interpret this market as produced by human beings as "exclusively self-interest maximizers, and the primary measure of self-interest as money. Thus Economics becomes a total science that explains everything. As the so-called 'rational choice theory,' it has invaded all the social sciences — especially political science and sociology" (p. 91; cf. p. 117).

Like other commentators we have heard, the authors are very critical of this point of view. They acknowledge that the market mechanism operates "in some ways through an autonomous logic"; they point out, however, that the very existence of the market depends upon "certain institutional arrangements" which have grown up in a particular historical society (p. 22). "It has become clear" in the modern world "that the market, left to itself, does not automatically result in human well-being" (p. 85). And with thinkers such as Paul Ormerod, they reject as "massively false" the understanding "that society, or at least that portion of it we call 'the economy,' is an automatic mechanism whose motive force is the self-interested action of millions of unrelated individuals," so that "strategic action is all that is required; the larger order will take care of itself" (pp. 97-98; cf. p. 278).

Integrating this evaluation into their general argument for a moral revitalization of institutions, they cite James Fallows: "People don't live in markets, they live in societies" (p. 109). Like Ormerod, they would recover the broader understanding of the founders of the discipline originally called "political economy" — implying an economy which lives in a world of "law and mores," of "moral claims of justice"; "moral and institutional" issues must provide the setting for the "technical" analysis of today's economist (p. 84).

Their second line of argument seeks to counter the influence of Enlightenment presuppositions in American culture — presuppositions which have alienated this culture from the traditional resources it must use if it is to find solutions to its present problems. As we have seen, Lockean individualism has created a "cultural tradition that assumes that culture, community, and history do not matter much in the long run" (p. 228; cf. pp. 120, 163). Henry Ford, the quintessential American, sums up this attitude in the much quoted words, "History is more or less bunk . . . the only history that is worth a tinker's damn is the history we made today."[5] Our authors acknowledge the value of the critical spirit of the Enlightenment sweeping away "the cobwebs of tradition and superstition" (p. 156), but they judge that the moment has come to seek a proper balance: "Now we need to imagine how we can use . . . (our) better understanding of our historical reality to enhance our capacities to reflect, debate, and act together, so that we can reform the institutions that we have come to take for granted but that no longer are working very well" (p. 85; cf. pp. 50, 126).

The argument of *The Good Society* appeals to J. B. Metz's theme of "collective memories," memories which are embodied in the life of "our families, schools, universities, churches, and synagogues," memories which give expression to "important, but often barely conscious, patterns of meaning and self-definition," which must be called upon if America is to respond to today's "challenge and change" (p. 42). Appeal is also made to Mumford's understanding of "the great gift of

5. *Chicago Tribune*, 25 May 1916.

civilization" as involving, for our Western tradition, a twofold reference: "a cultural tradition" on the one hand and "a vision of renewal that lures us forward" on the other (p. 86). Our authors continue, "without an orientation to past and future, Mumford argued, identity and meaning are not possible, and even personal freedom and pleasure are diminished." Survival in "the great global society of modernity" belongs to those communities which have found "the ability to preserve" these precarious "gifts."

For those who appreciate the achievements of modernity, this preservation cannot be a simple "restoration" of some of America's "overlapping cultural traditions," but their "reinterpretation and renegotiation" (p. 140). The exploration of reality initiated by the Enlightenment has led to a situation in which we "know more about different cultures from all of human history than we have ever known before"; we must now "make sense of our own uniquely modern form of culture and society, including the place in it of the natural sciences" (p. 173).

Today's knowledge of the cultural traditions of humanity makes it clear that "if we want to understand traditional cultures," we must take seriously the fact that "religious concerns are central to most of them" (p. 173). Because these thinkers see religious traditions as important bearers of the community's "collective memory," they view the privatization of religion in an ethos formed by Lockean assumptions as depriving American culture of an important resource. They identify with the views of Mary Hatch when she regrets the relegation of religion to "the private realm" (together with "art," "sexuality," and "moral feeling"). "When modern Christianity decided that it couldn't say anything true in substance about the public or political world," she comments, "it turned inward." This has led to a situation in which "the church doesn't incarnate religion" in the midst of modern culture: "It's not really 'the Body of Christ,' nor is it part of the public world" (pp. 206-7). The language of "covenant and communion," so important in the Judeo-Christian tradition, is forgotten; the "unique endowment" of the West's "biblical and theological heritage" plays no part in the formation of the vision inspiring civil society (p. 193); the "narrative ethics" which formed the generations of past ages is no longer part of ordinary experience (p. 208); the vision of history nurtured by a familiarity with "the Bible's meaning enmeshed

144

within the web of history and culture" is lost (p. 209). *The Good Society* illustrates this last point for Americans by recalling that the "Exodus story binds together all sorts of Americans from the beginning of our history to the present . . . a story that Americans from John Winthrop (first governor of the Massachusetts Bay Colony speaking in 1630) to Martin Luther King have told over and over again" (p. 247).

These examples give an edge to the book's contention that, as bearers of collective memory in the tradition of American culture, the churches are able to "conscientize" their "members' subjectivity" and to "confront the world with unconventional moral responsibilities" (p. 207).

The authors' third argument takes us to the heart of their concerns — as they attempt to articulate the wisdom which must provide an antidote to the inadequacies of the Lockean assumptions of American culture. These lessons concern the health and degeneration of the *institutions* which unite a political community; the meaning of the *common good,* indeed the meaning of *"good"* as applied to life and to society; the meaning of *freedom* and *solidarity* in a life-giving human community; the *values* which should be upheld in the life of a nation. Clearly, they raise what are essentially *philosophical* issues. By what is probably a deliberate choice, *The Good Society* makes its case in rhetorical rather than in formally philosophical terms. The point is made that rhetoric has "had an honored place in the educational curriculum for millennia, and was closely associated with the search for the common good in republican and democratic societies" (p. 145). As we have seen, they also urge the recovery of "an enlarged paradigm of knowledge, which recognizes the value of science, but acknowledges that other ways of knowing have equal dignity," thus giving "practical" or "moral reason," "art and literature" their proper place as the bearers of "deep moral insight" (p. 177). A properly philosophical discussion of the issues raised by the rhetoric of *The Good Society* will be undertaken presently.

The "conception of institutions," our authors write, "is central" to their book (p. 17). Institutions "mediate the relations between the self and the world"; they may be described as a social interaction "that operates under mutual expectation" on the part of participants (p. 287). Because institutions "mediate our ultimate moral (and religious) commitments" and are "premised on moral (and religious) understandings, what sociologists call ultimate values" (p. 288), they are "an indispensable source from which character is formed" in the shared life of a community (p. 6). In this common life "we create institutions and they also create us" (p. 12). Because "they affect or even create our identities as selves and as citizens," their "reinvigoration" is not "an idealistic whim but the only realistic basis on which we can move ahead as a free people" (p. 141). Although they are the community's "essential bearers of ideals and meanings," it is important to recognize that the embodiment of these ideals achieved by social institutions "is imperfect" — indeed, they sometimes become "corrupt" (p. 40).

It is interesting that, like most of the commentators we have considered, Bellah and his team are far more conscious of Weber's sociological analysis than that of the other great exponent of sociological positivism, Émile Durkheim (d. 1917). Both thinkers set out to interpret human society in terms of the "facts" which constitute it. For Weber, the elemental social fact is the action of the social monad, the individual citizen; the social fact central to Durkheim's analysis is the group mind at work in and through the individual. While Durkheim's approach has much that should make it congenial to the authors of *The Good Society* in their desire to stress the importance of "institutions" in the life of the political community, it is understandable that the fear of a drift toward totalitarianism makes modern authors wary of Durkheim's approach. The two thinkers' different options raise the question, however, of the arbitrariness of basic methodological principles on the part of sociological positivism.

The central argument of *The Good Society* is that the Lockean individualism which has shaped the assumptions behind American institutions, serving "as the central American value system," has proved inadequate to the task and that a reform of America's institutions through a change in the nation's central value system is called for (p. 288; cf. pp. 61, 80-81, 103, 293).

The rhetoric of the book invokes a cluster of notions which are seen by its authors as essential to the institutional renewal they are advocating. Rejecting the "value-free" approach to social science which has established itself in the ideology of modernity, they are concerned to affirm the place values should have in the shared life of the political community. "Seeking the good" and having a sound understanding of

146

"the good life" and "the good society" are the daunting challenges Americans must take up "in a dangerous, complicated, but possibly perfectible world" (p. 232). "Quality of life" must be the goal of institutional reform (p. 105). The values which shape the institutions of society should be "more than idiosyncratic personal opinions" (p. 119). Our authors applaud the dissatisfaction, not always fully articulated, of ordinary Americans with modernity's drift toward a utilitarian reductionism (p. 123). Value acceptance must provide the basis of an effective moral consciousness: "We believe it is necessary to bridge the gap between theoretical reason and moral reason," they declare; and they make it clear that in this they differ from the view which prevails in contemporary social science (p. 292). Value acceptance makes "responsibility" and "accountability" meaningful (p. 283). Weber's bureaucratic effectiveness leaves the essential question of value unanswered (p. 23). "The focus must be on justice in the broadest sense — that is giving what is due to both persons and the natural environment" (p. 143).

The Good Society constantly appeals to the "common good." The authors make no claim, however, that they or anyone else can propose the "pattern of a good society": "It is central to our notion of a good society that it is an open quest, actively involving all its members . . . the common good is the pursuit of the good in common" (p. 9). Properly understood, the common good is not limited to the concerns of a particular nation or people, but must embody the interests of the whole world community (p. 247).

Bellah and colleagues agree with the assumption so important to the society shaped by modernity, that freedom — "the most contagious idea in history" (p. 225) — is "an essential ingredient in a definition of a good society." They argue, however, that the meaning of this freedom needs to be probed more deeply. They disagree with the common Lockean assumption that freedom means "the right to be left alone." Such a notion is inadequate for the functioning of the society of late modernity; it must be widened to include "the right to participate in the economic and political decisions that affect our lives." In other words, freedom is the animating principle of the "institutions" which should be the shared expression of "what we really want and what we ought to want" (p. 9). The positive value of freedom can only find expression when it is realized "along with the other virtues, such as

147

care and responsibility" (p. 50). "A less constricted understanding of freedom and justice," our authors argue, "would enable us to see how they are connected with the common good" (p. 245). The reappropriation of resources of American culture will bring awareness that "deep within the American tradition" is embedded "the notion that freedom is not purely a human accomplishment but a divine gift that conveys profound responsibilities upon the recipient" (p. 246).

Thus the freedom so prized by modernity will only find its authentic expression if it is lived in an authentic solidarity with the community which bestows that freedom. The "interdependence" essential to the institutions *The Good Society* wishes to revitalize is constantly referred to throughout the book. It is this interdependence that will lead nations like the United States to recognize that "justice" in the fullest sense is a commitment to "solidarity and hope for the whole human species" (p. 143).

It is interesting to compare *The Good Society*'s critique of modern democratic societies with that, already referred to, made by John Ralston Saul in his *Unconscious Civilisation*.[6] Saul sums up the essential thesis of his text: "our civilisation" finds itself "locked in the grip of an ideology," which he names "corporatism"; because this ideology canonizes a partisan spirit and "leads to a worship of self-interest and a denial of the public good," it "denies and undermines the legitimacy of the individual as the citizen in a democracy" (p. 191).

Saul sees this social malady permeating our whole cultural tradition, reflecting the widespread acceptance of a distorted "individualism": "a narrow and superficial deformation of the Western idea" of individualism, which has amounted to "a hijacking of Western civilisation" (p. 2). Corporatism's individualistic self-interest was given "a sophisticated intellectual shape" in the nineteenth century, Saul notes, by the great sociologists Max Weber and Émile Durkheim (p. 28).

The partisan spirit of corporatism, Saul contends, gives rise to ideologies which dominate social awareness. His sharpest criticism is reserved for the corporatist ideology of economic rationalism, which reduces the citizen "to the status of a subject at the foot of the throne of the market place" (p. 80).

6. References which follow are to John Ralston Saul, *The Unconscious Civilisation* (Ringwood, Victoria: Penguin, 1997).

To this point Saul's analysis is at one with that of *The Good Society*. When he proposes a remedy to the situation, however, he parts company with Bellah and colleagues. Because he does not question the Lockean assumptions he shares with those whose views he wishes to contest, and because he has no clear understanding of the "common good" of human society, he does not come to grips with the real problem as the authors of *The Good Society* do.

It is notable that in his social analysis Saul constantly refers to "public good" and studiously avoids any use of the more familiar term "common good." This choice of language is significant. Saul's recognition of the "unconsciousness" and "conformity" engendered by *ideological* solidarity makes him distrustful of *any* form of social solidarity. This distrust is reflected in his careful — yet somewhat paradoxical — definition of the source of social responsibility's legitimacy as "the individual citizenry acting as a whole," after the manner of a jury (pp. 32, 172).

In reacting against the *misleading* solidarity established by ideological consensus, and having only a Lockean notion of society to appeal to, Saul fails to recognize that the society he is arguing for must be grounded in the *genuine* solidarity which transcends partisan factionalism. He fails, in fact, to recognize that the *public* good he wishes to promote is, of its nature, also the *common* good, which establishes the bond of fellowship fundamental to human society. This oversight is worth exploring further, since it reflects assumptions which today are very common.

Saul's position, when examined more closely, is ambiguous. On the one hand, he more than once applauds the twelfth-century recognition of the importance of "friendship and community" (p. 2), a recognition which saw "the individual as a reality in a community of friends within society" (p. 58); the fact that the "individual lives in society," Saul declares to be a "primary characteristic" of an authentic "individualism" (p. 77). On the other hand, however, the social analysis of *The Unconscious Civilisation* fails to rise above the perspective of what Bellah and the authors of *The Good Society* call "one of the most powerful ideologies ever invented, if not the most powerful," John Locke's interpretation of human society.

According to Locke, social solidarity only exists through a contractual compromise setting limits to the individual's pursuit of self-interest: as Bellah and colleagues explain it, "government exists to provide a minimum of order for individuals to accumulate property. All traditional restraints are rejected, and nothing is taken for granted that has not been voluntarily agreed to on the basis of reason."[7]

The two works of social analysis of Bellah and his companions, *Habits of the Heart* and *The Good Society*, should be well known to Saul. It is puzzling that he does not refer to them. Given the central place the criticism of ideology has in his analysis, it is ironic that Saul leaves himself open to the criticism that his view of society is shaped by an ideology!

The line of reasoning we are suggesting as an alternative to Saul's analysis is straightforward enough. Social solidarity has different forms. A *partisan* solidarity, which pursues the advantages of a particular group in disregard of the good of other members of society, must be distinguished from that solidarity which is established by the *collaborative order* which is essential to the living of a full human life.

Throughout his text we find a sprinkling of medieval references, but one familiar with medieval thought is led to ask whether Saul fully appreciates that thought. Thomas Aquinas speaks clearly and simply of the social solidarity to which we refer. Commenting on Aristotle's *Ethics* (1.1), he notes that "the unity which is the political community is only a unity of order."[8] He compares the achievement of social collaboration with the movement of a ship "which results from the combined action of the rowers." Singly, no rower could move the ship, but in an orderly collaboration they all achieve the movement. He is echoing a comparison made by Aristotle in his *Politics*.

Saul clearly recognizes that the essentials of a human way of life are only possible through a social collaboration. Making the distinction which is called for between different forms of solidarity would enable him to agree with Aquinas that the solidarity which is "civil society is the greatest thing which human reason is capable of constructing."[9]

Because he fails to make this distinction, Saul can only see social responsibility as the undertaking of an onerous and quixotic task.

7. Bellah et al., *The Good Society*, p. 67.
8. Commentary on *Nichomachean Ethics*, Book 1, Part 1, in *Aquinas: Selected Political Readings*, ed. A. P. D'Entrèves (Oxford: Blackwell, 1987), p. 97.
9. Commentary on *Politics*, Book 1, Part 1.

Acting as a responsible citizen who is alive to the partisan spirit of competing ideologies is, he must admit, "not a particularly pleasant or easy style of life" (p. 169); in the "equilibrium" of a democracy which is truly "citizen based," he can only promise a prospect of "permanent psychic discomfort" (p. 195). Once the solidarity of a genuine collaboration is appreciated for what it is, however, it gives rise to the enterprise satisfaction which is all-important to any collaborative effort. It is this satisfaction which is shared in the "political friendship" which is a key theme in Aristotle's social philosophy.

To one who accepts the reductionist principles of Locke, however, "political friendship" can mean only factionalism, or the stability of a group in a state of truce.

Saul's frequently repeated dichotomy between "self-interest" and "disinterest" reflects the inadequacy of his analysis. A proper understanding of the common good of social solidarity recognizes that it is *my* good as a citizen, to be fostered — beyond individualistic benefits — as the only way making possible for me a full and authentic human life.

*   *   *

The social order of modernity's democratic society — established upon the recognition of the rights of every citizen before the law, upon a constitutional law which declares publicly the rights and duties of its citizens, and upon the principle that the source of all authority to govern is the consent of those who are governed — is a truly remarkable achievement.

However, as we have seen, this achievement is not without its problems. Johann Baptist Metz speaks of the sense of helplessness experienced by ordinary citizens before a system of politics which seems to be caught up in serving the technological and economic processes of the modern world, and to be unable to control the "anonymous 'power systems'" which govern these processes. Like other commentators on modernity, he sees in the politics of modernity the danger of a drift toward totalitarian control, and he probably reflects a widespread mood when he suggests that the immediate concern of many citizens is "pure survival," or the "cunning animal adaptation" which is called for to use the processes of today's world to advantage. Moreover, behind this mood of uneasiness lies a theoretical uncertainty concerning the very foundations of democratic society. In his *Triumph of the West,* J. M. Roberts sees the notions of inalienable right and popular sovereignty as incompatible; Alasdair MacIntyre sees the concept of "natural right" as a "fiction" which cannot be rationally sustained. John Ralston Saul's *Unconscious Civilisation* is a spirited attempt to face real problems emerging for today's democratic societies.

Robert Bellah and his colleagues mount an eloquent defense of the foundations of a healthy political community. The positions they so ably uphold in rhetorical terms deserve to be evaluated philosophically. Our Western tradition does in fact possess the resources with which the foundations of modernity's democratic society can be maintained and consolidated. The methodological assumptions of modernity, however — measured by disinterested reason alone and disregarding the integrated manifold of cognitive modes previously taken for granted in our Western tradition, as bearers of collective memory and wisdom — made this work of consolidation difficult.

As Richard Tarnas explains, modernity's new outlook easily assumed that the methodology of the experimental sciences could be applied to the organization of society:

> The way was now open to envision and establish a new form of society, based on self-evident principles of individual liberty and rationality. For the strategies and principles that science has shown to be so useful for discovering truth in nature were clearly relevant to the social realm as well. Just as the antiquated Ptolemaic structure of the heavens . . . had been replaced by the rational simplicity of the Newtonian universe, so too could the antiquated structure of society . . . be replaced by new forms of government based not on supposed divine sanction and inherited traditional assumptions, but on rationally ascertainable individual rights and mutually beneficial social contracts.[10]

As we have seen, the political thought of John Locke, one of the first exponents of this methodological approach, was to have a decisive influence in the emergence of the democratic society of modernity. Of-

---

10. Richard Tarnas, *The Passion of the Western Mind: Understanding the Ideas That Have Shaped Our World View* (New York: Ballantine, 1993), p. 283.

fering a welcome alternative to the oppressive weight of tradition and the political establishments it upheld, Locke proposed a new system of political accountability. There can be no question of abandoning this achievement. It must be preserved and extended by integrating Locke's principles into a more adequate understanding of social reality.

One of the inadequacies of Locke's account of human society is his neglect of a fundamental distinction. We can only give a satisfactory account of the complex processes of society by distinguishing two different kinds of human association. One is *pre-deliberative,* and one is rationally *deliberated.* Ferdinand Tönnies, in a work published in 1887 under the title *Gemeinschaft und Gesellschaft,* appeals to this distinction. For Tönnies, *Gemeinschaft* (or "community") refers to a form of association into which the human agent is more or less instinctively drawn by the inclinations and needs of human nature. The tribal life of archaic societies is an obvious example. *Gesellschaft* (or "society"), on the other hand, is an association entered into according to deliberately defined terms. The political constitution envisaged by Locke is an obvious example of this. Though we may disagree with Tönnies when — in the evolutionary perspective of nineteenth-century "Progress" ideology — he saw the transition in the history of European society from *Gemeinschaft* to *Gesellschaft* as the expression of a law of history, it is not difficult to recognize that the distinction he made has applications far beyond what he suggested. Indeed, it is this distinction, and the fact that the two forms of association are complementary rather than in opposition, which underlies much of the argument of Bellah and his associates.

Sir Ernest Barker is one of the great names in political science. He began his professional career as an expert in the political thought of Plato and Aristotle and ended it accepting the chair of political science in war-ravaged Cologne (1947-48). Though he uses a different terminology, Barker appeals to the distinction we are making as he points to the limitations of the "social contract" theory of Locke:

> *Society* is not constituted, and never was constituted, on any basis of contract. Society is an all-purpose association — "in all science . . . in all art . . . in every virtue and in all perfection" — which transcends the notion of law, and has grown and exists of itself. In the strict sense of the word "social," there is not, and never has been, a

153

social contract. On the other hand, *the State,* as distinct from society, may fairly be conceived in terms of contract; and we may regard it as constituted on the basis of contract — though seldom (except after revolution, or, again, in the case of confederations) created by an act of contract. The State, as such, is a legal association, constituted by the action of its members in making a constitution (such an action sometimes, as in Great Britain, being along a line of time, rather than at a point of time), and therein and thereby contracting themselves into a body politic.[11]

In a work published in 1960,[12] John Courtney Murray, one of the most elegant minds America has produced, pursues an argument similar to that of the Bellah team. They cite him, and he may well have contributed to their thought. Murray made use of the same terminology as Barker in describing what he judged to be one of the presuppositions of the consensus which gave birth to the United States. He refers to "the principle that the state is distinct from society and limited in its offices towards society." He continues:

This principle . . . was inherent in the Great Tradition (having its origin in medieval times). Before it was cancelled out by the rise of the modern omnicompetent society-state, it had found expression in the distinction between the order of politics and the order of culture. . . . The American Proposition, in reviving the distinction between society and state, which had perished with the advance of absolutism, likewise renewed the principle of the incompetence of government in the field of opinion. Government submits itself to judgment by the truth of society; it is not itself a judge of the truth in society. (p. 35)[13]

11. *Social Contract: Essays by Locke, Hume, and Rousseau, with an Introduction by Sir Ernest Barker* (London: Oxford University Press, 1947), p. xv.

12. John Courtney Murray, *We Hold These Truths: Reflections on the American Proposition* (London: Sheed & Ward, 1960). References which follow are to this work.

13. Locke's political treatises were designed, as has already been noted, to counteract the pretensions of the theory of "the Divine Right of Kings," which appeared in the early modern period as a justification to an emerging absolutism in politics.

It is clear that the two forms of association we have distinguished — let us call them "community association" and "societal association" — are complementary in the life of a mature political community. Human culture is the common achievement of many generations. Participation in the community association which is the bearer of the traditions of human culture is not a matter of choice; it is something demanded for human survival and development. As it develops, a cultural tradition moves from the informal procedures and norms of community association to the articulation of the explicit norms which belong to societal association. To understand this development — as the texts of Barker and Murray make clear — is to recognize that the function of societal association is not one of replacing the community association, but of safeguarding and fostering its development. A proper understanding of this takes us a long way toward resolving many of the difficulties of contemporary democratic societies.

It was unfortunate that Locke's Enlightenment assumptions made it difficult for this relationship between community association (and its cultural achievements) and societal association to be properly appreciated. As Murray remarks, it is difficult for us to share the naive enthusiasm of the Enlightenment for the "law of nature" and the "state of nature" in which this law was envisaged as finding expression. For the Enlightenment tradition, however, these notions — immortalized in the novels of Defoe and Rousseau, and very different from what we might presume these phrases to mean — "had all the power of a myth" (p. 302). This "state of nature" was an imaginary construct, envisaging the condition of the human agent prior to the formation of human associations, the establishing of community law, and the customs of social life: "man appears with complete suddenness as a full-grown individual, a hard little atom in the midst of atoms equally hard, all solitary and self-enclosed, each a sociological monad. . . . In this absolute lordship, equality and independence consists in the Lockean idea of man's 'freedom,' a freedom that is natural and therefore inalienable save within the limits of his own free choice" (p. 303). According to Locke, the human agent only relinquishes this primordial freedom because it is "very unsecure" in the state of nature; this is done, Locke says, by entering into a social contract with others "for the mutual preservation of their lives, liberties, and estates, which I call by the general name property."[14]

Murray puts his finger on the nub of the problem which puzzles J. M. Roberts and Alasdair MacIntyre in their evaluation of the "natural" rights upheld by today's democratic society. Although Locke's ideology appears to establish the basis of the "natural" rights of citizens, its account of social relationship really leaves no place for the *ordo iuris,* the "order of right," an order which is intelligibly different from the order of physical agents. It is interesting to compare the position adopted by Rousseau in regard to this issue — as he represents the beginnings of romanticism's attempt to break out of the narrow constraints of Locke's Enlightenment methodology. Rousseau recognizes that the order of "right" is essentially different from the order of "might": "Strength is a physical attribute, and I fail to see how any moral sanction can attach to its effects . . . what validity can there be in a Right which ceases to exist when might changes hands? . . . the word Right adds nothing to the idea of might. It becomes, in this connection, completely meaningless."[15]

But, in the judgment of Barker, Rousseau does not succeed in providing a satisfactory philosophical vindication of this important insight. "Rousseau," Barker writes, "was not a philosopher" but "a *litterateur* of genius and acute sensibility." As Barker goes on to point out, this vindication clearly postulated acceptance in some terms of the concept of "natural law," but Rousseau's writings show that he "hardly knew" where he stood with regard to the natural law. On the one hand, "he needed it — for how could there be a legal thing like a contract of society unless there were a natural law in terms and under the sanction of which a contract could be made?" But on the other hand, "he disliked it; and he felt in his bones that the nation made the law, and not law the nation."[16]

The case Bellah and his associates have argued rhetorically is put in philosophical terms by Murray. He points out that "the idea of natural law" brings "vital resources" to a cultural tradition. This idea for Murray has an implied "metaphysical character," a "secure an-

14. Locke, *Second Treatise on Civil Government,* par. 123.
15. Rousseau, *The Social Contract,* bk. 1, chap. 3.
16. Barker, in *Social Contract,* pp. xxxv, xxxix.

chorage in the order of reality — the ultimate order of beings and purposes." "As a metaphysical idea," Murray writes, "the idea of natural law is timeless, and for that reason timely; for what is timeless is always timely" (p. 320). We must return to the philosophical issues Murray has raised, but before doing so we should note his criticism of Locke's position as unable to resolve the question of how "natural rights" are compatible with the demands of social solidarity and the sovereignty of the people.

Writing in 1960, Murray saw the world as confronted with a choice between the "old Liberal individualism" produced by Locke's ideology and a Marxist reaction to that position which reduced the freedom of the individual to a sharing in the freedom of the state "by pursuing its purposes, which are determined by the laws of dialectical materialism . . . the triumph of collective man over nature in a classless society" (p. 322). Both views are based on an acceptance, "as the ultimate reality," of "the material fact of power — in one case the power of the individual, in the other, the power of the collectivity," with the result that for each of these opposing ideologies society and the state are based upon "a metaphysics of force (if the phrase be not contradictory)" (p. 322). The order of right has not been explained satisfactorily if it is reduced to the order of might. But this, according to Murray, is what Locke has attempted to do:

> the individualism of Locke's law of nature results in a complete evacuation of the notion of the "rights" of man. It is quite evident that Locke's state of nature reveals no *ordo iuris*, and no rights in any recognizable moral sense. There is simply a pattern of power relationships — the absolute lordship of one individual balanced against the equally absolute lordship of others. Significantly, Locke uses the word "power" more frequently than the word "right" in describing the state of nature. Moreover, what the social contract does, in effect, is simply to transfer this system of power relationships into the civil state, with the sole but significant difference that there is now added to it a "third power," the public power of government. In the naked essence of Locke's thought, government is the arbiter of "right," only in the sense that it is a power to check power. And its use is "right" when behind it is the consent of the community, that is, the consent of the majority, that is, again (in

157

Locke's explanation of majority rule), "the greater force," in which is embodied "the power of the whole." (pp. 307-8)[17]

Murray is at one with the writers of *The Good Society* in pointing out that the great influence of Locke's ideology was to lead to a dislocation which deprived the political tradition of the United States of the access it might have had to the cultural resources of the Western tradition:

> the men who framed the American Bill of Rights understood history and tradition, and they understood nature in the light of both. They too were individualists, but not to the point of ignoring the social nature of man. They did their thinking within the tradition of freedom that was their heritage from England. Its roots were not in the top of anyone's brain but in history. Importantly, its roots were in the medieval notion of the *homo liber et legalis,* the man whose freedom rests on law, whose law was the age-old custom in which the nature of man expressed itself, and whose lawful freedoms were possessed in association with his fellows. The rights for which the colonists contended against the English Crown were basically the rights of Englishmen. And these were substantially the rights written into the Bill of Rights. (p. 38)

The alternative to the philosophical position appealed to by Murray to vindicate the order of right as the basis of human society is the value-free approach to social science discussed by Bellah and his colleagues. The essential argument against this approach must be the philosophical one, but it is worth considering the suggestion that such an approach will inevitably be shaped by particular values, even though they are not clearly recognized. According to Eric Voegelin, the values operative in the social science of positivism will be shaped by the Zeitgeist, by political preferences and personal idiosyncrasies, so that the past is often interpreted as a movement toward some accepted fashion in philosophy or politics. But this is not a satisfactory

---

17. See also Murray, p. 309, for Murray's comments on the "nominalism" which is fundamental to the philosophical principles with which Locke approached his task.

situation. As he puts it, "Uncritical opinion, private or public (*doxa* in the Platonic sense), cannot substitute for theory in science."[18]

Metz, too, has pointed to the fact that, though the Enlightenment's aim was the universal availability of information and a public reason which belonged to the whole of humanity, this movement became identified in fact with the outlook and interests of the bourgeoisie. The comments of the historian Christopher Dawson upon this situation may well tell us a lot about the problems faced by today's democratic societies:

> when the French Revolution and the fall of the old regime made the bourgeoisie the ruling class in the West, it retained its inherited characteristics, its attitude of hostile criticism towards the traditional order and its enlightened selfishness in the pursuit of its own interests. But although the bourgeois now possessed the substance of power, he never really accepted responsibility as the old ruler had done. . . . To the bourgeois politician the electorate is an accidental collection of voters; to the bourgeois industrialist his employees are an accidental collection of wage earners. The king and the priest, on the other hand, were united to their people by a bond of organic solidarity. They were not individuals standing over against other individuals, but part of the common social organism and representatives of a common spiritual order. The bourgeoisie upset the throne and the altar, but they put in their place nothing but themselves. Hence their regime cannot appeal to any higher sanction than that of self-interest. It is continually in a state of disintegration and flux. It is not a permanent form of social organization, but a transitional phase between two orders.[19]

It is only in terms of a metaphysical analysis — carried out in terms of what Murray calls "the ultimate order of beings and purposes" and validating an "order of right" — that the central issue of

18. Eric Voegelin, *The New Science of Politics* (Chicago: University of Chicago Press, 1960), p. 10.

19. Christopher Dawson, *Dynamics of World History*, ed. J. Mulloy (New York: Sheed & Ward, 1957), pp. 227-28. See Aquinas, *Summa theologiae* 2-2, q. 77, art. 4, for comments on *negotio*, or commerce, as having no in-built measure or finality.

human society can be satisfactorily addressed. Murray contrasts this approach with that of Locke:

> Our decisions, unlike those of the eighteenth century, cannot be purely political, because our reflection on the bases of society and the problem of its freedom and its order must be much more profound. And this in turn is so because these problems stand revealed to us in their depths; one cannot any longer, like John Locke, be superficial about them. Our reflection, therefore, on the problem of freedom, human rights, and political order must inevitably carry us to a metaphysical decision in regard of the nature of man. (p. 321)

In suggesting the use of metaphysical understanding, we run up, of course, against the assumptions of the "scientific" methodology of the Enlightenment. In facing this question, today's inquirer should ponder the observations of Voegelin. He notes that Max Weber's positivistic approach prevented this great mind from measuring its insights against the metaphysical tradition of earlier thought: "By the time the would-be critic has penetrated the meaning of metaphysics with sufficient thoroughness to make his criticism weighty," Voegelin observes, "he will have become a metaphysician himself. The attack on metaphysics can be undertaken with a good conscience only from the safe distance of imperfect knowledge."[20]

The *ordo iuris* of the Aristotelian tradition to which Murray refers understands human society as *a unity of order* among persons who have entered into *a solidarity based in their common purpose,* the good human life. The meaningfulness and acceptability of this understanding stands or falls upon the acceptance or rejection of an inherent purposefulness in human existence. As we have seen, the Enlightenment ideology rules out in principle the acceptance of such purposefulness in critical discussion. On the other hand, one after the other of our commentators has argued that the culture of modernity has much to gain from the rehabilitation of an understanding of finality as essential to the moral order which is the ultimate measure of human existence. Bellah and his associates see the value-free social science encouraged by Lockean assumptions as depriving American life of the rationale which is indis-

---

20. Voegelin, p. 20.

pensable if Americans are to find the meaning of the "good life" they are to share as a nation. Charles Taylor finds that it is impossible to give an account of moral experience without the recognition of "hyper-goods" as standards against which responsible human action is evaluated, and as establishing one's being "as a person." Just as the Enlightenment overturned the anthropocentrism which distorted the scientific interpretation of nature, so now, he argues, it must be recognized that the impersonal methodology of the science of the Enlightenment is not appropriate to the interpretation of what is irreducibly proper to human existence. Alasdair MacIntyre argues that contemporary philosophical approaches — having abandoned the notion of *telos,* taken for granted in antecedent cultural traditions — have found it impossible to render a satisfactory rational account of the moral order. He judges that the unity of a human life must be recovered through the recognition that it has "the unity of a narrative quest." What Taylor and MacIntyre argue for individual morality, Barker argues for the moral order which sustains society. For Barker, the institutions and laws of the state, "in themselves, are mere stocks and stones," their "true reality is not objective, but subjective"; he adds, "A law exists so far as it is a spiritual motive, apprehended and acted upon."[21]

The simplest vindication of the teleological interpretation of human society, it may be argued, is provided by the account this interpretation is able to give of the notions most cherished in contemporary political awareness. Before all else, it provides the key to an understanding of the central problem we mentioned above, the reconciliation of the notion of *natural and inalienable rights* with an authentic social *solidarity* and the effective *sovereignty of the people.* Not only are these basic principles of human society compatible, but an understanding of their relationship gives an eminently satisfactory meaning to modernity's ideals of *freedom* and *equality.* It is, moreover, in the reconciliation of individual rights and social solidarity that *the common good* becomes meaningful. It is through a realistic understanding of the common good that the role of government becomes intelligible, and *constitutional law* and *government by consent of the people* are vindicated.

21. Ernest Barker, *The Political Thought of Plato and Aristotle* (New York: Oxford University Press, 1959), p. 323.

Aristotle and Aquinas begin their account of human society by pointing out that the unity belonging to a political community is essentially "a unity of order."[22] To say that the human agent is by nature social is to say that all worthwhile human achievements are realized in collaboration with other human agents, that human development takes place in cultural solidarity. The goals adopted by the human agent are normally pursued in common with other human agents, and the benefits achieved — whether physical, emotional, intellectual, moral, or spiritual — are held in common in varying degrees with other human agents. This seeking of the good as a common good is the basis of social order. Social order is the collaborative order which is the precondition to all human development and achievements.

It is coordination which establishes human solidarity. In human communities in which reason has not become fully aware of itself, this coordination will be to a large extent pre-deliberative; in developed human societies, on the other hand, collaboration includes the explicit adoption of the rationally deliberated norms of constitutional law. As Barker puts it, "Society is an all-purpose association . . . which transcends the notion of law, and has grown and exists of itself. . . . The State, as such, is a legal association constituted by the action of its members in making a constitution."[23]

The account of human society which is based in the finality inherent in human existence in no way claims — it should be noted — that those who propose it can provide a blueprint for the perfect human society. The good to which human society is directed is *the human good*. The good which is the measure of human destiny defies neat definition;[24] it is pursued collaboratively in an open quest involving all members of society.[25] The fostering of this primordial common good should be compared, not to the framing of a carefully de-

---

22. Cf. Saint Thomas on Aristotle's *Ethics* 1.1. See also my *The Person and the Group: A Study in the Tradition of Aristotelian Realism of the Meaning of Human Society* (Milwaukee: Bruce, 1967), which is a detailed analysis of the implications of this understanding of social order.

23. Barker, in *Social Contract*, p. xv.

24. See, for instance, Karl Rahner, *Theological Investigations* (London: Darton, Longman & Todd, 1974), 1:300-302, 310-15.

25. Cf. Bellah et al., *The Good Society*, p. 19, already cited.

fined social contract, but to the work of a gardener who discovers the potentialities of his plants as he cares for them.

In other words, the conscious sharing of a human way of life, or claims by some participants in a particular society to possess something of the truth, in no way implies the imposition of a closed social system which is the enemy of the pluralism which has emerged in modernity's democratic society. Jacques Maritain sums up what this open quest implies: "Man finds himself by subordinating himself to the group, and the group attains its goal only by serving man and by realizing that man has secrets which escape the group and a vocation which the group does not encompass."[26] In the argument of his *Unconscious Civilisation,* Saul sees a claim to possess "the truth" as leading inevitably to a closed ideological solidarity. He fails to distinguish claims to possess "the truth" (conceived as a closed system) and claims to possess "something of the truth" (which merely imply the making of some contribution to humanity's common search for the truth).

The collaborative solidarity of human agents is grounded in intelligence.[27] The benefits peculiar to human existence, achieved by intelligence and free will, are of the *spiritual,* or immaterial, order. One's possession of the truth is in no way exclusive of possession by others; one's possession of the quality of justice in no way diminishes the possibility of possession of the same quality by other persons. What is more, although human association is necessary in the first instance because of the indigence of the isolated individual, this association of rational agents moves, of its nature, toward the formation of a collaborative solidarity in which the sharing of the benefits of creativity and spiritual achievement is its primary dynamism — as Maritain puts it: "But why is it that the person, as person, seeks to live in society? It does so, first, because of its very perfections, as person, and its

26. Jacques Maritain, *The Rights of Man and Natural Law* (New York: Scribner, 1943), p. 32.

27. It is significant that, unlike Aristotle and Aquinas, Locke does not see human sociability as grounded in rationality. He writes: "God having made man such a creature that, in his own judgment it was not good for him to be alone, put him under strong obligations of necessity, convenience, and inclination, to drive him into society, *as well as* fitted him with understanding and language to continue and enjoy it" (*Second Treatise,* par. 77, emphasis added).

inner urge to the communications of knowledge and love which require relationship with other persons . . . in response to the law of superabundance inscribed in the depths of being, life, intelligence, and love."[28]

It is at the level of *material* benefits that possession becomes exclusive, giving rise to the issue of property rights — a distribution of usage appropriated to some individuals rather than to others. For Aristotle and Aquinas this is an important but subsidiary issue of social order, to which reference will be made in what follows. For Locke, however (who has difficulty recognizing the immateriality which is the differential of intellection), all the human benefits with which his social order is concerned are contained under the rubric of "property." One is not surprised to find him drifting — as Murray points out — toward the physical term "power," in preference to the juridical term "right," in his description of the relationships constitutive of society.

Because the agents sharing in this solidarity of human society are persons pursuing their own destiny and finality, their solidarity is essentially different from that of infra-rational groups in collaboration. To suggest that they exist without qualification for the sake of the totality is the essence of totalitarianism. Animals on the other hand are by nature part of the whole (flock, hive, species, ecological economy) in which they exist, and whatever finality they have serves the finality of the whole to which they belong.

In the metaphysical perspective of Aristotle and Aquinas, it is the proper activities of intelligence and free will — different in kind from the knowledge and emotion of the order of sensation — which make it possible for a human person to participate in the achievements of social solidarity in a manner which is not possible for subrational beings. By reason of their materiality, subrational beings are incapable of participating in the achievements of the whole upon which they depend in any other manner than by totally subordinating themselves to its maintenance and spending themselves without qualification for its sake — acting out their role as *parts*. In contrast, the rational agent is capable of a higher

28. Jacques Maritain, *The Person and the Common Good* (New York: Scribner, 1947), pp. 37-38.

manner of communion in the best achievements of human society and participates in the solidarity of society for the sake of this communion. The intelligent agent's peculiar finality implies a dignity which demands that it not be reduced to the status of a mere part. Its qualified subordination to the totality is entered into for the sake of a personal sharing in the benefits of this communion.

Let us explain this further. Intelligence passes beyond the knowledge of particular material shapes, such as triangles, to the understanding of the mathematical necessities which are characteristic of triangularity, necessities which are of fundamental importance, for instance, in the constructions of contemporary engineering — the necessities which, as we have seen, scientists such as Paul Davies and John Barrow judge to be beyond the order of space and time proper to the material universe. It is an intellectual appreciation of the place of "fairness," or justice, in human dealings which provides the basis of a healthy human society. Such benefits as those of mathematical understanding and the practical appreciation of justice are in no way diminished by being shared. On the other hand, the material benefits necessary for human existence must be divided and diminished in being shared. The solidarity which is essential to human society has as its paramount purpose a communion in the goods proper to rational existence; the solidarity of infra-rational beings has as its purpose a service of the processes of the material cosmos.

The subordination of the person to the social totality, therefore, is not an unqualified subordination as in the case of infra-rational agents, but a qualified subordination, entered into by the human agent in order to participate in the achievements of social solidarity. Maritain sums up the point we are making — a point not appreciated by Locke — in these terms:

> The common good of society is neither a simple collection of private goods, nor a good belonging to the whole which (in the case of the species in relation to its individual members) draws the parts to itself, as if they were pure means to serve itself alone. The common good is the good *human* life of the multitude of persons; it is their communion in the good life; it is therefore common *to the whole and*

to its parts, on whom it flows back and who must all benefit from it.[29]

We have already cited the text in which Maritain expresses well the dialectical relationship between the person and the social group: the person finds an authentic existence in subordination to the group; the group fulfills its purpose by serving the person in an acknowledgment that the person has a vocation and destiny which cannot be contained within the collaborative unity which constitutes the group.

The recognition of finality is at the heart of the account I am proposing — the finality implied in my use and Maritain's use of notions such as "benefit" and "achievement." Let us explore the intelligible implications of finality more fully. As we have seen, MacIntyre argues that the accounts of the moral order given by the ideology of modernity suffer from the cultural dislocation which this ideology brought about in abandoning any notion of *telos* or purposefulness.[30] MacIntyre asks whether it is possible to have a *functional* understanding of anything, except in terms of purpose; using as simple illustrations "watch" and "farmer," he concludes that the "No 'ought' conclusion from 'is' premises" principle can only be upheld in reasoning that does not include functional concepts. Modernity's approach to morality upon this basis, MacIntyre points out, involves a radical break with the understanding of the moral order shared by classical antiquity and the Middle Ages, which presupposed "at least one central functional concept, the concept of *man* understood as having an essential nature and an essential purpose or function."[31]

The account of society being proposed understands the human agent as having a nature recognizably different in kind from that of infra-rational agents, and therefore as having a finality defined by the potentialities of that nature. The account I have given of the difference between the solidarity of a human society and that of infra-rational agents is grounded in these philosophical principles. It stands or falls with them. The ideology of modernity, on the other hand, in

---

29. Jacques Maritain, *Scholasticism and Politics* (New York: Scribner, 1947), pp. 39-40.

30. MacIntyre, p. 55.

31. MacIntyre, p. 58.

consciously rejecting a teleological view of human nature — indeed, any understanding of the human agent as having an essence which defines the agent's true purpose — is forced to find some other account of the difference between human society and the marvelous functioning of an ants' nest, if it is not to run the risk of drifting toward some form of totalitarianism.

The account I am giving of human society is greatly strengthened when we consider what it says concerning concepts fundamental to the society of modernity's self-understanding. It should already be clear that the acceptance of a finality which is the measure of human existence makes possible a reconciliation of the notion of natural or inalienable rights with an acceptance of solidarity as an essential dimension of human existence. We shall consider below the related question of the reconciliation of natural rights with the fundamental principle of the sovereignty of the people which gives expression to this solidarity.

To bring to light the full implications of the acceptance of human finality for an understanding of "natural right," let us extend MacIntyre's reasoning. This reasoning — using the example of "watch" and "farmer" — was that the value of a functional entity can be gauged according to the measure of success such an entity has in achieving the purpose implied in its essential function. This reasoning can be pursued at a more radical level: the essential value of different functional entities can be compared according to the different purposes they achieve. If, as the account of human society we are explaining affirms, the human agent's finality is to be understood in terms of absolutes (recall our examples of mathematical truth and the principle of justice), the value of the human agent is itself absolute. The recognition of "natural rights" is the recognition that — because the essential orientation of the human agent to the order of absolutes gives the human agent an absolute value — the human agent should never be made a *means* toward some common achievement of the whole. The "rights" of the human agent look to those dimensions of existence which should never be frustrated as society seeks the human good in solidarity. The human agent freely submits himself or herself to the demands of the common good, in order to be the beneficiary of the achievements of this common human good, and the "rights" it implies.

167

MacIntyre's assertion that the "natural right" of modernity is a "fiction" is puzzling. It may well be suggested that the application to the notion of *"right"* of the historical method he has used so effectively in his study of "virtue" would lead to the recognition that the notion of "right" is just as fundamental to the intelligibility of the moral order of human society as the notion of "virtue."

For this account of human society, therefore, *"the common good"* is not merely a reassuring buzzword expressing a more or less meaningless ideal. The analysis we have made makes its meaning clear. Human society is the coordination of personal activities to achieve and maintain the countless institutions which make possible an existence in keeping with the nature and destiny of human agents.[32] The culture shared by a human community provides benefits which are utterly beyond the capabilities of any one human agent; their maintenance requires the coordinated activities of innumerable beneficiaries, giving themselves to thousands of specialized occupations, each ministering to the complex requirements of a way of life. Without an immensely complicated coordination of human activities, a civilized way of life would disintegrate — in fact, history shows that such a disintegration has more than once taken place.

Once social collaboration is appreciated for what it is, it must be recognized that it gives rise to the *enterprise satisfaction* which is all-important to any collaborative effort. It is this satisfaction in the common enterprise of human society which is shared in the "political friendship" which is a key theme in Aristotle's social analysis. To those who accept the reductionist principles of Locke's social theory, it is clear that shared social life can only mean the factionalism condemned by John Ralston Saul, or the stability of a group in a state of truce. We see here one of the greatest weaknesses of modern democratic societies — the lack of a sense of enterprise satisfaction — because a clear, practical appreciation of the common good is lacking.

The pattern we have described and the common good it promotes are readily intelligible. The problem of reconciling natural right and the sovereignty of the people meets insoluble difficulties, however, if it is not recognized that this common good is the unifying

32. As we have seen, Bellah and associates make "institution" in this sense a central theme of *The Good Society* — cf. pp. 7-12, 287-88.

principle of human society in *all* its forms. Prior to the deliberated constitution of the societal association of "the state," this common good already constitutes the normative principle of a shared cultural tradition. The constitutional forms of the state do not *establish* the rights of the citizens in any unqualified sense; they establish the code which spells out in juridical terms the manner in which the inalienable rights of participants will be upheld in the life of a political community.[33]

This account of human society also makes eminently meaningful the *freedom* which is one of the cornerstones of the ideology of modernity. "Emancipation," as we have seen, is an epoch-making term; it has become the very slogan of modernity. This is readily understandable when the Enlightenment's positive achievement of critical awareness and accountability is compared with the spirit of previous cultures. But more than one observer of modernity has commented that this freedom is problematic if it has no accepted frame of reference. Our account makes, not some abstract blueprint, but the existential good which is essential to being human the measure of human freedom. In other words, the pursuit of one's personal good, as realized in solidarity with other members of a cultural and political tradition, gives rise to social responsibilities and norms. Within his Aristotelian perspective, Aquinas already anticipates such a notion of freedom in a common good: "In a free community possessing the right to enact its own laws the consent of the whole community in the observance of a certain custom has more value than the authority of the ruler whose power to enact laws derives from the fact that he represents the community."[34]

The fundamental *equality* of all citizens, taken for granted in the constitutional arrangements of modernity, is also readily intelligible within the perspective we are describing. It involves a nice relation-

---

33. It may be noted that the history of the recognition of "natural right" in our Western tradition is obscured to some degree by the fact that the Latin term *ius* served for both "right" and "law" in medieval usage. The communality involved in this terminology is reflected in what has just been stated in the text, that the "rights" of the citizen are declared in the "juridical" provisions of constitutional law and upheld in the administration of justice within the terms of the constitution.

34. Aquinas, *Summa theologiae* 2-2, q. 97, art. 3, ad 3.

ship between the freedom of the human agent and the demands of the common good. In the definition of right which he elaborates in this perspective, Aquinas writes: "the *right* or the *just* is a work that is adjusted to another person according to some kind of equality."[35]

Since every human agent is in principle sovereign in the pursuit of an absolute and transcendent destiny, every human *person*, whether adult or child, man or woman, simpleton or savant, cultured or uncultured, has absolute and equal value. This equality contrasts with the inequality which rules the world of *things*, which may be simply subordinated to one another, according to the place their intrinsic nature and purpose has in the material economy as a whole. This equality in human dignity belongs to all human agents, giving them equal claim in principle upon what makes possible the pursuit of a full human destiny. Clearly, it is a great injustice to prevent a citizen or a group of citizens from access to a share in the benefits which are essential to the human agent's intellectual and moral nature. In the order of material benefits, all citizens have equal right of access to these things.

With regard to the use of material things, Saint Thomas interprets the rights associated with "private property" as not absolute, but essentially qualified. While effective care of material things requires that they are normally appropriated, the freedom this appropriation implies must be exercised within the limits established by the demands of the common good, and must ultimately serve the natural right of all human beings to benefit from the material universe.[36]

It will be recognized that — in terms of concrete benefits to which one may claim access by right — social equality will often be not an absolute or arithmetic equality but a proportional equality, insofar as the material goods necessary to two different persons in the

35. Aquinas, *Summa theologiae* 2-2, q. 57, art. 2. Aquinas reiterates an assertion very modern in its ring: "all men are by nature equal" (cf. 2-2, q. 104, art. 5; 1, q. 109, art. 2, ad 3, etc.).

36. See my *Person and the Group,* pp. 143-45. For Aquinas, property right is a "positive" right (i.e., a right depending upon human enactment — in this case accepted forms of acquisition); it serves the more radical "natural" (i.e., inalienable) right to which reference has been made — the right to benefit from the resources of the material universe. The implications of responsibility for the environment are not difficult to recognize.

170

pursuit of their destiny may vary according to circumstance. To use a simple illustration, though a fully grown man and a child may both have a right to be fully clothed, the quantity of apparel needed by the man will be much greater than that required by the child. There are many parallels to this simple example, as persons belonging to different historical communities, with different talents and aspirations, different avocations and functions in the community pursue their human destiny within the cultural solidarity of the community to which they belong.

It must be noted, moreover, as the authors of *The Good Society* have insisted, that the natural rights of all men and women throughout the world require, as a matter of natural justice, that the way be genuinely open for the different cultural communities throughout the world, in their various socioeconomic circumstances, to pursue an authentic destiny for their participants. This issue is not fully faced up to by the world's powerful industrial countries and their financial institutions, in their dealings with less advantaged nations. The implications of property rights, as analyzed by Aquinas, should be recognized and taken more seriously by those responsible for international financial arrangements.

Modernity has made the contemporary world militantly aware that discrimination in the recognition of human rights on grounds of race, gender, creed, wealth, or any other count is a violation of this equality belonging to all human persons by nature. Our account of human society — within an Aristotelian perspective — provides an eminently intelligible philosophical basis for this conviction.

During the twentieth century the phrase "social justice" has established itself in common usage. It represents a reaction on the part of responsible social awareness to a cultural situation in which our Western tradition has been unduly influenced by Lockean individualism. The bourgeois mentality of modernity, which recognizes with great seriousness the justice involved in business transactions, is often insensitive to the fact that *the demands of the common good* give rise to obligations in justice, binding upon those whose initiatives shape the society in which they live.

For Aquinas, as we have seen, "right" and "justice" are correlatives: different orders of *right* give rise to different orders of obligation in *justice*. Individual rights give rise to two distinct forms of obligation in justice. The most obvious is the *commutative* justice which governs transactions between individuals. *Distributive* justice, the justice which must be exercised by those administering human society in the distribution of the burdens and privileges of citizenship, is also easily recognized.

The function of justice in a human community would not be adequately represented, however, if "social justice" were understood as no more than the conscientious observance of individual rights of others in the orders of commutative and distributive justice. Rights belong not only to individuals but also to persons in solidarity. All members of a human community are obliged to recognize the rights their fellow citizens have to a promotion of the public order which fosters the common human good. The Aristotelian tradition calls this latter form of justice "legal justice," an obvious reference to the fact that the law is the most notable expression of the demands of public order and the common good. It may also be called *general justice* insofar as it is a dimension of all activity within a life of human solidarity. MacIntyre's *After Virtue* provides a helpful background to what Aquinas says concerning this "general justice": "the good of any virtue, whether such virtue direct one in relation to the self, or in relation to certain other individual persons, is referable to the common good, to which justice directs: so that all acts of virtue can pertain to justice, insofar as it directs one to the common good. It is in this sense that justice is called a general virtue."[37]

The three cornerstones of modernity's democratic politics are the recognition of the inalienable rights of the citizen, the constitutional law which declares the fundamental norms whereby the common good will be upheld, and the principle that the consent of the people is the source of all authority to govern. We have already established that an Aristotelian perspective acknowledging the teleological dimension of human existence provides a vindication of the first of these principles, and its compatibility with the demands of social solidarity. We must now show how this perspective also provides a clear vindication of the other two principles.

From what has already been said, it is clear that the work of government within any political community is a service which assists the

37. Aquinas, *Summa theologiae* 2-2, q. 58, art. 5.

community toward the achievement of the common good. Since it is the members of the community who are first and foremost responsible for the common achievement and benefits in solidarity which constitute the common good, it is the community association at large which is responsible in a primordial sense for the governing of the community. We have used the term "community association" advisedly. Discussion of the nature and source of authority to govern easily becomes confused if it is not recognized that the provisions of what we have called "societal association" (or "the state") presuppose the reality of "community association" (what Sir Ernest Barker calls "the all-purpose association of Society").

The most fundamental government of the community belongs, therefore, to the community itself. The community may truly be said to govern itself, for instance, when — apart from any enactment of constitutional law — the members of the community achieve a moral unanimity in the practical recognition of many basic rights: natural rights such as a person's right to life, to association with fellow human beings, to enter into marriage and raise a family, to seek and propagate the truth, to acquire the material necessities of life. In a developed political community, the work of government, the enacting of the norms of social collaboration in the common good, is entrusted to the instrumentality of particular members suitably qualified, who act on behalf of the community. To such governing authorities are entrusted the drawing up of the terms of constitutional law, the enactment of policies and initiatives which shape the common life of the political community within the terms laid down by the constitution, and the administration of justice under the law. Properly understood, therefore, the instruments of government are an extension of the community's responsibility for its own common good. It clearly follows that it is the consent of the people expressed through plebiscites and elections as provided by the constitution which gives binding force to constitutional law and is the source of all authority to govern.

This Aristotelian interpretation of the foundation of government was, once more, clearly enunciated by Aquinas: "Law strictly understood has as its first and principal object the ordering of the common good. But to order affairs to the common good is the task either of the whole community or some . . . person who represents it. Thus the promulgation of law is the business either of the whole community or of that political person whose duty is the care of the common good."[38]

It is interesting, in the context of contemporary political discussion, to recognize that our account of human society upholds the principle of "small government" — not in the Lockean sense of an economic rationalism which seeks to minimize constraints upon the pursuit of individual advantage, but in a much more defensible sense. If the role of government is to serve as an instrument of the community in the pursuit of the human good in solidarity, the initiatives of government should be restricted to this instrumental function. What can be effectively undertaken by other free associations within the life of the community should not normally be undertaken by the instrumentalities of government.[39] Thus government instrumentalities provide an all-important *complement* to the initiatives of individuals and free associations in the promotion of the common good. A practical corollary of this is the recognition of the importance of nongovernment organizations in a healthy political community if the rich variety of the human good to be realized in solidarity is to flourish.[40]

The objective of the present chapter was the consolidation of the immense achievements of modernity in its establishing of today's democratic society. Commentators upon the culture of modernity have argued that some of the fundamental problems which have emerged in late modernity are related to the Enlightenment ideology's rejection of any notion of an inherent purposefulness in human existence. We have found that the acceptance of such purposefulness makes possible an account of human society which shows the most cherished themes of modernity's political awareness — inalienable

---

38. Aquinas, *Summa theologiae* 1-2, q. 90, art. 3.

39. Bellah and colleagues emphasize the importance of this "principle of subsidiarity" (cf. *The Good Society*, pp. 282-83). Perhaps the import of this principle would be more clearly indicated if it were called the "principle of autonomy."

40. The Club of Rome's report, *The First Global Revolution*, published in 1991, stressed the importance of nongovernment organizations in the life of the worldwide community in the situation which is emerging. (The churches' contribution, stressed in *The Good Society*, belongs to this order. Bellah and associates sum up something of the importance of this contribution — putting a community in touch with the collective memory which provides all-important cultural resources — with the phrase "the language of covenant and communion.")

rights, freedom, equality, popular sovereignty, and government by consent — to be interrelated in a way which is eminently intelligible. Modernity's democratic society will only flourish if these principles are upheld. Those who reject our account must provide an equally convincing vindication of these cherished principles. If they cannot do so, they must ask themselves whether their position amounts in the end to little more than a doctrinaire denial inspired by the ideology of the Enlightenment.

PART III

Toward a Christian
Affirmation of Modernity

CHAPTER 9

"Witness," the Only Adequate Medium of Existential Truth

IN THIS FINAL PART OF THE BOOK, I SHALL BE ADOPT-
ing the point of view of a Christian theologian. If Enlightenment sec-
ularists and proponents of Christian faith differ on many things, it
may seem that they should agree that the spirit of modernity and the
essential claims of Christian faith cannot be reconciled. I mean, in
these chapters, to contest this. I shall argue, not only that the essential
project of modernity and the fundamentals of Christian faith can be
reconciled, but also that their concerns converge in a way which is important for the future of humanity.

Modernity's wide-ranging investigations have provided information not previously available of the place of religion in the world's cultural traditions. At the same time, the methodological assumptions of
modernity have undermined expectations that religion might have anything to contribute to a critical understanding of our human situation.

This paradox, it will be recalled, is evident in the work of Max
Weber. Weber acknowledged that "religious forces, and the ethical
ideas of duty based upon them, have in the past always been among
the most important formative influences of conduct."[1] At the same

---

1. Cited in Lawrence Cahoone's anthology, *From Modernism to Postmodernism* (Cambridge, Mass.: Blackwell, 1996), p. 166.

time, however, the methodological positivism he adopted made it impossible for him to incorporate any serious evaluation of these religious values in his sociological analysis.

The same paradox is evident in contemporary scholarship. On the one hand, in the judgment of the great twentieth-century authority on comparative religion Mircea Eliade, the religious quest which has shaped the cultures of the world was not an effort to escape the everyday experience of the world, but an attempt to interpret the world of immediate experience in a manner which laid hold of its ultimate reality.[2] Indeed, in the judgment of British historian Christopher Dawson:

> Religion is the key of history. We cannot understand the inner form of a society unless we understand its religion. We cannot understand its cultural achievements unless we understand the religious beliefs behind them. In all ages the first creative works of a culture are due to religious inspiration and dedicated to a religious end. The temples of the gods are the most enduring works of man. Religion stands at the threshold of all the great literatures of the world. Philosophy is its offspring and is a child which constantly returns to its parent.[3]

But on the other hand, the Enlightenment's manner of distinguishing — within the perspective of positivism — various academic disciplines and their specific concerns has given rise to an outlook which set up a dichotomy between the realms of "the profane" (open to investigation by "objective" scientific procedures) and "the sacred" (belonging to the "subjective" order).

The development of this dichotomy within the outlook of modernity is not difficult to follow. Until the end of the eighteenth century, the outlook described by Eliade was taken for granted in our cultural tradition: "religion" was identified with a whole culture insofar as it came to terms with what was seen as ultimate in human exis-

---

2. Cf. Eliade's *The Sacred and the Profane* (New York: Harper & Row, 1961), pp. 63, 65, 94, 95, 100, etc.

3. Christopher Dawson, *Religion and Culture* (London: Sheed & Ward, 1949), p. 50; cf. Robert N. Bellah, Richard Madsen, William M. Sullivan, Ann Swidler, and Steven M. Tipton, *The Good Society* (New York: Random House, Vintage, 1992), p. 173: "[I]f we want to understand traditional cultures, we shall have to take seriously that religious concerns are central to most of them"; also p. 16.

tence; the order of the "sacred," with which religion was concerned, was seen as coextensive with life itself. From the beginning of the nineteenth century, however, under the influence of the Enlightenment's methodological assumption, "religion" came to mean a particular sphere of human activity, among others. Joseph D. Bettis describes this development:

> The attempt to describe religion as a separate and independent sphere of individual and human activity did not appear until near the beginning of the nineteenth century. Schleiermacher's *On Religion* was one of the first books to regard it as an isolable subject. Prior to that a religious tradition was identified with the cultural tradition that provided the fundamental means of individual and social identification. Traditionally, religion referred to the basic guiding images and principles of an individual and a culture. Religion was identical with style of life.[4]

The perspective that emerged in earlier chapters of this book allows us to recognize that the Enlightenment's differentiation of the spheres of religion ("the sacred") and the secular ("the profane") was an expression of modernity's concern to protect the legitimate autonomy of the secular order. We are also in a position to recognize that a reaction was entirely justified against medievalism's amalgamation of the orders of the secular and the sacred through the cultural process of "sacralization." In fact, the true spirit of modernity and a sound Christian theology find themselves in agreement, that the demise of medieval culture was inevitable.

Modernity's instinct that medieval culture compromised the authentic autonomy of the secular order was sound. For its part, Christian theology must recognize that an affirmation of the divine mystery through a "sacralizing" of human culture (making that culture's paramount function a symbolic reference to the transcendent) was a compromising of the affirmation of created reality given in the incarnation, the central tenet of Christian faith.

Both modernity and Christian theology now find themselves,

---

4. Joseph D. Bettis, *Phenomenology of Religion* (London: SCM, 1975), p. 170.

however, called to make immense adjustments. Modernity must recognize that achieving an authentic autonomy for the secular order does not require calling into question the claims of the world's religious traditions — in fact, modernity must recognize that religious awareness and the wisdom it brings make an all-important contribution to an authentic human existence.

For their part, those who promote the religious traditions of the world must reassess their task within the rich context provided by the research of modernity. In the remainder of this chapter we shall consider only one of the many issues this reassessment raises — the part played by "witness" in the interaction between the project of modernity and the world's religious traditions as they make possible a fuller appreciation of the existential truth which gives meaning to the human story.

Modernity's spirit of inquiry and accountability has provided an awareness of the various religious traditions of humanity which is unprecedented and rapidly increasing. This development has also brought an increasing interaction among these traditions. Not surprisingly, the interaction to this point has taken the form, for the most part, of contestation and rivalry. These traditions must move beyond this antagonistic relationship, however, if they are to make an effective contribution to existential truth.

Encounters between religious traditions which make *doctrinal teaching* the medium of their communication are rarely very productive, becoming little more than polite confrontations incapable, by reason of conflicting assumptions, of achieving any meaningful dialogue. This approach reflects, in fact, the emphasis given by the Enlightenment to propositional truth. Today, within Christian theology, it is being recognized that it has led to a neglect of other dimensions of human communication essential to the "witness" which is an effective sharing of existential truth.[5] Rising above the antagonistic relationship of doctrinal debate does not necessitate turning one's back upon what is proper to the teachings of one's own tradition. It merely calls for a recognition that religious traditions share in a common task on

---

5. We have already heard J. B. Metz making this criticism; cf. *Faith in History and Society* (New York: Seabury Crossroad, 1980; German original, 1977), pp. 3, 33, 131, 150.

behalf of humanity. Those who are committed to the great religious traditions of the world should communicate with one another by giving a witness to the existential truth to which their particular tradition has given access. Having found what is life-giving beyond the measures of mundane experience, they should greet as fellows those who have made a similar discovery. They should see them as enlightening collaborators in the task of bringing news of the transcendent measure of all existence to questing humanity.

In other words, the sharing which is appropriate between the world religions — and the interchange between their points of view and that shaped by the concerns of modernity — should be at the level, not of doctrine, but of *witness*. It is not difficult to recognize that, though it is outside the purview of the Enlightenment ideology, "witness" has a fundamental place in human communication and experience. By "witness," we refer to a communication which resonates with overtones of personal authenticity and existential discovery. It is normally "witness," in its many forms, which inspires those seeking to give meaning and value to their existence to join a cause, to share a vision, to take up an avocation; it inspires lovers to receive declarations of love and abiding fidelity with a trust which is beyond rational proof. In a certain sense, human "witness" reaches beyond the normal confines of human language. It is not surprising, therefore, to find that it has an important place in the life of religious traditions.[6]

An appreciation of the place of "witness" in the search for existential truth leads to the recognition that propositional formularies — necessary as they are for human communication[7] — are an inad-

---

6. C. A. J. Coady's painstaking study, *Testimony: A Philosophical Study* (New York: Oxford University Press, 1994), leaves one with the impression that "witness" is a neglected area of philosophical analysis. Though Coady criticizes the Enlightenment presuppositions which help to account for this, his own study is almost entirely confined to *propositional* testimony. He adopts a philosophical approach based in "procedural" rather than "substantive" reason (writing that philosophy's "conclusions seem so essentially unstable that many are tempted to hold that the subject consists of a set of skills rather than a body of truths," p. 61 n. 12).

7. For an enlightening treatment of the validity and limitations of propositional expressions of religious truth, see Bernard Lonergan's "The Origins of Christian Realism," in *A Second Collection* (London: Darton, Longman & Todd, 1974), pp. 239-61. S. Mark Heim's *Salvation: Truth and Difference in Religion*

equate medium for the full expression of existential truth. For Christian theology, *faith* is an existential meeting with the divine mystery, through the gift of the Spirit of God. Of its nature, such a meeting is beyond adequate expression in the language of human articulation. As a consequence, *doctrinal statements* are of limited significance as an expression of the full truth of faith. As Saint Paul tells the Corinthians, the reality of the divine mystery can be spoken of and known by faith, only "in a mirror dimly" (1 Cor. 13:12) — only through a language and finite concepts which can bring no more than an analogical expression of what is beyond the grasp of created concepts.[8]

For Christian theology, "witness" involves both faith's encounter with the divine mystery and a propositional or symbolic expression of this meeting: it is a human communication which derives its power from the fact that it resonates with existential discovery and authenticity. All the world's great religious traditions derive their enduring vitality from an analogous "witness." A meeting of religious traditions which seeks a sharing of access to existential truth, through a respectful exchange of "witness," should bring a sense of sharing in the same transcendent mystery. Such an exchange would also prepare the way for the contribution the wisdom of these traditions can make to our Western culture as it seeks to go beyond the ideological constraints of modernity.

Because "witness" is essential to the communication of religious awareness, it has always had a fundamental place in the life of the Christian tradition. It is a neglected topic, however, in Christian theology. Karl Barth is one theologian who has reflected profoundly upon the place of "witness" in Christian life. Let us conclude this chapter by outlining some of Barth's reflections upon this topic. They have

---

(Maryknoll, N.Y.: Orbis, 1995) takes up the "orientational pluralism" suggested by Nicholas Rescher in his *Strife of Systems: An Essay on the Grounds and Implications of Philosophical Diversity* (Pittsburgh: University of Pittsburgh Press, 1985), to which we referred in an earlier chapter, as having an analogous application to interfaith dialogue.

8. It should be noted here that, in a manner which is too infrequently adverted to by religious scholars, doctrine frequently shades off into *ideological* discourse — as the securities of a group come to be identified with particular hard-edged doctrinal positions.

implications for the dialogue which must take place between Christian faith and the concerns of modernity.

Barth's discussion of the place of the Scriptures in the Christian life is grounded in the notion of "witness." Barth discusses the question, "What does it mean to say we believe that the Bible is the Word of God?"[9] He rejects emphatically an interpretation of this statement which would give it a metaphorical sense — a sense in which the Scriptures would be understood as "a lesser, less potent, less ineffable and majestic word of God." "There is only one Word of God," he declares, "and that is the eternal Word of the Father which for our reconciliation became flesh like us and has now returned to the Father, to be present in His Church by the Holy Spirit" (pp. 512-13). The answer Barth gives to his question hinges on the function of "witness." Barth explains that the Scriptures may be identified with the eternal Word, because they are the bearers of a privileged and normative witness to the Word of God.[10] For reasons to which we have already referred, the communication of the eternal Word of the Father cannot take place through the "direct impartation" of doctrinal statements, to use the terms of Barth; it is encountered through the medium of a "witness," which brings an order of truth which cannot be adequately expressed in propositional form.

The words of this witness speak to us at two levels. Most immediately and obviously they address us in the propositional terms used by the scriptural authors. At another level, however, these statements resonate with the authenticity and existential discovery of faith's meeting with the expression of the ways of the living God at the heart of the religious tradition to which they give expression. The presence of the eternal Word in human history in Jesus of Nazareth is the essential and primordial measure of Christian faith; the eternal Word is not present, however, "on earth" in the Bible in the same manner as that Word is "in heaven": "in His eternal presence as the Word of

9. Karl Barth, *Church Dogmatics* I/2 (Edinburgh: T. & T. Clark, 1961), pp. 506-8, 512-14. References which follow are to this text.

10. Though he does not use the term, Barth's response to his question appeals to the figure of *metonymy:* "the use of the name of a thing for that of another associated with or suggested by it" — as described in Webster's dictionary. This figure is used, for instance, when a judge is given the title "Justice."

God He is concealed from us who now live on earth and in time. He is revealed only in the sign of His humanity, and especially in the witness of His prophets and apostles. By nature these signs are not heavenly-human, but earthly- and temporal-human" (p. 513).[11]

This "witness" — in those who give it and in those who receive it — is a function of the presence of the Spirit of God:

> if they are to act as signs, if the eternal presence of Christ is to be revealed to us in time, there is a constant need of the continuing work of the Holy Spirit in the Church and in its members which is always taking place in new acts . . . the very fact . . . that the promise speaks to us and that we are obedient in faith, is always before us as a question which has to be answered again and again by the work of the Holy Spirit. This is the event we look to if — here on earth in the Church non-triumphant, but militant — we confess that the Bible is God's Word. (pp. 513-14)

Barth's analysis has far-reaching implications. In the first place, it makes it possible to accept the Scriptures as a witness to the eternal Word and at the same time to take seriously the inadequacies of the biblical writings as the ongoing essays of human authors and their faith communities which are an integral part of human culture and history, witnessing to a meeting with the ways of God in the mystery of a self-disclosure which spans many centuries. Barth's illustrations of the two levels at work in the witness of the Scriptures are simple and clear: if we accept the words of the Scriptures as a "witness," we must acknowledge that they are put together by "fallible, erring men like ourselves." As such, they "can be subjected to all kinds of imma-

---

11. Elsewhere Barth describes the impact of the life of Jesus of Nazareth in terms which clearly imply the dynamic of "witness" we are referring to: "the man who even in our human situation and within our human history, has lived and lives and will live this eternal life, this Stranger whom we cannot overlook or remove . . . because as such He is at Home among us and like us and with us, belonging as we do to our human situation and history. It is because it is the life . . . of this near Neighbour even in all His otherness, that this life is called light, revelation and word . . . this life of a man like us . . . is a declaration . . . it is an address, promise and demand, a question and answer" (*Church Dogmatics* IV/3, first half [Edinburgh: T. & T. Clark, 1961], pp. 83-84).

nent criticism," bringing to light their "lacunae, inconsistencies and over-emphases"; believers may well be alienated, Barth declares, by the figures of Moses, James, and Paul, and "make little or nothing of large tracts of the Bible"; only the presence of God's Spirit in our meeting with this witness "can genuinely and seriously prevent us from taking offence at the Bible" (p. 507).

This appreciation of the limitations which may be present in the formularies which are the bearers of a genuine witness to the mystery of God makes possible a more inclusive attitude to expressions of truth outside our Christian tradition. The project of modernity, for instance, has brought to light issues which could not be adequately appreciated by the cultures reflected in the doctrinal positions of the biblical writings. The fact, for example, that this literature does not transcend the *patriarchal assumptions* of the biblical period confronts us with a particular form of "the scandal of particularity" which it was impossible for the divine condescension to avoid in making use of the economy of the incarnation. If we cannot share these assumptions, they should not obscure for us the essential witness of the Scriptures concerning the ways of God which invites us to leave behind all human discrimination and domination. The biblical literature's negative polemic against the *cosmic religions* should not prevent us from acknowledging the presence, in *every* human situation and culture, of the gracious God witnessed to in the Scriptures. The *exclusivism* which marks so much of what the Scriptures say as they attempt to come to terms with the mystery of *divine election,* and the call to service it brings to a particular people in the midst of all the peoples of the world, challenges us to make our own the inclusive point of view adopted by the witness of the life and death of Jesus of Nazareth.[12]

In this total perspective, all that the literature of the Scriptures contains is providentially "written down for our instruction, upon whom the end of the ages has come" (1 Cor. 10:11 RSV); we must look into the mirror of the Scriptures and learn the lessons which come from comparing the ongoing pedagogy they record with the truth given to the world in the witness they contain, finally expressed

---

12. See J. Jeremias, *Jesus' Promise to the Nations* (Philadelphia: Fortress, 1982); N. T. Wright, *Jesus and the Victory of God* (London: SPCK, 1996).

in the life, death, and resurrection of the eternal Word which the Scriptures proclaim.[13]

The perspective we are considering can contribute to the needs of our age in various ways. Christians are invited, for example, to acknowledge the possibility of a genuine meeting with the divine mystery in the other great religious traditions of the world. Clearly, the "inspiration" of the Spirit of God — which Barth has made an essential element in a witness which brings a meeting with the divine mystery — is not confined exclusively to the Scriptures which provide a normative testimony to Christian faith. What is unique to the Christian Scriptures is not the fact that through the presence — or "inspiration" — of the Holy Spirit they give a witness to the mystery of the living God. Such "inspiration" is a recurring reality in the life of the believing community. If Francis of Assisi, Dietrich Bonhoeffer, and John XXIII — to name but a few examples — have given to the world, through their witness and teaching, a glimpse of the ways of God revealed to the world in Jesus of Nazareth, this can only be because the "inspiration" of the Spirit of God, as described by Barth, was present in their lives and words. But Christians are invited to widen their horizons in another important way.

The perspective opened up by Barth's analysis looks beyond the confines of the Christian tradition. While this perspective recognizes that a life-giving witness to existential truth may be given in the other great world religions, it also invites a readiness to acknowledge the working of God's Spirit in the lore, literature, and arts of the world.

13. Norbert Lohfink, "The Inerrancy of Scripture," in his *The Christian Meaning of the Old Testament* (London: Burns & Oates, 1969), pp. 37-39, provides the background to this perspective, which is not familiar to many Christians: "Jesus, the apostles and the primitive Church made, with regard to the Jewish canon which they found before them, the decision that the Old Testament canon should form the enduring background history and document of the New Testament which had come in Christ. . . . The fact of Christ is like the key signature at the beginning of the score which determines everything that follows. . . . It makes a single book of the Old and New Testaments, not merely from the point of view of their transcendental divine author, but also with regard to its inherent purpose, an intentionally unified body of meaning, which is very complicated and manifold, but which cannot be broken up into independent parts. Only within this all-embracing unity is the sense of each individual statement finally determined."

Without losing their proper character, the sacred writings of the world religions, including the Christian Scriptures, are seen as integral to the entire heritage of humanity in its quest for existential truth. They provide an index — of great moment, but not exclusive — that must be applied in the evaluation of what makes up this heritage.

An acceptance of these principles by participants in the dialogue among the world religions which must surely take place in the coming age would make this dialogue far more productive for its participants, and far more encouraging for the culture of modernity as it seeks access to the truth beyond the narrowness of its originating ideology.

CHAPTER 10

Today's Comprehensive Context More Adequately Discloses the Implications of the Judeo-Christian "Differentiation of Consciousness"

THE PRECEDING CHAPTER CONSIDERED, IN GENERAL terms, the "witness" given by the world's religious traditions. The present chapter considers the particular witness of the Judeo-Christian tradition. It may well be argued that this tradition is still coming to a full understanding of its peculiar identity, its place in the totality of human experience, of which the inquiring spirit of modernity has made us aware. Though the "gospel," or "good news," has been a fundamental theme of Christianity's self-awareness since its very beginnings, it is only in our time that the full implications of this theme are being clarified. This clarification is brought by modernity's more adequate appreciation of the full range of human experience. At the same time, discussion taking place within Christian theology is bringing a greater appreciation of the implications of the message which is essential to the "differentiation of consciousness" defining our tradition.

One may well ask, in fact, whether a full appreciation of the import of the gospel was possible before the present era. The meaningfulness of a message is only fully grasped when one knows the situation which the message addresses. In our age, we have begun for the first time to appreciate the full range of human existence and experience which is addressed by the gospel message. This development opens the way to an unprecedented recognition of its full implications.

The revolutionary message of Judeo-Christian faith saw itself initially as a challenge to the mythological assumptions of the sacralized cultures which shaped the ancient world. It is not surprising therefore that this tradition has until the recent past tended to see itself as a counter-identity in confrontation with competing worldviews. Today, however, our appreciation of the full range of human experience enables us to see the "differentiation of consciousness" peculiar to the Judeo-Christian tradition as bringing a corrective which radically *complements,* rather than *replaces,* the outlooks of the world's cultures and their traditions of wisdom.

Eric Voegelin pioneered discussion along the lines we are proposing. In his *New Science of Politics,* he suggested that the "differentiation of consciousness" provides the key to an interpretation of the movement of history, and its distinct phases. Voegelin divided the history of our Western tradition into four periods: (1) a period shaped by a *"cosmological" principle;* (2) a period shaped by an *"anthropological" principle;* (3) a period shaped by a *"soteriological" principle;* and (4) a period shaped by what Voegelin calls a *"gnostic" principle.*

It is important for our present discussion to clarify the full implications of this progressive development. The emergence of a new differentiation of consciousness is not necessarily a *negation* of the outlook of the previous stage. Rather it should provide the previous outlook with a new and radical extension. Thus the anthropological principle does not abrogate the cosmological principle; it may be seen as complementing it by providing a more adequate understanding of the measure which was previously accepted. The fact that the divine measure symbolically recognized in the order of the cosmos is now grasped more directly does not necessarily abrogate what was essential to previous understanding. Similarly, the soteriological principle which shapes the Judeo-Christian consciousness, properly understood, provides a startlingly new and radical dimension to the anthropological principle. Extending this interpretation, one may well, in the last analysis, make a far more positive judgment than Voegelin himself does of the differentiation of consciousness which characterizes modernity. The *immanentizing of norms* brought by modernity may be seen, not as incompatible with what was essential to previous representations of truth, but as the achieving of a wholesome *autonomy* under the norms they represent. If this interpretation is correct, our

191

Western culture will be able, in the end, to give a proper expression to what has been achieved in this progressive differentiation of consciousness, while retaining what is essential to each of the successive representations of the truth it has known.

Coming to terms with the transcendent measure of the reality of experience has not been easy for humanity's cultural traditions. If modernity has attempted to immanentize its ultimate measure, most cultural traditions which have acknowledged a "divine" order have tended to misrepresent the transcendent nature of the divine measure through a "sacralization" of cultural processes. In the last chapter we pointed to the medieval instance of this. J. B. Metz has pointed to the fatal flaw in this outlook: "This view never allowed the world to become wholly secular because it never let God become wholly divine."[1] On the one hand, because the transcendent was called upon to validate a meaning for the cosmos which allayed the human agent's existential fear of chaos, the divinity was compromised by being seen as, first and foremost, a world-maintaining principle; on the other hand, the process of sacralization, interpreting mundane things and, in particular, nature itself as an immediate manifestation of the presence and power of God, invested mundane reality with a numinous radiance which prevented it from being appreciated for what it is in itself.

This process of *sacralization* must be recognized for what it is if we are to fully understand the *secularization* taking place in our modern Western culture. Sacralization and its reversal, secularization, are ideological processes of the kind our discussion has brought us to appreciate. Through the process of sacralization, the *cosmological* culture tended to embrace an ambiguous "divinization" of the world. The *anthropological* culture, as Metz points out in the work cited above, did not escape ambiguity in regard to this issue: calling in principle for what Voegelin calls a "de-divinization" of the cosmos, yet at the same time not achieving this in its hesitant attitude to the mythologies.[2] The *soteriological* culture is, when fully authentic, "de-

---

1. J. B. Metz, *Theology of the World* (New York: Herder & Herder, 1971), p. 34.
2. Cf. Eric Voegelin, *The New Science of Politics* (Chicago: University of Chicago Press, 1960), pp. 66, 69, 157. Plato's ambiguous attitude in this regard is well known. See G. Vlastos, "Socratic Piety," in chap. 6 *passim* of his *Socrates: Ironist and Moral Philosopher* (Cambridge: Cambridge University Press, 1991).

divinizing."[3] It is lear, however, that until the recent past it has retained a residual tendency to "divinization": the Christian culture of the medieval period and later — according to interpreters such as Mircea Eliade, M.-D. Chenu, H. U. von Balthasar, Y. Congar, and J. B. Metz[4] — did not completely avoid the tendency to sacralize or "divinize" cultural realities in an uncritical way which was not in keeping with the true genius of Christian faith and the liberating message of the gospel it proclaimed.[5] If one accepts Voegelin's account of it, the *gnostic* culture of modernity can be interpreted as tending toward a pseudodivinization of mundane reality.[6]

Voegelin's analysis has clear implications concerning the emergence with full clarity of the gospel message within the comprehensive context of human history, a message which claims to bring a truth which has been the object of humanity's great quest — at once absolutely transcendent and inseparable from the authentic human existence. It also helps us understand the factors which have tended to obscure the full implications of this challenging truth and its absolute transcendence.

In his study *Theology and Literature,* T. R. Wright goes to the heart of the claim which is essential to Christian faith: "the Christian claim is that one particular story, centred upon Christ, tells us the universal truth about history."[7] In other words, the biblical story which reaches its climax in the life, death, and exaltation of Jesus of Nazareth discloses a truth about human existence which is universal. In the light of the biblical story, we can find the ultimate significance of our own stories. And conversely, the story of each of us can shed light on the ongoing story of the Christian people as a whole, the church. We are confronted once again with the function of narrative as the medium of existential truth.

---

3. Cf. Voegelin, p. 101.

4. Cf. my *Christian Mystery in the Secular Age* (Westminster, Md.: Christian Classics, 1991) — on Eliade, pp. 5 and 7; on Chenu, pp. 9, 43, 297 n; on von Balthasar, p. 10; on Congar, p. 14; on Metz, pp. 12-14.

5. Cf. *Christian Mystery,* pp. 144-45, 34, 41. See also H. Schürmann, "N.T. Notes on the Question of 'Desacralisation': The Point of Contact for the Sacral within the Context of the N.T. Revelation," *Theology Digest* 17 (1969): 7-9.

6. Cf. Voegelin, pp. 124-25 (referred to in chap. 1) and pp. 148-49.

7. T. R. Wright, *Theology and Literature* (Oxford: Blackwell, 1989), p. 84.

The story of my work as a theologian could probably best be told as the story of a progressive exploration of what "the gospel" means and its relationship to human experience. Like so many important terms, the word "gospel" tends to be denatured by overuse. For that reason I hesitated to use it in giving a title to this chapter. I can only hope that the narrative of my own theological journey brings to light the full significance of this term — which predates the Christian movement itself, already finding substance and expression in the prophetic tradition of Israel. I am convinced that a renewed appreciation of the gospel given to the world in Jesus Christ is imperative if the community of Christian faith is to take up effectively the challenges of the coming age. In particular, it is only in a common faith in the gospel that the movement toward Christian unity will be able to overcome its present frustrations.

I vividly remember what was in fact the starting point of my journey into an understanding of the Christian gospel, as I prepared my first theology lectures forty years ago. How was I to find a focus, I asked myself, which could give life and interest to the courses which had been assigned to me? Somehow the truth I must communicate to my students in interpreting the Christian faith must come to them as more than dry theological theorems; the truth I was interpreting should touch them with life and hope at the deepest level of their existence and personhood. I have often looked back at that moment and recognized that, though I did not use the term "gospel," I had instinctively turned to an interpretation of Christian faith which was focused through the recognition that the truth it brought came as "good news," as a medium of existential truth.

A few years later I shared in the new recognition brought by the Second Vatican Council, that "the gospel spirit" and "gospel values" must be the soul of the program of renewal initiated by the council. If we glimpsed the profound import of these notions, they were difficult to pin down theologically. Though I had begun to seek a formulation for a theology of the Christian gospel, I tended to be inhibited by the fact that Catholic theology had not seen this as an important focus of attention.[8]

8. The tentative nature of the title I gave to an article I published in 1979 is significant: "Towards a Theology of the Good News," *Australian Catholic Record*

By the time I took part in the first meeting of the regrouping of the Anglican–Roman Catholic International Commission (ARCIC II) at Venice in 1983, I was convinced that the essential focus of the Christian gospel should be a reference to God: the good news brought by Christ concerned *who God is shown to be for us* in what God does for us in Christ. I was invited to give a paper at this initial meeting exploring ways in which the ecclesiologies of our two communions could be reconciled. In my paper I analyzed the life of the church as related in all its aspects to the good news of God which it must bring to the world. I suggested that all ecumenical dialogue should take place within the essential dialogue of Christian faith, in which believers are together humbled before the gospel. In discussions carried on in this spirit, I suggested, all other issues would be seen in a new light. Though I was congratulated after I had given my paper, my essential suggestion was immediately set aside. As the commission got on with its work, we soon found ourselves caught up in the old game of theological diplomacy which I had hoped — somewhat idealistically, I suppose — to avoid.

I made another attempt to establish a gospel perspective later in the work of ARCIC II. We were beginning to discuss the questions which loomed large in the disputes of the sixteenth century, concerning grace and justification. I suggested that we together acknowledge that theological interpreters had "laid clumsy hands upon the mysteries of God" and seek to make a common confession of the gospel mystery which could serve as the starting point of our

---

56 (1979): 235-46. My work in adult education had brought home to me in the 1970s the fact that many of our people were burdened with the notion of an angry and demanding God; my article "Sinful Man before the Living God: Has Our Teaching Done Justice to the Message of the Scriptures?" *Australian Catholic Record* 60 (1983): 252-73, written at the time I was preparing to accompany Australian bishops attending the synod which was to discuss the sacrament of reconciliation, helped focus my reflections. Five years later a more confident theology was taking shape in my *Sign and Promise* (London: Collins, 1988), pp. 73-78 ("United in the Gospel and Humbled before the Gospel"). In time I came to appreciate that this neglect constituted a serious deficiency in Catholic theology, being in part an unfortunate reaction which failed to appreciate the Reformers' emphasis upon the gospel theme: cf. my *Christian Mystery*, pp. 115-22 ("The Essential Message of the Gospel Embodied in the Christ-Event").

195

discussions. The outcome was the same. From time to time my words were recalled approvingly, but our work of theological diplomacy continued.

When I joined the Australian dialogue of Lutheran and Roman Catholic churches in 1992, my thought concerning the essentials of an adequate theology of the gospel had become clearer, and it was to be confirmed in a work of collaboration with fellow Christians whose tradition had long been centered on the gospel.

When I prepared my paper for the initial meeting of ARCIC II, as I have said, I had become convinced that a satisfactory theology of the Christian gospel must find its focus in the divine mystery: the truth owned by Christian faith is "good news" because it brings an assurance of what the living God is shown to be, beyond all the distortions and uncertainties which have burdened human awareness, in God's intervention in human history in Jesus Christ.

This insight — that the essential message of the gospel is a revelation of the ways of God which overturns humanity's distortions and fears — is confirmed by Christian theology's interpretation of the meaning of "faith."

The German theologian Walter Kasper takes us to the source of the gospel message, summarizing the meaning of "faith" for Jesus of Nazareth as he is remembered in the New Testament accounts: "Faith is open to something other, something new, something to come. . . . It is the description of the essence of faith to say: faith is participation in the omnipotence of God. . . . Faith is existence in receptivity and obedience."[9]

Paul of Tarsus was the first great interpreter of the Christian gospel and the "faith" with which it is received. According to Paul, an intervention of God and his Son has revealed the "mystery" of God's design for creation; this revelation is the very basis of the great innovation of Christian existence. This new order is the expression of what Paul calls God's "justice" — the power, inmost being, generosity, and mercy which are God's, even independently of creation.

For Paul, "faith" constitutes an access to this divine "justice" and its expression in Jesus Christ: "the righteousness of God is the di-

---

9. Walter Kasper, *Jesus the Christ* (London: Burns & Oates, 1976), pp. 81-82.

vine principle of the Christian order, and faith is the corresponding human attitude."[10]

M.-D. Chenu points to the revolution this gospel truth brings to humanity's quest for a right relationship to the divine, comparing and contrasting the dynamisms of "religion" and "faith." For Chenu, religion has its origins in a "pre-reflexive" wisdom of archaic cultures which recognizes the existence and fundamental importance of the divine, and creates a way of life which is a "lived acknowledgment of a divine Being." Faith, on the other hand, is not the act of humanity seeking to establish a right relationship with the divine mystery, but "the act of response to and of communion with a personal God, who on his own initiative enters into conversation with [us] and establishes a communion in love." Chenu then sums up the way the truth owned by Christian faith is *a truth of God that is lived before it is told:* "In accord with the logic of love, this God enters into the life of the 'other' and" becomes human "in order to bring this act to its full reality. Divinization thus comes by means of a humanization. All this may seem to the unbeliever nothing but myth or illusion, but it is the very object of faith and governs its design and structure."[11] In order to make his point, Chenu has set up a contrast between "religion" and "faith." Our comments above concerning the progressive differentiation of consciousness should alert us, however, to the fact that they are not ultimately opposed to one another, but able to be integrated in a balanced human existence.[12]

Hans Urs von Balthasar sums up in memorable words the essential message of the gospel, as the revelation of the ways of God to struggling humanity, the revelation of "the dazzling darkness and divine beauty of a love which gives itself without remainder, and which, in Jesus Christ, is poured out in the world in the form of human powerlessness."[13]

10. Lucien Cerfaux, *The Spiritual Journey of Saint Paul* (New York: Sheed & Ward, 1968), p. 125.

11. Cf. M.-D. Chenu, "The Need for a Theology of the World," in *The Great Ideas Today (1967),* ed. R. Hutchins and M. Adler (Chicago: Britannica, 1967), pp. 55-68, quotes p. 58.

12. See my "Is Religion the Enemy of Faith?" *Theological Studies* 45 (1984): 254-74.

13. Cf. Hans Urs von Balthasar, *The Glory of God* (Edinburgh: T. & T. Clark, 1984), vol. 2, introduction.

The community of Christian faith has been disrupted by the fact that the polarization which followed the sixteenth-century Reformation brought a divergence of approaches to the gospel truth. The dialogue in recent decades between Lutherans and Roman Catholics has shown not only that this divergence can be overcome, but also that a renewed understanding of the gospel provides the basis of a promising ecumenical convergence. Catholic and Protestant awareness can find profound agreement concerning the *essential message* of the gospel. The divergence which has taken place since the sixteenth century concerns the *mediums through which this essential message has found expression* in the life of God's people. A recognition of the variety of these mediums helps us appreciate and overcome this divergence.

Catholic awareness of the gospel, we may well acknowledge, has suffered from the weakness of being too diffuse and lacking in focus. The positive side of this awareness was the soundness of an instinctive recognition that the divine truth, which is lived before it is told, and which comes as a word of life and love to every human situation, would be compromised if it were exclusively identified with a particular "message." This approach, however, made it difficult for Catholics to recognize the prophetic validity and significance of a Protestant awareness which — as it called for the renewal of the Christian church — took its stand upon a clear gospel message.[14]

The tradition of theological awareness which derived from Martin Luther had a very definite focus upon this gospel message. It ran the danger, however, of not being open with the passing of time to the recognition that the divine truth of the gospel demands a variety of prophetic voices in different human situations.

The perspective provided by today's biblical and theological awareness makes it comparatively easy for ecumenical dialogue to move from the contrasting positions I have described onto a common ground which makes possible a shared confession of faith in the gos-

---

14. I have often quoted the judgment of the Catholic theologian and ecumenist Louis Bouyer, that Protestantism must take its place in a reconciled community of Christian faith "as a prophetic movement of permanent significance and import" (*The Church of God* [Chicago: Franciscan Herald, 1983], p. 146; see also the conclusion of his *Spirit and Forms of Protestantism* [London, 1963], pp. 222, 225).

pel. This common confession recognizes that the ultimate truth of God becomes "good news" as it is refracted through a series of mediums: (1) the Savior himself ("we proclaim Christ crucified" [1 Cor. 1:23]); (2) the "story" which is given the privileged name "gospel" in the New Testament; (3) the proclamation which was dear to Paul and other apostles before the evangelists did their work (Rom. 3:21-26; Gal. 1:6; etc.); (4) the eucharistic mystery, in which we "proclaim the Lord's death until he comes" (1 Cor. 11:26 NRSV).

Reflection will show that this list is not exclusive. In particular, I shall suggest below that we should add *the cosmos* as a universal medium of the gospel truth.

As we understand the ways in which these various mediums mediate the transcendent gospel of God's self-giving "without remainder," we shall recognize how profoundly they are linked. We will not do justice to the gospel truth if we concentrate too exclusively upon one or the other of the mediums which make up a total economy.

It goes without saying that the incarnate Word is the ultimate embodiment of the good news. He is the word of love from the heart of God to a tragic humanity, "poured out in the world in the form of human powerlessness": "in these last days he has spoken to us by a Son . . . the reflection of God's glory and the exact imprint of God's very being" (Heb. 1:2-3 NRSV). As we come to appreciate that the human truth of each of us is embodied in our stories, we find a deeper appreciation of the manner in which the life and death of Jesus was the expression of the gospel truth. As von Balthasar writes, "Jesus interprets God" not through "an inert, mechanical alphabet simply used to put the absolute into words"; he "speaks with his whole existence of flesh and blood." Through the Holy Spirit, the whole drama of Jesus' life "was the eternal Father's self-offering and self-interpretation."[15]

Von Balthasar was an admirer of the theological achievement of Karl Barth, and there is little doubt that we can hear in his words an echo of Barth, for whom "the event of the existence of Jesus Christ in the form of a life-history" is a "self-attesting reality."[16] Barth sums up

15. Hans Urs von Balthasar, *Does Jesus Know Us? Do We Know Him?* (San Francisco: Ignatius, 1983), pp. 83-84.
16. Karl Barth, *Church Dogmatics* IV/3, first half (Edinburgh: T. & T. Clark, 1962), p. 55.

the challenge this story brings to every human existence in the words we cited in the previous chapter: "It is because it is the life . . . of this near Neighbour even in all His otherness, that this life is called light, revelation and word . . . this life of a man like us . . . is a declaration . . . it is an address, promise and demand, a question and answer."[17]

In retrospect we may recognize that it was inevitable that with the passing of time the story of this life would be remembered and recorded, as the truth of God which it lived out in our midst was fully recognized and honored. It is probably no coincidence that the New Testament texts which were to be honored in a unique way by the name "Gospel" came into existence in the period following the death of the great apostles. The testimony of those who gave witness to their meeting with the risen Lord, as the revelation of all that God had achieved for the world in him, had provided a unique point of reference for the originating moment of Christian experience and the "witness" it called for. Their removal from the scene created a completely new situation. It was, it seems, the genius of Mark which recognized that what was remembered of Jesus constituted a story which could speak for itself with the sovereign power of "God's Word," calling later generations of Christians to meet the Lord and become his disciples.[18]

In my work *Making Australia,* I pointed to an irony in our history which constitutes a challenge to those who witness to Christian faith in this country. On the one hand, the Christian denominations in

17. Barth, *Church Dogmatics* IV/3, pp. 83-84.
18. "The idea of collecting the traditions about Jesus into a story whose order and arrangement itself would provide, with a minimum of editorial comment, the context for understanding and interpreting those traditions is apparently the invention of Mark himself. That insight is a key to understanding the way in which . . . (he) composed the Gospel. Rather than choosing a form in which incident was interlaced with comment on the way the incident was to be understood, Mark chose to let the traditions speak for themselves. It was the interpretative context that was to be the key, not the author's own theological expositions. In that way the traditions would remain free to make their original points, but the way they were arranged and juxtaposed would provide the clue as to the overall context within which those points were to be understood" (P. Achtemeier, "Mark as Interpreter of the Jesus Tradition," *Interpretation* 32 [1978]: 340). Cf. also J. Rohde, *Rediscovering the Teaching of the Evangelists* (London, 1968), pp. 128-29; E. Schweitzer, "The Portrayal of the Life of Faith in the Gospel of Mark," *Interpretation* 32 (1978): 387-99.

Australia have concentrated their attention upon *doctrines,* doctrines which often tended to find expression in the *ideologies* which sustained the group identity of particular denominations. On the other hand, there have existed in our midst visionaries who, though they felt alienated from denominational Christianity, found the measure of the dreams and hopes they held for our young nation in the *gospel story.*[19]

Joseph Furphy, for example, the author of *Such Is Life,* a novel which explored Australia's prospects at the end of the nineteenth century, was a marginalized Christian. When he died, his family was perplexed as to how to arrange his Christian burial. Yet, at the beginning of this century, he looked for the measure of his Australian hopes in "the charter of the kingdom (preached by Jesus) — in the sunshiny Sermon on the Mount."[20] Furphy certainly understood this charter as "good news" for humanity; he continues: "History marks a point in time when first the Humanity of God touches the divine aspiration in man. . . . 'The Soul, naturally Christian' responds to this touch, even though blindly and erratically, and so from generation to generation the multitudes stand waiting to welcome the Gospel of Humanity with psalms and hosannas as of old." Furphy entered deeply into the lessons contained in the life of Jesus — more deeply, one would say, than many of the churchmen he bitterly criticized. Musing upon a swagman who has died alone on the track as representing the "nameless flotsam of humanity," he writes: "Few and feeble are his friends on earth; and the One who, like him, was wearied with his journey, and, like him, had not where to lay his head, is gone, according to His own parable, into a far country . . . the Light of the world, the God-in-man, the only God we can ever know, is by His own authority represented for all time by the poorest of the poor."[21]

Henry Lawson, who helped establish within the legend which had been an important expression of our national identity a realism which takes seriously the challenges of Australian life, also looks to the gospel story for the measure of Australian hopes. According to histo-

19. Cf. John Thornhill, *Making Australia* (Newtown, New South Wales: Millennium, 1992), pp. 195-200.

20. Joseph Furphy, *Such Is Life: Being Certain Extracts from the Diary of Tom Collins* (Sydney: Angus & Robertson, 1945; original ed., 1905), pp. 111-12; cf. also p. 107.

21. Furphy, p. 107.

rian Manning Clark, "In Lawson's mind there was always somewhere in the Australian bush someone who was behaving in a Christ-like manner."[22] A bush preacher speaks for Lawson in one of the most moving pages of his writings. He had

> long since abandoned hope that either man or place could ever be different. He did not promise "better times" to a people whose crops were ruined by drought, to a people . . . starved off their selections and forced to work as hirelings for wages, leaving behind them a dusty patch in the scrub. He spoke to them about life as they knew it, about their secret longings for something better, and of how they would have to suffer before they could achieve anything in Australia. He told them there was beauty in their lives, yes and even in their harsh, uncouth land, if only they would look for it. He spoke to them about the evils of self-pity and not forgiving men their trespasses, and remaining hard of heart.[23]

In his search for Australia's hopes, Manning Clark, Australia's best-known historian, adopted the same measure: "the image of Christ . . . the image that he said those things by the side of the waters of Galilee."[24]

The next medium is proclamation. We have suggested that it is unfortunate that Protestantism's awareness of the Christian gospel has been too narrowly focused upon the proclamation of a specific message. This is surely related to Martin Luther's emphasis upon the "gospel" theme of the New Testament in his program of renewal. The very notion of "good news" immediately suggests the proclamation of a message. Luther's suggestion that the biblical message of the "good news" of God's unconditional graciousness would bring hope and joy to an age in which many people labored under the sense of helplessness and alienation from God was a truly prophetic contribution. One of the most tragic aspects of the sixteenth-century upheaval was the failure on the part of his Catholic opponents to recognize the impor-

22. Manning Clark, *In Search of Henry Lawson* (North Sydney: Macmillan, 1978), p. 97.

23. Clark's summary, given in Thornhill, *Making Australia*, p. 199.

24. In one of his last interviews, *Sydney Morning Herald: Good Weekend Magazine,* 23 September 1989, p. 76.

tance of his "gospel" message.[25] On the other hand, it was unfortunate that, as historical circumstances changed, Protestant awareness was not able to recognize that the gospel cannot be exclusively identified with a particular message. The import of the truth of God given in Jesus Christ will only be properly expressed when its "dazzling darkness" is interpreted for vastly different human situations by a great variety of prophetic voices who, like Luther, give expression to what the goodness and love which "gives itself without remainder" made present in our world in Jesus Christ means for these situations.

The Report of the Joint Lutheran–Roman Catholic Study Commission, "The Gospel and the Church," issued in Malta in 1971,[26] takes up the question of the context which is essential to the meaningfulness of the gospel message. Having made a common confession of faith (par. 42: "Here is our confession of faith: in his love for the world God enters into history and makes it part of his saving act. This has always been part of belief in the incarnation"), the report stresses the importance of the "world" as providing this context:

> Although the gospel cannot be derived from the world, it must nevertheless be recognised that it is concretised only in specific and ever-changing circumstances. It becomes the *viva vox evangelii* (living voice of the gospel) only when it is formulated and expressed through the power of the Holy Spirit, in reference to the ever new questions raised by men of today (Cf. Vatican II, Pastoral Constitution on the Church in the Modern World, 44). Only when the gospel is proclaimed for such specific situations do we grasp its saving character. Thus the world not only provides opportunities for communication of the gospel, but it also has a hermeneutical function. It is this very world which to a certain extent enriches us with a deeper understanding of the fullness of the gospel. (par. 43)

25. In what follows I am indebted to Peter Manns's *Martin Luther* (New York: Crossroad, 1983). Manns, a Catholic historian, made his mark at the Third International Congress for Luther Research (1966). References which follow are to this text.

26. Cf. *Growth in Agreement: Reports and Agreed Statements of Ecumenical Conversations on a World Level,* ed. Harding Meyer and Lukas Vischer (New York: Paulist Press, 1972), pp. 168-89.

The culture of modernity provides an enlarged context with immense potential to disclose the implications of gospel truth which Christian awareness is only beginning to appreciate.

This insight — that the culture which defines a human situation provides the context within which the gospel becomes meaningful — provided the key essential to my project, in *Making Australia,* of exploring the "political theology" which must express for Australians the relevance of Christian faith to the experience we share. As I wrote in *Making Australia:*

> As the Christian movement has sought to give this gospel truth to the world, two models of evangelisation have emerged which have a recognisable relationship to the claims of Christian faith. . . . One emphasises the divine self-giving which constitutes the ultimate objective content of the "good news"; the other looks to human subjectivity as it is called by the gospel truth to an ultimate authenticity and fulfilment. An analysis of their implications leads to the conclusion that these two models are of their nature complementary. They will prove inadequate and ineffectual if those who make use of them fail to recognise their complementarity and the dialectic that should bring about a vital interchange between them. The gospel truth can only present itself as good news if it addresses humanity at the deepest level of personhood and need.[27]

As my investigations in *Making Australia* show, the resources of our Australian culture — such things as our egalitarian ideal in all its ambiguities, our "battler" spirit, and the remarkable relationship with the unique environment of our continent (something we white Australians are coming to share more consciously with Aboriginal Australians) — can help us make a life-giving meeting with the gospel story and with the divine truth it brings into our midst.[28]

Let us return to Martin Luther's contribution to the understanding of the Christian gospel. According to Peter Manns, the genius of Luther's approach is shown in the way he allowed the Scriptures to speak through their own idiom and rhetoric (p. 45). This

27. Thornhill, *Making Australia,* p. 193.
28. Cf. Thornhill, *Making Australia,* pp. 204-14.

approach brought to light the link between the gospel message Luther was stressing and the gospel story: "He found his way back to the beginnings of a biblical theology in which the story of Abraham or of Christ happens anew for every reader" (p. 120). It is widely recognized that Luther made a significant contribution to the theology of the cross. The climactic moment of the believer's meeting with the gospel story is given for him in the message of the cross. There he found the ultimate basis of the gospel message he brought to his age: "His theology of love has his theology of the cross as its immediate precondition . . . in the cross of His Son, God hides Himself and His work and also His love and grace under their opposite" (p. 50).

An appreciation of the relationship between the biblical story, on the one hand, and Christian witness and proclamation on the other, in Luther's understanding of the Christian gospel, could well provide an important basis for the ecumenical discussions which must take place between Catholic and Protestant traditions in the future. Peter Manns's study of Luther concludes: "What is exciting about Luther is that he bursts the framework of the old Church without thereby leaving it, and that he does not establish a 'new church' whose 'reformist configuration' would be a function of its rejection of Catholicism" (p. 50).

Unfortunately, sixteenth-century Catholics were incapable of appreciating the potential value of Luther's contribution to Christian awareness. One searches in vain in the *Indices* of the published documents of the Council of Trent for any echo of the "gospel" theme which was giving such a powerful impetus to the Protestant movement. In fact, *"evangelium"* seems to appear only once in the *index rerum*.[29]

Trent's remarkable text on the relationship between Scripture and tradition which was taken up by the Second Vatican Council's *Constitution on Divine Revelation* would seem at first sight to contradict what has just been said.[30] This text takes as its pivotal idea the "gospel," and outlines the complex economy through which the gospel is given. Having its origin in the life and teaching of the Savior himself, it becomes a message to be proclaimed by the apostles as "a source of all saving truth"; through the work of the Spirit it finds enduring expression in the Scriptures and the church's living tradition.

29. *Acta* of the Council of Trent (Goerresiana edition), vol. 5, p. 96.
30. Cf. *Dei verbum*, par. 7.

However, when one investigates the manner in which this text was formulated and looks for later discussion which showed an appreciation of the way it could help resolve the crisis which had developed, one is disappointed. The Catholic theologian John Driedo, whose controversy with the emerging Protestant position had led him to recognize the central importance of the gospel theme, published in 1533 a work which outlined the position Trent was to adopt. Seripando, the Servite general, was familiar with Driedo's work and introduced his outline into the council's discussions. The papal legate, Cervini, saw the value of Driedo's approach for Trent's purposes.[31] Subsequent discussion indicates, however, that the importance of Driedo's analysis of the gospel theme for the life of the church was lost on those who had incorporated it into the council's teaching.

We have pointed to Christianity's eucharistic mystery as one of the mediating principles of gospel truth. There are important lessons to ponder here as one considers the relationship between the Eucharist and the gospel of God's self-giving "without remainder." One of the most moving moments of our Australian Lutheran–Roman Catholic dialogue took place in 1994, when one of our Lutheran brothers declared that the dialogue had led him to recognize the eucharistic mystery as "the sweetest gospel of all."

It is heartening to know that these words are representative of a widespread recognition of the place of the Eucharist in Christian life and witness, which is one of the important outcomes of the ecumenical conversations taking place in our time. In his work *Models of the Church*, Avery Dulles cites Karl Barth's reflections on the place the Eucharist has had in Christian worship. Comparing the worship of the Catholic and Protestant traditions, Barth observed that in the Catholic liturgy, "the poorest of sermonettes is transformed by the saving radiance of the eucharistic miracle." "How evident, obvious, well-ordered, and possible," Barth comments, "is the way of God to man and of man to God which leads from this centre." On the other hand, Barth regretted developments within the Protestant tradition which eclipsed the place of the Eucharist as a moment of meeting with the gospel truth: "[I]t is very clear that the Reformation wished to see something better substituted

31. Cf. H. Jedin, *A History of the Council of Trent* (London: Thomas Nelson, 1961), 2:73, and the *Acta* of the Council of Trent, vol. 5, p. 11; vol. 1, pp. 484-85.

for the mass it abolished, and that it expected that better thing would be — our preaching of the Word. The *verbum visibile,* the objectively clarified preaching of the Word, is the only sacrament left to us. The Reformers sternly took from us everything but the Bible."[32]

Looking back from where we stand today, we Catholics can recognize that Protestantism's enthusiasm for the "gospel" theme as it finds expression in the Scriptures led to a reaction which made it difficult for us to give the Scriptures the place they deserve in the life of the church. We may also recognize that when we made the Eucharist one of the great touchstones of our Catholic faith in the wintertime of recent centuries, we were following a very valid instinct. For it is in the Eucharist that the gospel truth which is lived before it is told, that the truth which is to be found in the "dazzling darkness" of a divine love which gives itself without remainder, finds an incomparable expression. In this mystery, through a gesture which goes beyond what can be communicated in words, Jesus unites us to himself in the movement of his self-giving to the Father for the sake of the world.[33]

The final medium of the gospel we wish to consider — the cosmos — is of obvious importance for countries like our own Australia which are seeking to appreciate more fully the cultural heritage of their indigenous peoples. It is not difficult to recognize that the essential message of the gospel sheds light — in retrospect, as it were — upon the situation of those many generations who had no possibility of meeting the divine mystery except through its self-expression in the cosmos. Australia's indigenous people are a remarkable example of a people with a culture shaped by Voegelin's "cosmic principle."

32. A. Dulles, *Models of the Church* (New York: Doubleday, 1974), pp. 159-60, citing K. Barth, *The Word of God and the Word of Man.* Dulles goes on to cite the views of Karl Rahner and Joseph Ratzinger on the essential unity of "word" and "sacrament," expressing the hope that "it may be possible for Protestants and Catholics to get beyond their sterile dispute as to whether word or sacrament is primary" (pp. 161-62).

33. I have attempted to analyze the meaning of this gesture of Jesus for those who sat with him at table in my article "The Eucharistic Gesture of Jesus: What Did It Mean to Those Who Shared His Table Fellowship?" *Australian Catholic Record* 68 (1991): 395-405. Though it was not my concern in writing this article, the analysis which emerged brings to light the essential link between this gesture of Jesus and the truth embodied in the lived story of his human existence and the death in which it reached its tragic climax.

Christian theology must recognize that the "love which gives without remainder" does not begin with Abraham. What was inaugurated in the life of the people of Israel — called to be "a light to the nations" (Isa. 42:6; 49:6) — was the *revelation* of that love. As we have seen, Paul recognized that the mystery of God's generosity existed before creation itself. The Second Vatican Council therefore does not hesitate to lay aside the exclusivism which has dominated Christian theology's understanding of the situation of those who have had no opportunity of meeting the gospel truth, teaching that, since "the vocation of humanity is one and divine," every man and woman born into this world has — "in a manner known only to God" — the possibility of sharing in the mystery of God's self-expression in Jesus Christ.[34]

Our understanding of human history and human experience as a whole brings out more clearly the implications of the gospel truth. In chapter 2 we discussed the Western tradition's "discovery" of the mind — the historical development of our culture has been shaped in large part by the emergence of a reflective awareness of understanding and reason. It may be argued that something similar has taken place and is taking place with regard to the "good news" which is the essential concern of Christian faith. Just as intelligence was taken for granted before a reflective appreciation of it was achieved by the Greeks, so too Christian awareness has for the most part taken the gospel for granted, or has interpreted it in inadequate terms. In the future, it may well be recognized that the overall development of the Christian movement has been shaped by the progressive emergence of an adequate appreciation of the gospel as the essential constitutive of Christianity, and of the way in which it speaks to humanity's age-old quest for existential truth.

*   *   *

Witness, as we have seen, resonates with personal authenticity and existential discovery. The witness the Judeo-Christian tradition must give to the world will only be effective if it is the expression of an existence shaped by the ways of the gospel. J. B. Metz takes up this chal-

34. *Gaudium et spes,* par. 22.

lenge in his *Faith in History and Society.*[35] He relates what he has to say to modernity's "universal theory of emancipation," which he judges to be "dangerously abstract and contradictory" if it does not acknowledge a "soteriology" (p. 127). This acknowledgment is concretized through the gospel's narrative form as "the memory of the crucified Lord" — as "a dangerous memory of freedom in the social systems of our technological civilisation" (p. 109); it can provide our world with a new understanding of politics which — confronted by humanity's solidarity in a "history of suffering" — finds "new possibilities and new criteria for the mastering of technological and economic processes" (p. 105).

The gospel's dangerous memory of our solidarity in human suffering challenges modernity, Metz writes, to acknowledge the impoverishment it has suffered "in expelling God from the centre of history" and replacing "God the Saviour" with "man the emancipator" as "the universal subject of history" (p. 124). Citing Max Weber and others, Metz notes the radical nature of the challenge brought by the gospel's "commandment of love" to a "society of exchange" which has placed a "ban on love" — a challenge to replace "the principle of exchange" with a spirit of genuine "solidarity" (p. 231).

The position Metz wishes to uphold is summed up in his definition of "faith" as "a praxis in history and society that is to be understood as hope in solidarity in the God of Jesus as a God of the living and the dead who calls all . . . to be subjects in his presence" (p. 73). As we have noted, Metz sees contemporary theology as reflecting the spirit of the Enlightenment in being too wedded to rational abstractions (p. 33); his presentation of the gospel in terms of "subject" and "narrative" is intended to provide an antidote to this neglect of the full existential impact of the Christian message (cf. p. 57).

The church as a whole, Metz tells us, must face the challenge of giving a genuine gospel witness if it is not to "sink to the level of an unnecessary religious paraphrase of modern processes in the world." If the church does not own the inclusive spirit of the gospel, it is in danger of becoming "a sect in the theological sense," concerned only

---

35. Johann Baptist Metz, *Faith in History and Society* (New York: Seabury Crossroad, 1980; German original, 1977). References which follow are to this text.

for "traditional sectarian orthodoxy," a "closed church" facing the broader world with a "sectarian attitude" (p. 97). We shall discuss this openness further in the next chapter.

Readers who are sensitive to the spirit of the Christian gospel may well have recognized an echo of that spirit in Václav Havel's suggestions that Europe's true greatness may be found in setting aside the triumphalism and power of the past and assuming a more modest servant role in its relationship to the broader world. Concluding the address quoted in chapter 4, he makes explicit reference to the ultimate expression of the gospel in human history: "Europe will only be able to bear the cross of this world, and thus follow the example of Him in whom it has believed for two thousand years, and in whose name it has committed so much evil, if it first pauses and reflects upon itself, when — in the best sense of the word — it lives up to the potential inherent in the twilight to which it owes its name."

CHAPTER 11

The Authentic Role of Catholicism: Providing a Home for Existential Truth in All Its Forms

TO THOSE WHO SEEK TO UNDERSTAND WHAT THEY own as their Catholic identity and heritage, the answers of yesterday no longer serve. We live in an age in which traditional ways and institutions are being called into question. The developments of recent decades have removed factors which played an important part in shaping a sense of Catholic identity in many parts of the world. A genuine fellowship among separated Christians has replaced yesterday's sectarian rivalry. In countries like Australia, rising generations of Catholics no longer see themselves as an aggrieved minority, something which in the past fostered countercultural mechanisms within the Catholic community.

In this climate, however, the real issue of Catholic identity comes into a clearer focus. Until the recent past, the stance of Catholicism has been one which was adopted perforce, in reaction to a succession of overwhelming historical situations which could not be fully understood by those involved: the apparent triumph of the Constantinian establishment, for instance; the social chaos of the Dark Ages; the tragic confrontation of the sixteenth century; and the modern world's awkwardness as it laid claim to a proper autonomy for the secular order.

Fortunately, however, at this moment when the Second Vatican Council has called Catholicism to meet the challenge of the present age by finding the church's true identity beyond the outlooks it has adopted in the past, it is possible for the Christian church to look back upon this history with a certain detachment and to recognize the lessons it has to offer.

We propose to explore Catholic identity at two levels, each of which shows its relationship to the existential truth which has become a central reference point in our discussion. First we shall discuss the question at the level of theological principle, then at the level of experience of Catholicism as a historical phenomenon. These two approaches shed light one upon the other.

At the level of theological principle, it may be argued, the basic truth of Christianity demands the continuing existence in human history of a tradition which witnesses to "the faith that was once for all entrusted to the saints" (Jude 3 NRSV). The validity of such a tradition implies the continuing existence of a community which is its bearer. This faith takes its stand upon the conviction that the truth it offers belongs to every age. Relying upon the Savior's promise, "I am with you always, to the end of the age" (Matt. 28:20 NRSV), it is convinced that the telling of the gospel story, and the celebration of what Christ has given to the world in the sacramental rites, will bring to the world the message of Christian faith until the end of human history. The ultimate claim of the Catholic communion is that, through the presence of the Spirit — despite continuing human frailty and folly — there still exists a bearer of this truth, because it has renounced none of the gifts of God through which this truth has been given to the world since the apostolic beginnings.

The Second Vatican Council gave expression to this unique claim when it declared that "the unique Church of Christ" which is confessed in the creed "subsists in the Catholic Church, which is presided over by the successor of Peter and by the bishops who are in union with that successor" (*Lumen gentium,* par. 8). The council's use of the esoteric term "subsists" reflects a clarification which was an important outcome of the discussion which produced this conciliar text. This discussion rejected a proposed wording which would have simply identified the church confessed in the creed with the Roman Catholic Church of history. The new terminology intended to make the identification in a nonexclusive way: while the Roman Catholic Church claims to retain all the elements contributing to the communion which is constitutive of the church owned by Christian faith, it acknowledges at the same time that these elements are found outside the Roman Catholic Church.

In fact, the council goes on immediately to affirm that "many elements of sanctification and of truth can be found outside" the Roman Catholic Church. It follows that those who do not belong to the fullness of the Roman Catholic communion may be truly said to belong to the church — through the gifts of the Spirit whereby they share in the tradition which hands on the Christian faith and give witness to that faith in the world. We may conclude, therefore, that the "Catholicism" we are to discuss, if it is acknowledged to be found in the Roman Catholic communion, transcends that communion and is shared in by all who witness to Christ in the world. Indeed, our discussion will lead us to the conclusion that "Catholicism," properly understood, is not a partisan sign of contradiction, but a royal way forward for an authentic ecumenism.[1]

Rosemary Haughton brought the theological principles we have outlined down to earth in her seminal work, *The Catholic Thing,* sketching a rich historical panorama peopled with a great variety of individuals and movements illustrating aspects and expressions of the "something else," as she calls the uniqueness of the Catholic tradition. She makes it clear, moreover, that this "Catholicism" is not to be found exclusively in the Roman Catholic communion. Indeed, it may be obscured within the life of that communion:

> Western culture has reached a point at which precisely that "something else" is vital for its sanity, let alone its salvation. It must be

---

1. In what follows we shall speak of the unique genius which we wish to identify and evaluate — what Rosemary Haughton calls "the Catholic thing" — using a capital letter, "Catholicism." Making the same distinction, Avery Dulles explains: "In the 20th century it has become necessary to distinguish between 'Catholic' with a lower-case and an upper-case 'c,' the former being associated with the noun 'catholicity' and the latter with 'Catholicism.' In the present essay I shall attempt to illumine this distinction, show the close affinity between the two meanings of the term 'catholic,' and give some indications of the relationship between Catholicism and Roman Catholicism" ("Catholicity and Catholicism," *Theology Digest* 34 [1987]: 203). See also Dulles, *The Catholicity of the Church* (Oxford: Clarendon, 1985), for a comprehensive discussion of our question.

clear . . . that by this "something else" I do not mean something that necessarily happens in the context of the Catholic Church as a recognizable body with an ascertainable membership. I do indeed mean that it is present in the visible Catholic Church, but the "something else" is not going on only there.[2]

The theological understanding we are seeking achieves a new focus when we recognize that the "elements" constitutive of the church's communion, to which *Lumen gentium* refers, have an essential unity. It is the Savior himself — the living expression of the gospel truth — who is the principle of this unity. The community of Christian faith exists for one thing only: to bring the gospel of God's "giving without remainder" to every age.

If "the Catholic thing" has reality through an age-old *tradition* in the common possession of these "elements," if it is an ongoing "enterprise," as Haughton puts it, its essential genius derives from the fact that this tradition and enterprise is sustained by the Spirit of God in order that the Savior may be given as a living presence in every age and culture, in every human situation. Walter Kasper's words, summing up the unique mystery encountered in Jesus of Nazareth, provide an important point of reference in our discussion of the genius of Catholicism, for if what we are saying is true, what the Savior stands for is also what Catholicism stands for.

In Jesus we finally come face to face with God. His life is the answer to the question "Who is God?" Jesus does not fit into any category. Neither ancient nor modern, nor Old Testament categories are adequate to understand him. He is and remains a mystery. . . . He is interested in only one thing, but interested in it totally: God's coming rule in love. He is interested in God and human beings, in God's history with human beings. That is his mission. We get closer to the mystery of his person only when we look into that mission.[3]

2. Rosemary Haughton, *The Catholic Thing* (Springfield, Ill.: Templegate, 1979), p. 8.
3. Walter Kasper, *Jesus the Christ* (London: Burns & Oates, 1977), p. 70.

Against the background of these theological principles, it is enlightening to consider the characteristics of Catholicism as a historical phenomenon. Two such characteristics come to mind: first, a *wholeness* which is hospitable to all that is life-giving before God, and secondly, a *realism* which owns unhesitatingly the truth of God in Christ, even though it overturns the expectations of human calculation. This realism has various aspects, as we shall see, each of which evidences the presence of the divine truth in Christ, a truth which draws all things to be measured by its inexhaustible standard.

Because of the wholeness we speak of, whatever is life-giving in Christian experience finds its true home in that tradition of shared life which — for all its lukewarmness and complacency — has renounced nothing of the gifts of God through which the Savior becomes a living presence in each age and brings to every human situation the divine truth expressed in our world by his life, death, and resurrection. More than this, as the great dialogue of the world religions will show, everything life-giving before God in their traditions of wisdom and religion should find a welcome within that tradition.

It is impossible to define what is *proper* to Catholicism except with reference to the integral Christian mystery and the inclusiveness of God's ways expressed in Jesus Christ. All that is authentic to Christian faith, all that is authentic in humanity's relationship with the divine, the tradition of Catholicism is prepared to hold *in common* with those who own these things, wherever they may be. As the bearer of all that constitutes communion in the mystery of Christ, the Catholic tradition is the true home of all that is life-giving in God.

It follows from this, of course, that the truest expression of Catholicism will be a generous hospitality which acknowledges with humble gratitude not only the contribution the shared traditions of separated Christians can make to the enriching of our common life in Christian faith, but also all that is valid in the religious traditions of the world. If this hospitality is real, the true genius of Catholicism will become not a partisan stand, but a royal road to Christian unity, and beyond Christian unity to the full expression of the unity of all the world's peoples.

This wholeness has a scope, of course, which takes in far more than the ecumenical issues we have used to illustrate it to this point. Because sharing in "the Catholic thing" is essentially an owning of the hospitality of the mystery of Christ as an expression of the hospitality of God, those who accept one another in the communion of Catholicism are an extraordinarily varied lot. As Haughton points out, in speaking of the Catholic communion we must not forget "that it is the *whole* Catholic thing — saints and sinners, Popes and housewives, bigots and simpletons and scholars — all these carry the message from one generation to another, the message which the great (and lesser) radicals recognize and revitalize."[4]

And how varied already are Catholicism's heroes and the traditions of Christian life and sanctity which they contribute to the expression of the wholeness of the Catholic tradition: Paul and John, Ambrose and Benedict, Athanasius and Anselm, Clare and Teresa, Ignatius and Philip Neri, Aquinas and Newman. The list is endless. What unites them all and what must animate the spirit of hospitality shown by Catholicism in every age is nothing more or less than a concern that all show themselves to be true followers of the same Christ.[5]

The other characteristic expressing the hospitality of Catholicism is its *realism*. As I join in worship and prayer with fellow believers, a mood akin to astonishment sometimes overtakes me as I listen to what is being expressed and taken for granted: things which all human calculation, left to itself, would judge preposterous nonsense; and to these things the assembly — learned and unlettered — gives prayerful assent, as defining the very meaning of human existence. French theologian M.-D. Chenu sums up the astounding claims of which we are speaking in a passage cited above:

> Faith is not the action of a man ascending toward the Divine. It is the act of response to and of communion with a personal God, who on his own initiative enters into conversation with men and establishes a communion in love. In accord with the logic of love, this God enters into the life of the "other" and makes himself man in order to bring this act to its full reality. Divinization thus comes by

4. Haughton, p. 171.
5. As has often been pointed out, the historically occasioned doctrinal definitions of Catholicism do not provide any adequate expression of the genius we are discussing. The outsider who sought to understand the Catholic tradition by the study of the doctrinal pronouncements found in Denzinger's *Enchiridion Symbolorum* would be left perplexed!

means of a humanization. All this may seem to the unbeliever nothing but myth or illusion, but it is the very object of faith and governs its design and structure.[6]

Facing the challenge brought by this living out of a positive relationship with all that is human — it must be acknowledged — Catholicism as a historical phenomenon has often known the temptation to a cultural compromise which has obscured the essential truth it is called to give to the world. This failure of Catholicism, however, contrasts with the exaggerated purism which has often characterized the Protestant tradition — an unfortunate by-product of the prophetic rhetoric which is its essential genius. The hospitality which Catholicism learns through an identification with the ways of God leads it to enter into dialogue with the realities of the age in which it lives. Because the designs of God to which it must witness involve *the whole human person,* the truest self of Catholicism has provided a setting within which the best in human culture has flourished.

Karl Barth recognized these tendencies within Catholicism and Protestantism. When asked in an interview during the first days of the Vatican Council whether the Roman Catholic or Protestant form of worship was closer to that of primitive Christianity, Barth replied, "Neither of them. Catholic worship is too florid, too loaded. And our own worship, though refining itself, has become too reminiscent of the synagogue. One might say that the great temptation of Protestantism is Judaism, whereas the great temptation of the Catholic Church would be paganism."

Going on in this interview to speak appreciatively of the liturgical renewal which was beginning to take place in the Roman Catholic Church, in accordance with the council's decisions — bringing "a new balance . . . between the role of preaching and the role of the sacrament" and having "the congregation take Communion at the same table as the priest, which considerably strengthens its communal aspect" — Barth pointed the way once again to that wholeness which

6. M.-D. Chenu, "The Need for a Theology of the World," in *The Great Ideas Today (1967),* ed. R. Hutchins and M. Adler (Chicago: Britannica, 1967), p. 58.

makes the Catholic tradition's truest self-expression the home where all genuine Christian impulses will flourish in their fullness.[7]

At another level it is this commitment, to bringing the whole reality of human existence to a sharing in the mystery of what God has done for the world in Christ, that makes the genius of Catholicism meet every human culture, not as something alien, but as a soil in which it can flourish as truly as it has in the Semitic and Western cultures which to this moment in history have provided its principal settings.

The dramatic increase in comparative cultural awareness in the recent past — one of the great achievements of modernity — constitutes an invitation to the Catholic tradition to pursue more courageously and confidently its immense potential in this regard, so that the community of Christian faith may show to the world that the apparently insuperable barriers which divide humanity can be overcome in a fellowship and solidarity which is found in Christ. It would be tragic if the inward-looking preoccupations which tend to absorb the attention of the Christian church in this challenging period of change and renewal should lead us to lose sight of the vision which is the expression of the true genius of Catholicism.

Catholicism's involvement with the whole person, its openness to the world's cultures, and its fruitful relationship with high culture and its arts remind us of another form of realism which is expressive of the genius we are describing. Understandably, it has been typical of religious fundamentalist traditions in their effort to give witness to what is most noble in human existence to seek a total dissociation from evil. This flight introduces considerable tensions into a cultural community in the process of coming to terms with its own moral and spiritual ambiguities, as the sectarian exclusivism which so frequently shows itself within religious traditions, Christian and non-Christian alike, makes abundantly clear. The truest self of Catholicism, however, takes another path, as Catholicism's relationship with modern literature serves to illustrate.

We pointed out above that the epic form has practically no place in contemporary literature; the strong direction taken by the story line of the *epic* reflects a culture in which commonly held beliefs are se-

7. As reported in the *Tablet*, 2 March 1963, p. 236.

curely integrated into the world it has established. In modernity's age of disillusionment, it is the *novel* which expresses humanity's cultural mood and continuing search for existential truth: "The novel is the epic of a world that has been abandoned by God."[8] The influence of Catholicism in the contemporary Western novel has often been re-marked upon. As a secularized Western culture struggles to find a meaning for human existence beyond disillusionment with the inade-quate ideals and ideologies which have sustained it in the past, the Catholic tradition has provided significant resources for writers who have set out to explore the darkness and struggles of the human heart. One thinks, for instance, of writers coming from such different back-grounds as François Mauriac, Evelyn Waugh, Flannery O'Connor, Graham Greene, and Shusaku Endo, all of whom make use of Ca-tholicism's vision of faith in their explorations of human existence.

The realism of Catholicism's attitude to human evil expressed by these novelists is remarkable. It is a realism which coexists with the compromises of those who make up the Catholic community, most of whom, it can be said, "have enough of ordinary inertia, timidity and greed to keep from becoming altogether delighted at plans to open up their cosy, familiar Church to the vigorous breeze of the Spirit."[9] In the end, however, this frailty does not lead to a watering down of the exalted ideals of the ways of God proclaimed by Jesus of Nazareth. Nor does it give rise to the reaction of sectarian exclusiveness. In-stead, the Catholic tradition acknowledges the evil which is part of the human story and seeks to identify with the mysterious ways of God in God's dealings with the real world of struggling humanity.

In a memorable page of his *Introduction to Christianity,* Joseph Ratzinger captures this attitude and relates it to the attitudes of the One to whom the Catholic tradition is called to give witness as the liv-ing expression of the gospel truth:

> In the human dream of a perfect world, holiness is always visualised as untouchability by sin and evil, as something unmixed with the latter; there always remains in some form or other a tendency to

---

8. György Lukács, cited by T. R. Wright, *Theology and Literature* (Oxford: Blackwell, 1989), p. 111.
9. Haughton, p. 171.

think in terms of black and white, a tendency to cut out and reject mercilessly the current form of the negative (which can be conceived in widely varying terms). . . . That is why the aspect of Christ's holiness that upset his contemporaries was the complete absence of this condemnatory note — fire did not fall on the unworthy nor were the zealous allowed to pull up the weeds which they saw growing luxuriantly on all sides. On the contrary, this holiness expressed itself precisely as mingling with the sinners whom Jesus drew into his vicinity; as mingling to the point where he himself was made "to be sin" and bore the curse of the law in execution as a criminal — complete community of fate with the lost (cf. 2 Cor 5:21; Gal 3:13). He has drawn sin to himself, made it his lot and so revealed what true "holiness" is: not separation but union, not judgment but redeeming love. Is the Church not simply the continuation of God's deliberate plunge into human wretchedness; is it not simply the continuation of Jesus' habit of sitting at table with sinners, of his mingling with the misery of sin to the point where he actually seems to sink under its weight? Is there not revealed in the unholiness of the Church, as opposed to man's expectation of purity, God's true holiness, which is love, love which does not keep its distance in a sort of aristocratic, untouchable purity but mixes with the dirt of the world, in order thus to overcome it?[10]

The true genius of Catholicism makes it the bearer of the tradition which shows itself to be the home of every truly Christian blessing and every inspiration bestowed by the Spirit of God. It has a realism which does not hesitate to take seriously all that is human, even the ambiguities and tragedies of our human story. These attitudes derive from the truth which found expression in the one in whom God's ways were made incarnate in our midst "in the form of human powerlessness."

The characteristics we have discussed belong to that which is best in the shared life of the Roman Catholic Church. With the Second Vatican Council, however, we must make it clear that there is no question of simply identifying "the Catholic thing" with Roman Catholicism. Much that is in the life of our church, we must sadly ac-

10. Joseph Ratzinger, *Introduction to Christianity* (London: Search, 1969), pp. 264-65.

knowledge, is not inspired by this life principle. And by the grace of the Spirit, this life principle can find genuine and varied expression outside the Roman Catholic communion. From this it follows that Catholicism properly understood is not some exclusive possession of the Roman Catholic Church as a partisan organization in history, but a common possession of all who share in humanity's existential truth. Far from being a divisive principle, it can become the royal road to a unity which is God's design for our human family.

But more remains to be said. The Catholic communion of which we speak has an identity which to this point we have refrained from introducing: what the New Testament began by calling "the way," it soon spoke of as a mystery of unprecedented sharing *(koinonia)* and revered as the church *(ekklesia),* which is the bride of Christ. Those who have come to appreciate fully the Catholic Church which is the object of Christian faith revere her as their mother.

During the time of its pilgrimage, this bride of Christ knows the challenge of maintaining the quality of her relationship with the Savior,[11] a challenge made all the more poignant by all that is implied by the qualities we have discussed. On the royal road to unity which all Christians should share, our reflection must take us beyond superficial issues to the depths of the mystery of the church and that union with Christ which is the source of her life.

It is one of the signs of maturity in the love of sons or daughters for their mother that they are able to accept her for what she truly is, and still love her dearly. The mature Christian believer must come to such an attitude. The human aspect of the church of the creed — in the end, there is no other! — may cause us disappointment and irritation at times. She may seem a rather starchy old lady, content to go about her business decked out in outmoded fashions; at times she

---

11. More than once in his writings, Yves Congar has pointed out that unless the "body of Christ" theme of Paul maintains the association it had for Paul with the "espousal" theme, it can give rise to an exaggerated "continuing incarnationism" which is a scandal to separated Christians. As Congar points out, the maintaining of the bond of espousal constitutes a lifelong challenge, and this challenge sheds light on the condition of the church in its relationship to the Lord in its time of pilgrimage. Rosemary Haughton makes a similar point, in *The Catholic Thing* (pp. 9-10, etc.), with her figure of the twin sisters — "Mother Church" and "Sophia" — who are like two personae giving expression to the church's life.

seems to weary of her journey and her long period of waiting, and to be tempted to settle down in a man-made bastion, out of touch with the march of the world's history. But those who have come to love her recognize in the depths of her life a divine presence and vitality, and qualities which are the gift of the Spouse who has given himself to her in everlasting fidelity, and they gratefully own her as their mother.

A complete description of Catholicism must include reference to the Petrine office. We have delayed our consideration of the papacy to this point, when the relationship between Catholicism and mother church has become clear. We have done this in order to avoid giving the impression that the papacy is the life principle of Catholicism, as many Christians — Catholics and non-Catholics alike — would presume. On the contrary, the office of Peter, exercised in the midst of the college of which it is the principle of unity, *presupposes* "the Catholic thing" we have been discussing. It is its servant, calling all believers to share the common faith which is the gift of the Spirit, recognizing and encouraging the prophetic voices which are in their midst, articulating the church's common faith, giving expression to the call to wholeness which is essential to the Catholic spirit, and extending that hospitality which is its true expression, as its most devoted and effective servant.

*   *   *

An authentic Catholic outlook is sympathetic to late modernity's dissatisfaction with "meta-narratives" which claim to explain a totalized reality. The realism of Catholicism acknowledges that its interpretation of human existence implies no blueprint of the future developments of human history. It agrees with the historian John O'Malley, who was quoted in chapter 7, that historical interpretations, including Christian ones, have too readily claimed what was really a time-conditioned cultural or theological construct to be an "over-arching divine plan." As Voegelin has reminded us, "uncertainty is the very essence of Christianity," so that any "attempt at constructing an eidos of history" is doomed to failure.[12] Whatever the value of the theologi-

12. Eric Voegelin, *The New Science of Politics* (Chicago: University of Chicago Press, 1960), pp. 121-22.

cal syntheses of those geniuses of the past who have sought to bring to light in history some "over-arching divine plan," the renewal of faith which is called for — if the needs of late modernity are to be addressed — must not seek to ground its interpretation of the human situation in any such construct.

But does that leave us any blueprint? What we have come to understand of the relationship between narrative and existential truth may provide the answer to this question. Narrative provides an access to the existential truth which is the measure of our being human. The dialogue of successive generations with the narratives of the biblical literature and with the ongoing experience of the people of God down through the ages provides an access to the truth of the gospel, the revelation made in God's dealings with that people: of what the ways of God are shown to be, beyond all the distortions and uncertainties of humanity's religious quest, in a word of *who-God-is*. This gospel cannot be identified with any "over-arching divine plan" which is accessible to us, because it is measured by the divine freedom and places us on the threshold of a divine mystery which is unspeakable.

What we are saying is related to the relationship between *the gospel* and *doctrine* discussed in an earlier chapter — a relationship which severely relativizes doctrinal statements. Without an awareness of the truth of the gospel as the measure of authentic human existence, doctrine can easily become the expression and instrument of a human institutionalization rather than the message of life and hope it should be for the world. The church too must heed the warning of Max Weber: if our concerns are shaped by institutional values rather than the values essential to the gospel truth itself, the church of history runs the danger of finding itself more and more imprisoned in an "iron cage of bureaucratic rationality ." The only overarching plan for the world is that which is in the keeping of the divine mystery. It will never be contained in any doctrinal system.

Already in 1935, Jacques Maritain adopted this open-ended point of view as he looked into the distant future of humanity:

> [O]ne may hold that this third age will primarily see the general liquidation of (a closed) post-medieval humanism, and none knows for how many centuries this will yet endure. I am in no wise imagining it will be any golden age, as do some millenarian dreamers. Man

223

will remain what in himself he is, but under a temporal regime, a
new historic heaven, destined also to come to an end, for all the
things of time wear out in time: it is only under that regime that
there will begin the flowering-time of integral humanism, of that
humanism of the Incarnation . . . which carries the sign of no theoc-
racy other than the gentle dominion of God's love.[13]

Presupposed in the mind of Maritain, as he looks forward to the
"flowering-time of integral humanism," is not some overarching plan
of history, but the conviction that — since in "an effective realisation
or refraction of the Gospel in the socio-temporal sphere, we are still
truly in a prehistoric age!"[14] — Christian hope may always look forward to the realization of what is really possible in the drama of history, even if it cannot adequately describe future developments, com-
mensurate with the unplumbed dimensions of human existence.

13. Jacques Maritain, *True Humanism* (London: Geoffrey Bles, 1954), pp.
238-39.
14. Maritain, p. 237.

APPENDIX

Aquinas on Understanding
That Is Aware of Itself

THE ACHIEVEMENT OF THOMAS AQUINAS, THE GREAT-
est mind of the Middle Ages, was virtually unknown to the founders of
modern thought. How would Aquinas respond to the problems of modernity? He would certainly question the Cartesian starting point of
modern thought — not only the constricted methodology Descartes gave
to modernity, but also the "methodological doubt" which set the tone for
much that was to follow. With Aristotle, Aquinas was aware of the fallacy
of calling for a demonstration of *all* assertions. Such a fallacy calls up an
infinite series which leaves the inquirer no closer to the possibility of
demonstration. All demonstration must be grounded, in the end, upon
what is evident-in-itself. The question is, therefore, the identification of
the self-evident starting point of rational inquiry.

For Aquinas this point is certainly not the Cartesian *cogito*. Richard Tarnas puts very simply the problem inherent in Descartes's starting point — a problem which has bedeviled the philosophical tradition
it was to engender: "if the only reality that the human mind has direct
access to is its own experience, then the world apprehended by the
mind is only the mind's interpretation of the world."[1] Aquinas would

1. Richard Tarnas, "The Transfiguration of the Western Mind," *Cross Currents* (fall 1989): 259.

protest that this is a very big "if"! He himself adopted an epistemological position which, far from being naive, was the outcome of a penetrating analysis, recorded in countless of his writings.[2] This position has as its starting point the recognition that *reality* is more evident to the human inquirer than *thought about reality* — of which the inquirer is only aware in a second moment of *reflexive* understanding.

The self-evident starting point of human inquiry, for Aquinas, therefore, is the knower's presence to reality, a unique order of event. The astounding implications of this event must be acknowledged and explored if a satisfactory account of intellectual inquiry is to be given. Aristotle before him had recognized the challenging nature of the starting point which confronted the Greek mind that had become aware of itself: the irreducible event of objective knowledge. In the last analysis, knowledge is an event different from all other orders of event, because — in some manner — what is immanent to the knower is the *known object itself,* not some *mere likeness* of what is known. In Aristotle's often quoted epigram, the knower becomes the known, and the mind is such that — in some manner — the whole order of the universe can be present within it.[3]

We are far removed from the starting point of Descartes. Paradoxically, Descartes's interpretation of his all-important *"cogito"* compromises the unique nature of the event in which knowledge is realized — reducing it to the order of physical events. Aquinas, on the other hand, accepts as self-evident the *sui generis* character of the knowledge event; his epistemological analysis is the exploration of its unavoidable implications.

Aquinas sided with Aristotle, of course, in his criticism of Plato's doctrine of universal "ideas" as explaining what takes place in abstract thought. With Aristotle, he saw the real world as made up, ultimately, of *individual substances,* realities distinct and separate from one another. These individual substances, however, are characterized by qualities and other characteristics which are held in common with other individual substances. These qualities and characteristics mani-

2. See, for ample evidence of this, Bernard Lonergan, *La notion de verbe dans les écrits de Saint Thomas d'Aquin* (Paris: Beauchesne, 1967).

3. Cf. Richard Tarnas, *The Passion of the Western Mind: Understanding the Ideas That Have Shaped Our World View* (New York: Ballantine, 1993), p. 187.

fest the *natures* of individual substances. For Aristotle, the unity of the universal concept which grasps the communality to be found in many individual substances does not derive, as Plato claimed, from some transcendent "idea." Rather, it is achieved by a process of *abstraction* which understands the communality of *nature* manifested through qualities and characteristics accessible to the human inquirer.[4]

For Aristotle and Aquinas, the human agent, while clearly belonging to the material order, transcends it. This is made clear by its manner of operating (through understanding and free will), which clearly transcends the conditions of materiality. Aquinas followed Aristotle in holding that the *universal and necessary* condition in which an abstract nature is grasped in understanding is due to the *spiritual* (or immaterial) manner of operating of the mind. In understanding, what is known is removed from the conditions of *particularity and contingency* which it has in the reality of the *material world*.[5] Human knowledge integrates the material and immaterial orders: knowledge has its origin in the *sensory* experience of concrete particulars in their material condition; from this knowledge of particular natures the knowledge of universals is abstracted by *intelligence*. Ultimately, for Aquinas, such abstract knowledge of natures is an indirect participation in the original pattern of created things in the mind of God.[6] In this way he preserved the central insight of Plato's metaphysical system.

It should be noted that the severe limitations implied in the assertion made by Aristotle and Aquinas, that the "natures" of things can be abstractly understood, will become clear when the details of Aquinas's position concerning the methodology of the various intellectual disciplines are explained.

While Aquinas built upon the achievement of Aristotle, he surpassed it in a remarkable way. Presupposed in Aristotle's metaphysical analysis was the recognition that the *real* includes not only *actuality* but also *potentiality* (according to Aristotle's illustration, neither the blind person nor the sleeping person *actually* sees; sight, however, is *real* in the sleeping person, not in the blind person). Aristotle's metaphysical analysis made *"substance"* its central point of reference,

4. Cf. Tarnas, *Passion*, p. 56; on Aquinas, see also pp. 183-84.
5. Cf. Tarnas, *Passion*, p. 187.
6. Cf. Tarnas, *Passion*, pp. 185-86.

as the paramount instance of actuality given in the real world. He distinguished "primary" substance (that given in the real world) and "secondary" substance (that which is grasped in an abstract universal concept).

Aquinas advances this analysis by distinguishing, within the actual order, an essential principle *(essentia)* and an existential principle *(esse)* — a distinction not clearly made in Greek language and thought.[7] The meaningfulness of *what*-something-*is* must be distinguished from the meaningfulness of *whether*-something-*is* (i.e., whether it has extramental reality). Aquinas pointed to the absolute uniqueness and ultimacy of *esse* in the order of actuality: as "the actuality of all actualities and the perfection of all perfections" *(De potentia* q. 7, art. 2 ad 9). He thus made *esse* the ultimate reference point of the metaphysical analysis which advanced the work of Aristotle.

One important implication of this analysis should be mentioned. The actuality brought by *esse* is not known *in itself* by the human inquirer, but through the limited (finite) essential principle through which it is realized. To know *esse* in itself would be to know the infinite divine actuality. Thus, in the metaphysics of Aquinas, this dazzlingly mysterious intelligible is like a divine signature upon the works of creation.

The metaphysical distinction of *essentia* and *esse* made it possible for Aquinas to elaborate an epistemology which is a distinct advance upon the thought of Aristotle. For Aquinas, the *sui generis* event of intellectual knowledge is a manner of *being.* The *being* of our experience has as its constitutive elements an *essential principle* and the *actuality of* "*esse.*" If the unique event of knowledge makes the "natures" (or *essences*) of the real immediately present to the knower, Aquinas sees this as happening through their having a new manner of existence *(esse).*

Since the actuality of *esse* leaves the essential order, as such, unaffected, the *sui generis* event of knowledge can make the knower present to the natures of the real world in themselves, not in some *simulacrum* which, absolutely speaking, is other than these natures — the position late medieval nominalists and, after them, Descartes were to adopt.

---

7. See Gregory Vlastos, *Socrates: Ironist and Moral Philosopher* (Cambridge: Cambridge University Press, 1991), p. 74 n. 137, and additional note 2.3, pp. 254-55.

Tarnas points to the far-reaching implications of this metaphysical and epistemological analysis:

> Aquinas went beyond the Aristotelians' tendency to view nature as existing apart from God, arguing that a deeper philosophical understanding of the meaning of existence would fully connect the created world with God. To accomplish this Aquinas reintroduced the Platonic notion of "participation" in this new context. Created things have true substantial reality because they participate in Existence, which is from God, the infinite self-subsistent ground of all being. . . . The essence of each thing, its specific kind of being, is the measure of its participation in the real existence communicated to it by God. What a thing is and the fact that it is at all are two distinct aspects of any created being. In God alone is there absolute simplicity, for what God is and the fact of his being are one and the same: God is "be-ing" itself — unlimited, absolute, beyond definition. Thus every creature is a compound of essence and existence, while God alone is not a compound, for his essence is existence per se. Creatures *have* existence; God *is* existence. Existence for creatures is not self-given, and therein lay Aquinas' fundamental philosophical tenet: the absolute contingency of the finite world on an infinite giver of being.[8]

Aquinas's understanding of the differentiation of scientific knowledges is grounded in the epistemological principles we have outlined. For him *universals are abstracted* from a sense knowledge of concrete individuals. In his commentary on a text of the sixth-century writer Boethius, *De trinitate,*[9] Aquinas in fact distinguishes three kinds of abstract thought, as giving rise to three distinct orders of intellectual discipline, each with its own proper methodology. Let us describe the essentials of each of these.

---

8. Tarnas, *Passion,* pp. 182-83.

9. Cf. St. Thomas Aquinas, *The Division and Methods of the Sciences,* ed. A. Maurer (Toronto: Pontifical Institute of Medieval Studies, 1958). It should come as no surprise, not only that modern thought has a very *different approach* to the question from that of Aquinas, but also that the *terminology* used has changed — as Maurer explains in his long introduction to Aquinas's treatise. Page references which follow are to this text.

The *mathematical methodology* analyzed by Aquinas is straight-forward enough. The *nature* which mathematics abstracts is that of *quantity* (p. xix), the first and most evident property of material reality. The transparency of the nature of quantity gives rise to the comparative ease and certainty with which mathematics proceeds. In fact, Aquinas judged that of the three methodologies he discusses, that of mathematics is the most certain.[10] Indeed, he warns against the temptation arising from this outstanding clarity, of wanting to make the methodology of mathematics normative for all intellectual inquiry (pp. xxvi-xxvii). This temptation was, in fact, to play an important part in the shaping of the intellectual climate of modernity, as we have seen.

Aquinas discusses the abstraction of what he calls *"natural science,"* or what scholastic thought today calls *"natural philosophy"* (to avoid confusion caused by today's understanding of what is meant by the term "science"). The following points, made by Armand Maurer,[11] summarize the essentials of Saint Thomas's teaching concerning this order of inquiry. (1) Natural philosophy makes an absolute (abstract) consideration of the natures (or essences) to be found in the physical world, abstracting these natures from the endless particular and concrete individuals in which they are realized (p. xviii). (2) These natures can only be known from the observation of the effects of which they are the causes: the methodology called for is a reasoning from effect to cause (p. xxx). (3) The conclusions of natural philosophy — depending as they do upon a reasoned understanding based upon the data available — have a qualified certainty, calling for constant reappraisal (p. xxxii). (4) Aquinas was aware of scientific inquiry which combines the methodology we have just described with mathematics[12] — he called studies of this kind "intermediate sciences" (pp. 33, 35, xxvi). (5) We must now recognize that the an-

---

10. The only mathematics known to Aquinas were arithmetic and Euclidean geometry (p. xix). The quantity he identified as the concern of mathematics, therefore, was that which has reality as belonging to concrete material natures. His principles are readily extended, however, to later mathematics in its understanding of quantity as a pure abstraction.

11. The editor of the version of the Aquinas text we are citing.

12. The study of optics was beginning in his day, and since Pythagoras of ancient Greece, the mathematical regularities of harmonics had been noted.

cients and medievals were excessively optimistic in their use of this methodology, endowing the doctrines of past thinkers with an authority to which they were not entitled, given the qualified nature of the proper methodology of natural philosophy — as Maurer observes, "the corpse of medieval physics is there to warn us" of the dangers in store for those who neglect this qualified status of the many of the conclusions of natural philosophy (p. xi). This shortcoming was to have far-reaching consequences in the development of Western thought, as we have seen.

As we have seen in chapter 1, this lack of the critical awareness we take for granted today is strikingly evident in the interpretation of astronomical data. As Maurer points out, "The tragedy was that the revolt against medieval physics" which emerged as an important formative influence of Western modernity "turned against, not only the bad physics of the Middle Ages, but against philosophy itself" (p. xii). The "scientific" project which emerged as central to modernity's quest for truth adopted a very different approach from that of Aquinas. Whereas the "natural science" of Aquinas sought to identify the *natures* which constitute mundane reality, as manifested in the regularities which characterize the functioning of these natures, later Western thought came to consider "natures" as no more than medieval fantasies. If it is true to its Cartesian principles, modern "scientific" thought makes no claim to an understanding of reality. It registers and investigates the regularities to be found in the observation of reality, interpreting its findings through the formulation of "theories" which are tested by further empirical verification and mathematical analysis.

Aquinas recognized that the methodology of *metaphysics,* the third discipline he distinguishes, is concerned with a universal very different from the "natures" considered by natural philosophy and mathematics — namely, "being as such" or "reality as such."[13] What is it that is common to *all* reality, whereby it is put outside nothingness? It is this ultimate dimension of reality which is the concern of the abstract thought of metaphysical understanding. Maurer discusses the subtle question of what differentiates the subject of meta-

---

13. As we have seen above, reality is understood by Aquinas as constituted by two intelligible principles, *nature* (or *essence*) and the act of *existence (esse).*

physical thinking from the subjects of natural philosophy and mathematics in the understanding of Aquinas (pp. xxii-xxvii). For our purposes, however, it is sufficient to recognize that, whereas the other two methodologies "abstract" *natures* from their particularized conditions in reality, metaphysics can only achieve its object by an understanding which grasps the relationship which *natures* (or essences) have with the principle or formality which confers on them an existence outside nothingness *(esse, the act of existing)*. The relationship between *essence* and *existence* is grasped, for Aquinas, in the act of judgment — which assigns essences to the order of existence. He considers therefore that since natural philosophy and mathematics, on the one hand, have as their subject matters *natures* or essences and metaphysics, on the other hand, has as its subject *the relationship between essence and existence,* the "abstractions" whereby their respective subject matters are grasped are essentially different.

Metaphysical understanding, it is clear, has great theological significance for Saint Thomas: it is the ultimate formality conferred by the *act of existing* which establishes the communality between God and creation.[14] It is this metaphysical communality which gives the discourse of faith and theology whatever limited validity it has. It is important to recognize, in this context, what has been called the "agnosticism" of Aquinas, which is summarized by John Courtney Murray in these terms:

> [O]ne aspect of St. Thomas' achievement calls for comment . . . his pervasive concern throughout the whole of his probing inquiry into the problem of God, to protect against prying scrutiny the mystery of the divine transcendence. This is the basic biblical truth, that God is the Holy One, whose Name is ineffable. St. Thomas states the truth in metaphysical form: "One thing about God remains completely unknown in this life, namely, what God is" (*In Rom.,* c. 1, lect. 6). He states the truth so often that some of his commentators have become uncomfortable at the patent poverty of the knowledge of God that he permits to man in this life. . . . St. Thomas adheres rigidly to what Sertillanges has called an "agnosti-

---

14. The position of Aquinas is well summarized in a passage of Tarnas already cited, *Passion*, pp. 182-83.

cism of definition." In the end, our presence to God is to One Un-known: "ei quasi ignoto coniungamur" (*Summa theol.* pars I, q.12, art.13 ad 1). We do not know what He is, to whom we are present and who is present to us. We only know what He is not. The philosophical assertion is as apodictic as the biblical assertion that God is the Holy One, who hides Himself.[15]

There can be little doubt that the principal reason the intellectual achievement of Aquinas has not been made accessible to contemporary thinkers is because his followers have tended to present this achievement as a *closed, self-sufficient system.* This approach is at odds with the intention of Aquinas himself, who would see his metaphysical *principles,* not as the components of a system, but as the soul of a methodology able to be employed in the exploration of reality at every phase of humanity's expanding historical and cultural awareness. Among contemporary scholars, Bernard Lonergan has been outstanding in the promotion of this more authentic approach.

15. John Courtney Murray, "The Problem of God in St. Thomas," *Theological Studies* 23 (1962): 14-15.

INDEX

Abstraction: Aristotle on, 227; Aquinas on, 229-31
Adams, Phillip, 32
"Aggiornamento," 126
"Agnosticism of definition": Aquinas on, 232
Alienations (of modernity), 41
Anaxagoras, 18
"Anthropological principle," 13
Aquinas, Saint Thomas, 18, 23, 27, 33, 225-33 *passim;* on government's mandate, 173-74; on property rights, 164, 170; on social solidarity, 150, 162, 169
Aristotle, 23, 110; Aquinas on, 226-28; cosmology of, 20-21, 47; MacIntyre on, 68, 72; on moral awareness, precritical, 72; social theory of, 150, 162
Aron, Raymond, 71
Astronomical theory, 8, 231
Auerbach, Erich, 111-12
Australia, 99, 102, 104-5, 108, 201-2

Authority: of competence, 93; to govern, 173-74
Autonomous self. *See* Monad subject
Autonomy of secular order, 4-5, 14, 23, 181, 192

Bacon, Francis, 10, 20, 49n.10, 61
Balthasar, Hans Urs von, 193, 197, 199
"Banality, apotheosis of," 92
Barker, Sir Ernest, 72n.6, 153-54, 161
Barrow, John, 33, 165
Barth, Karl, 184, 199, 206, 217
Beauty care, 81
Bellah, Robert (et al.), 36-37, 105, Ch. 8 *passim;* on "hermeneutics of recovery," 53
Bellow, Saul, 133
Berkeley, George, 41
Berlin, James, 139
Bloom, Harold, 116-17
Bok, Derek, 138